PREFACE.

THE materials for the lives of Samuel and Saul are found only in the First Book of Samuel, the First Book of Chronicles, and in some few notices in the New Testament. The ancient monuments afford no help, except in so far as they have tended to settle the chronology of the Exodus and the reign of Solomon, and consequently of events reckoned from those eras. Of late years such a mass of illustrative matter, historical, geographical, and connected with manners and customs, has been collected, that the writer's task is greatly facilitated, and he has rather to select and employ existing materials than to busy himself with independent investigation. I have largely availed myself of such aids, and gladly own my obligations to the commentaries of Bishop Ellicott, Mr. Kirkpatrick, and especially of Dean Payne Smith in "The Pulpit Commentary." I have also found some aid in three recent continental publications, viz., the commentary of Clair in " La Sainte Bible avec Commentaires," of Hummelauer in " Cursus Scripturæ sacræ," and of Klostermann in " Kurzgefasster Kommentar."

As the Life of David forms a separate number of this series of " Men of the Bible," I have touched but lightly on some particulars wherein he and Saul are concerned. The reader will find a fuller account in " David : his Life and Times."

CONTENTS.

CHAPTER I.

                                                     PAGE

SAMUEL'S YOUTH 1

Ramathaim-Zophim—Elkanah; his wives; attends the annual festival—Shiloh—The Judges—Eli and his sons—Hannah's vow—Nazirism—Samuel born, dedicated at the Tabernacle—Scripture canticles—Hannah's *Magnificat*—Women of the Tabernacle—Samuel's early training—Sins of Eli's sons—The prophet's warning.

CHAPTER II.

FIRST REVELATION TO SAMUEL. CAPTURE AND RESTORATION OF THE ARK 28

Life of Samuel at Shiloh—The doom of Eli revealed to Samuel—Samuel accredited as Prophet, meaning of the term—Condition of Israel and need of reformation—Oppression by the Philistines—Rebellion of the Israelites—Battle of Aphek—Defeat of the Israelites—Capture of the Ark—Death of Eli—Tabernacle removed to Nob—Shiloh destroyed—The ark taken to Ashdod—Dagon—Philistines plagued—Ark sent to Gath, to Ekron—Divinations—Propitiatory offerings—Ark returned to the Israelites at Bethshemesh; placed at Kirjath-Jearim.

CHAPTER III.

SAMUEL, JUDGE AND PROPHET 59

Samuel's efforts at reformation—Samuel recognied as Judge—Assembles the people at Mizpah—National repentance—Insurrection—Philistines defeated at Ebenezer—Effects of the victory—Theocratic government—Samuel's judicial circuit—He establishes "Schools of the Prophets"—Chronology of his life—Samuel's sons—The people demand a king—Samuel, by God's command, acquiesces in their request, but warns them of the consequences—The people persist in their demand.

CHAPTER IV.

SAUL ANOINTED KING 79

Saul; his genealogy—Is advised to consult Samuel at Ramah concerning the loss of his father's asses—The high-place—

CONTENTS.

Samuel warned of the coming of the destined king, receives Saul with high honour—Intimates his future lot—Privately anoints him king—Meaning of such unction—Samuel gives Saul three signs, and a premonition as a trial of faith—Saul returns home—Keeps his own counsel—Is publicly chosen king at Mizpah—Divination by lot—Saul's early policy.

CHAPTER V.

SAUL'S FIRST VICTORY 99

The Ammonites, they attack Jabesh-Gilead; offer ignominious terms to the inhabitants—Saul hears of the distress, summons all Israel, makes a forced march and relieves Jabesh-Gilead—His wise forbearance and magnanimity.

CHAPTER VI.

SAMUEL ABDICATES 109

Renewal of the monarchy—Samuel abrogates the office of Judge, defends his past career, shows that nothing in it excused the demand for a king—His words confirmed by a portent, endorsed by acclamation—He promises to intercede for the people.

CHAPTER VII.

SAUL'S FIRST REJECTION 117

Chronology of Saul's reign—Saul chooses a body-guard—Michmash—Jonathan destroys the column at Geba—Philistines prepare for war with overwhelming force—Saul retreats to Gilgal—Israelites disheartened—Trial of Saul's faith—His failure and disobedience—His sin explained—He is punished by rejection—A successor is announced—Samuel leaves Saul.

CHAPTER VIII.

BATTLE OF MICHMASH 129

Saul at Geba—The Philistines devastate the land—Jonathan and his armour-bearer attack their garrison—The Philistines, panic-stricken, fly—Saul joins in the pursuit—Great slaughter of the Philistines—Saul's rash vow, broken unwittingly by Jonathan—The violater discovered by lot—Jonathan rescued from death by the people.

CHAPTER IX.

SAUL'S FINAL REJECTION 144

The family of Saul—He gathers a chosen band of warriors—His successful wars—The Amalekites—Saul ordered to destroy them utterly—A trial of obedience—The Ban—Great destruction of the Amalekites—Saul spares Agag and the best of the spoil—Samuel warned of Saul's disobedience, taxes him with his sin; pronounces his final rejection—Slays Agag—Abandons Saul finally.

CONTENTS. vii

CHAPTER X.

A SUCCESSOR ANOINTED 158

Samuel sent to Bethlehem—Anoints David—Condition of Saul—David summoned to soothe him with music—Philistines invade Judah—Valley of Elah—Goliath challenges the Israelites—David accepts the challenge, kills the giant—Defeat and slaughter of the Philistines—Saul takes David into his service—Friendship of David and Jonathan.

CHAPTER XI.

SAUL'S JEALOUSY AND MANIA 168

Saul is jealous of David—Progress of his malady—Saul threatens David's life—Employs him on military expeditions—Gives him his daughter in marriage on condition of his slaying one hundred Philistines—Plots against his life—Relents for a while at Jonathan's intercession—Soon resumes his evil purpose—Tries to kill David—David saved by Michal—Flees to Samuel at Ramah—Saul sends to arrest him—Naioth—The messengers prophesy—Saul goes himself to Ramah and prophesies.

CHAPTER XII.

SAUL'S PERSECUTION OF DAVID 178

Saul's intention towards David tested at the Festival of the New Moon, and proved to be murderous—Jonathan informs David, who flees to Nob, is received and fed by Ahimelech—Doeg is present, informs Saul of what happened there—Massacre of the priests at Nob—Saul pursues David to Ziph—Disaffection in the land—Saul nearly entraps David at Maon—Is spared by David at Engedi—Affected by David's forbearance, Saul professes reconciliation.

CHAPTER XIII.

THE DEATH OF SAMUEL 190

Samuel dies—His funeral and tomb—His services to Israel—His character—His difficulties—His accomplished work.

CHAPTER XIV.

THE DEATH OF SAUL 198

Saul again pursues David to Hachilah—His life spared a second time by David—Saul's compunction—Philistines invade the country with large forces—Saul encamps at Gilboa—Can obtain no Divine counsel—Consults a witch at Endor, is answered by the spirit of Samuel—Warned of his approaching defeat and death—Returns to his camp—Battle of Gilboa—Defeat of Israel—Death of Saul and his sons—Their bodies affixed to the walls of Bethshan, removed and buried by the men of Jabesh-Gilead—News of the catastrophe brought to David—His conduct thereupon—His funeral elegy—Summary of Saul's character.

CHAPTER I.

SAMUEL'S YOUTH.

Ramathaim-Zophim—Elkanah; his wives; attends annual festival—Shiloh—The Judges—Eli and his sons—Hannah's vow—Nazirism—Samuel born; dedicated at the Tabernacle—Scripture canticles—Hannah's *Magnificat*—Women of the Tabernacle—Samuel's early training—Sins of Eli's sons—The prophet's warning.

SOME few miles north of Jerusalem, on the borders of the territory of Benjamin, stood the town of Ramathaim-Zophim, better known under the name of Ramah, and still more familiar in the form of Arimathæa, the home of that Joseph who was deemed worthy to have the privilege of laying in his own tomb the body of Jesus. The exact site of the place is unknown; but though situated in Benjamin, it is said in our record to lie in Mount Ephraim because the limestone ridge so called extended far south, beyond the limits of the tribe whence it derived its appellation.[1] Ramathaim, which means "The Two Ramahs," or Heights, was so called because it was built on two hills, and the word Zophim was added to distinguish it from other towns which bore the same name. Where there was an upper and a lower city, or where more than one village or town were combined under one designation, this name was often a dual or plural form. Familiar instances are Athenæ, Thebæ, Mycenæ. The addition of Zophim was derived from the original founder of the place. In remote times there had been a man of some eminence named Zuph, who had given his name to the whole district

[1] Dean Payne Smith, "Pulpit Commentary."

(1 Sam. ix. 5), and his descendants, the Zophim, had made Ramah their chief dwelling.[1] The head of this family, at the time when our history opens, some twelve centuries before the Christian era, was one Elkanah, a Levite of the line of Kohath, but who, his ancestors having originally dwelt in Ephraim, (Josh. xxi. 20), was considered to belong to that tribe, and is called (1 Sam. i. 1) an Ephrathite or Ephraimite. He was a man of wealth and high position, living on his own property and apparently not officiating as a Levite, and in the exercise of his discretion had married two wives, Hannah and Peninnah, the second wife being taken when all hope of having a son by the first was abandoned. Although no one who studied the record of the first institution of marriage could doubt that man was intended to have but one wife, yet polygamy was not forbidden in the Mosaic law, and those who practised it did not offend against any formal enactment. Like slavery, it had long and widely prevailed when the Sinaitic covenant was made, and the legislator accepted the custom and only took care to regulate and limit its practice. But infringements of the law of nature bring their own punishment. We first read of this violation of the primeval ordinance in the case of that descendant of Cain, the rude and ruffianly Lamech, who, in the ancient song which Moses has preserved (Gen. iv. 23, 24), boasts of his corporal strength, fearing neither God nor man, and trusting to his own right arm for defence and attack. Elkanah's home life was spoiled by the bickering and contention of his wives. His first wife was probably Hannah, "Grace," whose name recalls the sister of the Carthaginian Queen Dido, the old prophetess in the Temple (Luke ii. 36), and the mother of the Virgin Mary. She was a pious, amiable, unselfish woman, one who, in men's judgment, would have been thought a fit person to have brought up children in the nurture and admonition of the Lord; but she had to endure the hard fate of barrenness. What a terrible calamity this was considered by Hebrew women we may gather from the passionate appeal of Rachel to her husband Jacob: "Give me children, or else I die" (Gen. xxx. 1). No such

[1] Blunt, *in loc.*, translates the compound word, "The double high place of the Zuphite family," and considers that Ramah itself was built on the side of a hill, and that the high place was above the town, at the top of the eminence, being now represented by Neby-Samwil, four miles north-west of Jerusalem.

SAMUEL'S YOUTH.

impatience was found in Hannah. She is meek and calm even under the grossest provocation. Despairing of offspring from his first consort, Elkanah takes a second wife, Peninnah, " Pearl," or, as we might call her, Margaret, and by her becomes the father of numerous sons and daughters. Vain of her maternity, despising one who was denied the blessing of children, and jealous of the love with which her husband regarded her rival, Peninnah lost no opportunity of deriding and reviling Hannah both in public and in private. Elkanah was a religious and sensible man, and did not visit his disappointment on Hannah, but, rising superior to the common sentiment of his time and nation, regarded his childless wife with special favour, and showed her unusual tokens of regard. Far from losing her husband's love, as she might naturally have feared, Hannah becomes doubly dear to him; and when he finds her weeping at the insults offered by Peninnah, and unable to eat her food by reason of grief at heart, he comforts her in the tenderest fashion. "Hannah," he says, "why weepest thou? and why eatest thou not? and why is thy heart grieved? am not I better to thee than ten sons?" Thus was Hannah's grief consoled, and the unmerited reproach under which she laboured was made easier to endure. She learned to bear her burden, to acknowledge that she was tried in the same manner as her great ancestresses, Sarah and Rebekah, and to acquiesce in the dispensation, waiting patiently for the issue.

It had been ordered originally that all male Israelites were yearly to attend the three great festivals at the central place of worship. They were to appear before the Lord at the feasts of the Passover, Pentecost, and Tabernacles.[1] But this rule had never been observed, and certainly in the unsettled times which succeeded the death of Joshua had fallen into desuetude, and one public attendance in the year was thought sufficient even by religious and scrupulous people. This, too, seems to have been the rule in later times. Elkanah used to go up yearly to the house of the Lord of Hosts to worship and to sacrifice. Amid the laxity and corruption that existed, when men did what was right in their own eyes, and neither coercive authority nor public opinion enforced any close observance of Mosaic enactments, yet the Law was well known, and obeyed, as far as practicable, by the devout families in the land. Though women were not

[1] Exod. xxiii. 14-17.

required to make this pilgrimage, Elkanah took his wives with him on these occasions, as the Virgin Mary accompanied Joseph when he made his annual journey to Jerusalem to celebrate the Passover.[1] Piety rejoices to do more than bare duty requires. What particular festival it was which was thus solemnly observed we are not told; but it was most probably the Passover, that great national holy day which no pious and patriotic Hebrew would willingly forego. This feast the family of the good Elkanah celebrated before the ark in the place which God had chosen.

The tabernacle was now established at Shiloh, where originally it had been pitched by Joshua, and which during all the time of the Judges had been the centre of religious worship. If, as may have been the case, it was temporarily moved to some other locality, as Bethel and Mizpah, it always returned to Shiloh, and this place was regarded as the national sanctuary unto which all Israel resorted to meet the Lord of Hosts. It was, indeed, a site well fitted for this purpose, not for its beauty, which in those days would have been no consideration, nor for its strength, for it was by no means a naturally strong position, but for its seclusion and accessibility.[2] Its very name, "Place of Rest," gives the clue to its suitableness for being the home of the shrine of the covenant people; and appertaining to the powerful tribe of Ephraim it was as secure from danger as any place in the whole country. Its position is described carefully in Judges xxi. 19 as being "on the north side of Bethel, on the east side of the highway that goeth up from Bethel to Shechem, and on the south of Lebonah." These *data* have served to identify Shiloh with the modern Seilun, a village a little to the east of the main road from Bethel to Nablus, the ancient Shechem, and "covering a small hill, which is separated from the higher mountain on the north by a deep narrow valley, coming from the east, and running down towards El-Lubban (Lebonah). On the east and west of the hill are two small, though much wider valleys, running down north into the former."[3] The hill itself has been cut down on the north side to form a level surface some eighty feet wide by four hundred long, and on the plateau thus obtained the tabernacle was probably erected. "No spot in Central Palestine," says Dr. Geikie, "could be more secluded than this early sanctuary; nothing more featureless than

---

[1] Luke ii. 41.   [2] Stanley, "Jewish Church," i 278.
[3] Robinson, "Biblical Researches," iii. 85 ff, ed. 1841.

SAMUEL'S YOUTH.

the landscape around; so featureless, indeed, the landscape, and so secluded the spot, that from the time of St. Jerome till its re-discovery by Dr. Robinson in 1838, the very site was forgotten and unknown." According to rabbinical tradition, there was no regular edifice raised for the reception of the ark or substituted for the tent of meeting; a low stone wall surrounding a small enclosure, and covered with the tabernacle curtains, was the structure which sufficed to contain the symbols of the Lord's presence among His people. Round this erection a town had gradually grown, the entrance to which was guarded by a stone gateway, with its seats and open area, after the manner of Eastern cities. But the whole community still retained something of a nomadic character, and was called, in familar speech, the Camp of Shiloh. Here, under the vine-clad hills which rise like an amphitheatre around the sacred spot, flocked the maidens to celebrate with dance and song the joyous Feast of Tabernacles; here assembled the heads of tribes for solemn council; and here, too, as time went on and Israel declined more and more to heathen customs, gathered the devotees of shameless profligacy, who polluted the worship of Jehovah with their impure practices.

The period of the Judges had been a time of anarchy and confusion. With no central authority to organize the various tribes into one commonwealth, with no regular government, the people, acting without concert and doing what was right in their own eyes, were continually endangering their own safety, committing great crimes, and provoking the wrath of the Lord. Then when the necessity of the times called forth some hero to their rescue, they willingly followed his guidance, and won for themselves a temporary peace. But these successes were only local in their effects: and very commonly, while one portion of the Holy Land was enjoying rest and prosperity, in another quarter the colonists were oppressed and afflicted, crushed by the enemies whom they had culpably neglected to exterminate. The date of Samson's judgeship is not determined, but it probably coincided with the latter days of Eli. But he, though a man of wonderful personal prowess, was not fit to be a ruler and leader in difficult times; and if he gave an example to his contemporaries of successful resistance to powerful antagonists, he produced no permanent effect on the condition of the country, and left behind him nothing but the memory of impracticable exploits and useless victories. There was need of one who was a statesman as well as a warrior to take the lead at this crisis of national affairs. The Philistines, sometimes repulsed or defeated, never yet subdued, and inspired with the deadliest hatred against the Hebrews, had turned all their energies to the destruction of the invaders. They themselves of late years had greatly increased in power, owing to constant immigrations from their old home in Crete, whence also they obtained supplies of arms of quality far superior to any procurable by the Hebrews. Thus they were able to contest the possession of the country under very favourable conditions, and Israel had to contend for its very existence in the face of these formidable opponents. What might check the downward course of the Chosen People, and prevent their total subjection? The judgeship, founded on personal courage, and proceeding from the people, had proved incapable of effecting any permanent amelioration; there remained another expedient by which the threatened ruin of the community might be arrested.[1] What if the judicial office, combined with the sacerdotal, might prove to be the very force needed to confederate the nation in a strong and efficacious union, which would enable it to offer resistance to all aggression and to regain lost ground? The experiment had never yet been tried. None of the judges had been of priestly descent. At this time the high-priesthood was held by Eli, the head, not of the elder branch of Aaron's family, that of Eleazar, but of the house of Ithamar, the younger son of Aaron. The circumstances which led to this transference of the headship from the one to the other are nowhere related, and various reasons have been invented to account for the change.[2] But the office appertained to the family rather than to the individual; the right of primogeniture did not necessarily obtain in this matter; and any eligible member who had raised himself to eminence might well supersede the claims of supposed birthright, and take the first place when a vacancy occurred. This, doubtless, was what happened in the case of Eli. That it was no usurpation or unauthorized intrusion on his part may be gathered from the message brought to him by the man of God (1 Sam. iii. 27 ff.), who

[1] Ewald, "History of Israel," ii. 181, English translation.

[2] Rabbinical tradition asserts that the transfer took place on account of the part taken by Phinehas in the sacrifice of Jephthah's daughter (Stanley, 'Jewish Church," i. 375).

SAMUEL'S YOUTH.

makes no complaint of his tenure of the office, but only of the evil administration of it by his sons. There may have been no member of the elder branch of sufficient years or ability to assume the office; or, as is very probable, Eli had in his earlier days proved himself a great warrior or a competent leader, and was raised to his high post by general acclamation. The position of judge, to which his services had elevated him during the days of Samson, naturally pointed him out as a fit person to fill the office of high priest when unoccupied. Nor was this dignity at that time of any special consideration. The strict adherents of the traditional religion were few and of small political importance, so that there was no competition for the post, and any member of the Aaronic family who had made himself a name would be readily acknowledged as chief. If it seems impossible to connect Eli's character, as it appears in Holy Scripture, with any idea of heroism and energy, we must remember that when he is brought before us he is already an old man. He died at the age of ninety-eight, after judging Israel for forty years, so that his judgeship must have commenced when he was nearly sixty years old, and he may naturally have begun to show the ravages of time. The zeal and activity of youth had degenerated into apathy and coldness; the strenuous efforts which youthful spirits, animated by piety and patriotism, had enabled him to make, were perhaps no longer needed, and he sank into a lazy, phlegmatic indifference, which led to disastrous consequences in his family. Disabled by the infirmities of age from performing all the duties of his office, he had delegated the priestly functions to his sons, retaining in his own hands the judicial business. These sons, Hophni and Phinehas by name, by no means followed the steps of their good father, who, whatever were his shortcomings, was a righteous and religious man. They were licentious, unscrupulous reprobates, who prostituted their high office to the basest purposes, and introduced into the sanctuary of Shiloh the most degraded practices of heathendom. But their father restrained them not effectually. Lazy, indolent, and indulgent, he satisfies his conscience by administering a mild rebuke; and though they were priests bound to set an example of piety and purity, and he as judge was bound to carry out the denunciation of the law against sinners, he visits their grave offences with no punishment, and lets the scandal continue.

On one of the occasions when Elkanah and his family went

up to worship at Shiloh the attention of Eli was drawn to Hannah. It was at such times that Peninnah took the opportunity of openly deriding her barrenness and vaunting her own maternity. Elkanah indeed gave his childless wife larger portions of the sacrificial victims than he did to Peninnah, showing in every possible way his affection. But nothing could compensate for the desired joy of motherhood; and after the solemn sacrificial meal, which she had attended, though she had little appetite for banquet or pleasure in such festivity, she wended her way sadly to the sanctuary to pour out her heart unto God. Kneeling down in the inner court, she prayed unto the Lord and wept sore, and these were the words she spake: "O Lord of hosts, if Thou wilt indeed look on the affliction of thine handmaid, and remember me, and not forget thine handmaid, but wilt give unto thine handmaid a man child, then I will give him unto the Lord all the days of his life, and there shall no razor come upon his head." This was her vow if her request was granted. The son she prayed for should be dedicated to God's service, not as a mere Levite whose duties commenced from the twenty-fifth year and ceased at the fiftieth,[1] but all his days, from boyhood to the close of life. And more than this, he should be a perpetual Nazirite, his flowing hair, untouched by razor, should mark him out as set apart from common life, and consecrated to the Lord.

This institution of Nazirism was not a new thing.[2] Although we have no record of any Nazirite before Samson who made himself a name in history, yet it seems evident that the observance was in existence before the time of Moses, and that he merely gave it the sanction of law and regulated its practice.[3] It sprang from that religious zeal which, not content with performing the ordinary duties of piety, seeks for stricter modes of self-dedication, analogous to what is known in the Christian Church as "counsels of perfection," the endeavour to execute the precept of Christ, "Be ye perfect, even as your Father which is in heaven is perfect." In mediæval theology the counsels took the form of a threefold vow, answering to the threefold temptation arising from the world, the flesh, and the devil. Chastity, poverty, and obedience, opposed the dangers that threatened the soul from the lust of the flesh, the lust of the

---
[1] Numb. iv. 3; viii. 24, 25. [2] Ewald, "History of Israel," ii. 168 ff.
[3] Numb. vi. 2-21.

eye, and the pride of life. The Nazirite vow was also threefold. The devotee was bound to abstain from all intoxicating liquor, to let the hair grow, and to avoid all ceremonial defilement by contact with a dead body, even that of his nearest relation. Such a vow undertaken by parents for a child must have had a powerful influence on that child's career. Separated from common life, raised above his fellows, specially dedicated to God, the Nazirite deemed himself designated for some peculiar work, and gave himself up to this object as his chief aim, without distraction or disquieting interests. Thus Samson, though very far from being a faultless character, pursued one great design all his days. His sole purpose was to vex and harass the Philistines; his life and death were devoted to this single end. Hannah in making her vow (in which, according to the Mosaic precept,[1] her husband must have concurred) dedicated her son to a life-long service in the Tabernacle; but God had other and higher work for him than the discharge of mere ritual functions. The unborn child was destined for more extensive and conspicuous labours; in him the Levite should be merged in the Judge and the Prophet.

Long time did Hannah continue in prayer, prostrate before the Lord. From his chair of state, placed at the entrance of the court of the Tabernacle, or, as it is called (1 Sam. i. 9), "the palace of Jehovah," Eli marked this sorrowful woman, and, reasoning doubtless from a sad experience, misjudged her harshly. She was praying silently; no words came from her lips; "she spake to her heart." Such earnest, silent, devotion was quite unusual. Spoken prayer was the rule then as it is now among uncultured people. It needs great faith in the Unseen to believe that God hears and answers the unuttered aspirations of the worshipper. Men think that they shall be heard for their much speaking. Eli's experience had not led him to understand that prayer could be offered without speech; and painfully aware of the lax morality of his people, and the disorders which often accompanied the sacrificial feast, he immediately concluded that Hannah was drunken, that her unusual conduct, her quivering lips from which no sound issued, her streaming eyes, her flushed cheeks, were the tokens of intemperance. Coarsely he calls to her from his pontifical

[1] Numb. xxx. 6-15.

throne, and bids her go and sleep off the effects of her debauch, and not to bring her disgraceful condition under the very eye of the Lord. "How long," he cries, "how long wilt thou be drunken? Put away thy wine from thee." Hannah was accustomed to be misjudged, and had learned to be patient under injury. Eli's unfeeling suspicion does not anger her. She answers calmly, at once by voice and manner repelling the unworthy accusation, while showing all due reverence to her venerable rebuker. "No, my lord," she says, "I am a woman of a heavy heart; I have drunk neither wine nor strong drink, but I poured out my soul before the Lord. Count not thine handmaid for a worthless woman; for out of the abundance of my complaint and my provocation have I spoken hitherto." It was the continual cruelty of Peninnah that had driven her forth in sorrow of soul to commune with God in His house. Eli at once perceived his mistake, and retracted the injurious charge. Nay, more, he gives her gracious words, and comforts her, adding his own desire and assurance that her prayer, whatever it may be, would be accepted by the most High. "Go in peace, and the God of Israel grant thy petition that thou hast asked of Him." Comforted by these words, to which the dignity of Eli's office and the venerableness of his age gave weight, and lightened of her burden by casting it down at the Lord's feet in earnest prayer, Hannah rose up and went on her way. She returned to the family feast, composed and cheerful, no longer sad of countenance, but ready to take her part in the solemn festival and to eat her portion with joy and thankfulness.

The celebration of the festival being now ended, Elkanah and his family rose early next morning, and having paid their devotions unto the Lord, returned to their home at Ramathaim-Zophim. Hannah, though no express promise had been given to her, had confidence in the general assurance of God's favour and readiness to hear prayer; she had arrived nearly at the faith taught by the Lord Jesus in after time: "What things soever ye desire, when ye pray, believe that ye receive them, and ye shall have them" (Mark xi. 24). So it was with her. The Lord remembered and answered her prayer. She conceived and bare a son, and in grateful memory of the Lord's goodness she named him Samuel, "Heard of God." She had asked for a son with earnest, persevering supplication, and he should carry with him all his life the memorial of the gracious answer which she had received.¹ When the time came round for the yearly visit to Shiloh, Elkanah went up as usual to offer the annual sacrifice, and to pay the vow which he had made in case his beloved wife should be blessed with a child. Hannah however remained at home, for she said she would not go up till the boy was weaned, when she would take him with her to appear before the Lord, and thenceforward to abide in His presence for ever. The weaning of children was delayed till the second or third year. Among the Persians boys were suckled for two years and two months, girls for two years.² In 2 Macc. vii. 27 the mother of the seven brethren martyred by Antiochus speaks of having given her son suck for three years; and this seems to have been the usual period of lactation in those days. It appears, too, that children were taken into the Temple service at three years of age;³ and possibly the number of victims offered at Samuel's dedication points to the same conclusion. Thus their beloved son grew up under his pious mother's care in the peaceful home at Ramah. His physical needs were supplied by her watchful tenderness; his spiritual training was not neglected. In his infant soul were sown the seeds of holy thoughts; from the dawn of reason his mind was turned to the Lord, whose gift he was; the child of prayer was early taught to commune with God. And his father co-operated in all things with his mother. Elkanah did not merely acquiesce in his wife's vow, but helped her to carry it out effectually by his actions and his prayers. "Do what seemeth thee good," he says to her: "tarry till thou have weaned him; only the Lord establish His word," that is the word delivered by Eli, the high priest, when he had comforted Hannah with the solemn address, "the God of Israel grant thee thy petition." Tradition says that some direct revelation respecting the future destiny of Samuel was given. Thus Rashi writes: "The *Bath-kol* (daughter of the voice) went forth, saying, There shall arise a just one whose name shall be Samuel. Then every mother who bore a son called him Samuel; but when they saw his actions, they said, 'This is not Samuel.' But when this one

---

¹ Philo ("Quod Deus Immut.", ό 2) interprets the name to mean, "appointed for God," adding, "She having received him restores him to the Giver, judging nothing as a good belonging to herself which is not Divine grace."

² Kalisch on 1 Sam. i. 23.   ³ See 2 Chron. xxxi. 16.

was born, they said, 'This is that Samuel,' and this is what the Scripture means when it says, 'The Lord confirmed his word that Samuel may be that just one.'"[1] We need not accept this Rabbinical gloss, and Elkanah probably refers only to what had passed between Eli and Hannah, of which we have only the substance in our text, omitting further details of the mother's vow and the more distinct promise of its acceptance and fulfilment.

And now arrived the time when the child should be openly dedicated to the service of the Sanctuary. He is taken by his parents to Shiloh. Once more Hannah stands before the Lord, not empty-handed this time, not weeping and sorrow-stricken, but rejoicing in heart, filled with a great purpose, bearing with her the son for whom she had poured out her soul in prayer. She comes into the presence of Eli, who with his dim sight recognizes not in this inspired happy countenance the face of of the tearful suppliant whom he had comforted three years ago. "Oh, my lord," she cries, "as thy soul liveth, my lord, I am the woman that stood by Thee here praying unto the Lord. For this child I prayed, and the Lord hath given me my petition which I asked of Him; therefore, also, I have given back what was asked unto the Lord; as long as he liveth he is asked for the Lord."

Yes, indeed, she had made a humble request, but not for herself; she had prayed for something which she might devote to the service of Jehovah. And now she brings the long-desired child, and with due offerings solemnly dedicates him. Three bullocks and an ephah of fine flour and a skin of wine were then presented before the Tabernacle. Two of the animals were Elkanah's annual sacrifice; the third bullock was for the special burnt-offering that accompanied the consecration of Samuel to Jehovah.[2] And the good father ratified the act, and himself with all his household worshipped the Lord there.

[1] Bishop Ellicott, Comm. *in loc*.

[2] The LXX. instead of "three bullocks," read "a bullock of three years old," as Gen. xv. 9. This reminds one of the consecration of the irregular priesthood in the evil days of Jeroboam (2 Chron. xiii. 9). But the present Hebrew text is probably correct, as an ephah of meal was about the proper quantity for the meat-offering that accompanied the sacrifice of three bullocks, three-tenths being the ordered offering for one victim (Num. xxviii. 12 ff. See also viii. 7 ff.)

SAMUEL'S YOUTH.

This vow of Hannah, does it seem strange to us and unnatural, a piece of needless self-sacrifice, the act of a bigoted and hard-natured mother? Nay, surely, very far from that. Hannah was a tender, simple, guileless woman. There is nothing exaggerated, nothing forced in her character.[1] All her impulses are controlled by her quiet faith and genuine piety. It is natural to her to testify her gratitude by the surrender of what is dearest; she cannot offer to the Lord of that which costs her nothing. The comfort of her child's presence she willingly puts aside that she may make a worthy offering; she foregoes the sweet endearment of his love that she may express her thankfulness without a selfish thought to mar its completeness. A vow is a high form of self-surrender, and has its appointed place in the religious life. If it was allowed in concession to the sentiments of an age of imperfect religious development, it certainly conduced to definiteness in conduct and strictness in practice. The great lawgiver saw that the custom of making vows existed and could not prudently be suppressed; it appealed to a feeling inherent in human nature; it arose from a principle which in itself was praiseworthy, the offering of the best to God. It was therefore to be regulated and modified, not abrogated. The present was an age of vows; not only do we read of Samson being dedicated to God as a Nazirite; there is the oath taken in the Benjamite war; there is Jephthah's vow.[2] Such an undertaking gives a conscious strength and tenacity to a purpose, even as Hannibal was inspired to wage unceasing warfare against Rome by the oath which he took at the altar in his father's presence. The moral support of such a covenant or promise is very great; and in a place and time where it was practised and highly regarded, God sanctioned the usage, and deigned to mould it to His own ends. In the present case, Hannah's vow co-operated with God's design for the reformation of Israel; the voluntary obligation which she incurred helped to place in the required position one who, upheld by his dedication and consecrated to a single purpose, could contribute all his life and energies to executing a high mission.

Hannah had marked with sorrow Israel's declension from the

[1] I here acknowledge with gratitude my obligation to Niemeyer's "Charakteristik der Bibel" for many hints as to the character of those with whom I have had to deal in these biographies.

[2] Judges xi. 30, xxi. 5.

right path ; the anarchy and confusion around her, the degradation of the priesthood, the absence of all true religion in the majority of the nation, had filled her heart with poignant regrets. She saw that a great reformation was needed, if the people were to retain the favour of God, and vanquish their enemies. And to carry out this reformation required a leader, holy, single-hearted, devoted. Such an one she hoped to see in the son so earnestly desired, so wonderfully bestowed. He should be dedicated to God all his life; he should be a Nazirite very different from Samson ; not such an example as the sons of Eli should he set ; he should carry on the office of judge in a different spirit from that which Eli displayed. According to Jewish law, every first-born son belonged to the Lord, and had to be redeemed by substitution. Hannah of set purpose refused to redeem her boy, but returned him a living sacrifice to Jehovah, that from his infancy upwards he might be known to be so dedicated, and might conciliate men's regard and win their reverence as one who had always and continuously served the Lord.

For the mercy and loving-kindness which the Lord had showed unto her, Hannah utters her thanksgiving in a song which reaches far beyond the occasion which gives it birth, and rises into the region of prophecy, echoed by seers in succeeding ages till it culminates in the *Magnificat* of the Blessed Virgin Mary when she celebrates the birth of the Messiah. The Christian Church early caught the prophetic element in this Canticle, and employed it in public worship ; it was sung at Matins in the English office. Attempts have been made to assign this song to a later age, as being, except in one allusion, not particularly applicable to the circumstances under which it is said to have been composed, and as being more likely to have been produced at the time of some great national victory, as, for instance, that of David over Goliath. This criticism arises from the failure to recognize the true character of such utterances. They are never simply egotistical ; they always expand from the particular occasion into something greater, wider, the love and care of God for all His creatures, the extension of His kingdom, the glory of Messiah's reign. As Bishop Wordsworth finely says, speaking of Sacred Poetry[1] : " Like a pebble cast into a clear and calm lake, it sends forth concentric rings of waves, ever enlarging towards the margin, so that the par-

---

[1] Comm. on 1 Sam. ii. 1.

ticular mercy to the individual produces ever-expanding undulations of praise." These songs of holy women begin with Sarah's exultation at the birth of Isaac (Gen. xxi. 6, 7), when, in allusion to the name of her son and to the joy which through his great descendant should fill all the earth, she cries: "God hath made me to laugh; every one that heareth will laugh with me." This was her *Magnificat*. Then comes the triumphant hymn of Miriam, after the passage of the Red Sea and the victory over the Egyptians (Exod. xv.) This is followed by the Song of Deborah (Judges v.), who in fervid poetry praises the Lord for the deliverance of the people by a woman's hand. The great events which these women celebrated were types and foreshadowings of the triumphs of Messiah, and as such were dimly recognized by those who sung of them. Of the same character were the recorded songs of Moses, David, and Hezekiah; they are prophetic and Messianic. Such is this ode of Hannah's. She saw beyond the immediate present, and in the mercy displayed in her own case, she recognized the Divine economy in the government of the world, and a promise of future blessing not on individuals only, but on her nation also. He who took care of the poor and needy, and raised up the lowly to high estate, would equally protect and exalt His people now downtrodden and sore oppressed. What had happened to her was a pledge of God's dealing with Israel; her own deliverance was a type of the salvation wrought by God throughout the world's history. In her prophetic spirit she foresaw a great change in the government of the chosen people; the theocracy administered by leaders and judges was to give place to a more settled and permanent form of rule. Knowing from the promises made to the patriarchs, and from many expressions and stipulations in the Pentateuch, that Israel was destined to be a Kingdom, she sings of a King whom God would one day bestow upon His people, who should unite and rule them, and to whom the Lord would give strength and success. And in this monarch she foresaw the Lord's Anointed, some one greater than David and Solomon, even the Messiah. She expressed her confidence in the realization of the promises connected with royal dominion in Israel, which were now beginning to stir in the hearts of the people; but the Spirit who spoke by her signified a more glorious accomplishment than was commonly expected; and we, by the light of later history, can read in her pregnant words intimations of a mighty future, the coming of King Messiah and the glories of His kingdom. In this light the ode was regarded by the early Christian Church.[1] The Fathers generally see in Hannah a type of the Church, and in her words a prophetic announcement of the victories of Christ. And Jewish expositors held the same opinion,[2] which is further supported by the use made of this song by Zechariah and the Virgin Mary in the New Testament. The former in the *Benedictus* and the latter in the *Magnificat* found themselves upon Hannah's Thanksgiving, and show how it was regarded by pious Israelites.[3] Such songs were preserved among the people, handed down by oral tradition, employed in public worship, committed to writing in course of time, and inserted in the sacred books by their several compilers and editors, as worthy expressions of the religious life, of the hopes and aspirations of the faithful in Israel. Thus then the happy mother sang :—

" 1. My heart exulteth in the Lord,
My horn is exalted in the Lord,
My mouth is opened wide over mine enemies,
Because I rejoice in Thy salvation.

2. There is none holy as the Lord ;
For there is none beside Thee,
Neither is there any rock like our God.

3. Talk no more so exceedingly proudly ;
Let not arrogancy come out of your mouth ;
For the Lord is a God of knowledge,
And by Him actions are weighed.

4. The heroes of the bow are confounded,
And they that stumbled are girded with strength.

5. They that were full have hired out themselves for bread,
And they that were hungry are at ease ;
Yea, the barren hath borne seven,
And she that hath many children languisheth.

6. The Lord killeth and maketh alive,
He bringeth down to the grave, and He doth bring up.

7. The Lord maketh poor and maketh rich,
He bringeth low, also He lifteth up.

8. He raiseth up the poor out of the dust,
He lifteth up the needy from the dunghill,

---

[1] St. Aug "De Civit." xxii. 4. S Cypr. "De Orat. Dom." 140 See more *ap* Corn. a Lap. *in loc*.
[2] See Targ. of Jonathan and Kimchi *in loc.*
[3] Luke i. 46 ff. 68 ff.

SAMUEL'S YOUTH.

> o make them sit with princes,
> And enjoy the throne of glory;
> For the pillars of the earth are the Lord's,
> And He hath set the world upon them.
>
> 9. He keepeth the feet of His holy ones,
> But the wicked are put to silence in darkness;
> For not by strength doth man prevail.
> 10. The adversaries of the Lord are confounded;
> Against them in heaven doth He thunder;
> The Lord judgeth the ends of the earth,
> That He may give strength unto His king,
> And exalt the horn of His anointed."

Let us see what this song of thanksgiving means. Hannah begins by expressing the holy joy that filled her heart, and the strength which she felt in the consciousness that God had heard her, and had changed her earthly lot. This feeling opened her lips in praise, and constrained her to utter her gratitude to the Lord, to whom all her blessings were owed (ver. 1). He alone is absolutely holy, He alone lives in Himself, unchangeable, majestic, secure, the Rock, on whom she rests in perfect trust (ver. 2). Then with a glance at Peninnah's insolent provocation, she bids the wicked tremble at His holiness, who knows and judges all human actions (ver. 3). See, she says, the working of this attribute of God in the vicissitudes of human events. Heroes who rejoice in their strength are shattered and brought to shame; the weak and powerless are made mighty for battle (ver. 4). The rich and wealthy become hirelings for a daily wage; the once famished cease from labour and keep holiday. She who, like me, was barren and bare not, is blessed with children in perfection, and the fruitful mother pines away because she has lost her sons and hath none to comfort her in her old age (ver. 5).[1] Death and life are from the Lord; He brings to the brink of the grave and rescues therefrom at His good pleasure (ver. 6). Poverty and riches are at His disposal; He bringeth some low, He lifteth others on high (ver. 7). He raiseth the poor from the very dust, and the needy from the lowest degradation, to give them a seat among princes, and to make them enjoy the throne of glory.[2] And this He does because He is the Creator and Upholder of the universe (ver. 8). Therefore the righteous have nothing to fear. He guards every

[1] Comp. Psa. cxiii. 2, Jer. xv. 9.   [2] Comp. Psa. cxiii. 7, 8.

step of the earthly course of the pious, and punishes the wicked in the silence of the grave, in distress and calamity; for they had but natural strength to rely upon, and no man in his own power can meet the storms of life (ver. 9). All who contend with the Lord are confounded and sore vexed. Jehovah seated in heaven utters the sentence, the voice of His thunder; He judges the whole earth to its remotest quarters, and He will perfect the kingdom which He hath founded in Israel, raising up a King in His own good time, Who shall be endowed with irresistible might and be the universal Saviour (ver. 10).

When the celebration of the festival was completed, Elkanah and his wives returned to their home at Ramah, leaving their child Samuel behind in Eli's care. The disturbing element in this pious household was now removed; the childless wife could no longer be reviled; her reproach among women was at an end. So the quiet home life flowed on, and as years passed, other children were born to Hannah; the prattle of little voices made music in her ears, and three sons and two daughters gladdened the hearts of the faithful parents. A Jewish legend, with a kind of poetical justice in view, relates how the birth of each of Hannah's children was accompanied by the death of one of Peninnah's; but it would have been scant equity thus to punish the father for his wife's natural exultation, ill-natured though it was; nor can we conceive that the good Hannah would have felt happiness in her own maternity, if it had brought such sorrow to her rival. The later life of these children has left no mark on the page of history, and nothing whatever is known about them.

And now see the little Samuel, a gentle child of some three years old, in the holy house of Shiloh under the training of the old high priest and his assistants. These were not all rough men, of lax habits and doubtful piety, which unhappily was the character of many of the officiants at the sanctuary. There were women, too, who had regular duties to perform in connection with the Tabernacle; and to their care, doubtless, the boy was entrusted.[1] What exactly was the service which these women ren-

---

[1] See 1 Sam. ii. 22 "The women that assembled at the door of the Tabernacle," where the words ought to be rendered "The women that did service at the door," &c., as in Exod. xxxviii. 8. The expression is used of formal, military service, and would show that they had their office and work duly regulated.

dered is nowhere stated. It seems plain that they had been originally appointed by Moses, as we read of the women who did service at the Tabernacle offering their mirrors for the material of the great laver (Exod. xxxviii. 8) ; and the institution continued unto the destruction of the Temple. Intimations of this fact occasionally appear in Scripture. Not improbably the women who publicly celebrated the victories of Hebrew heroes, as Barak and David, belonged to this class. To such there may be an allusion in Psa. lxviii. 11 : " The Lord giveth the word ; the women that publish the tidings are a great host." It is not unlikely that Anna the prophetess was one of them ; and the widows and deaconesses of the early Christian Church may have been the natural successors of this primitive order. That they assisted in the liturgical portions of Divine service is not probable ; their duties would be such as more especially appertained to female work in a household, the cooking of the sacrificial food, the cleansing of the vessels, the care of children, the spinning, embroidering, and washing of the curtains and hangings of the sanctuary. We know that in after years, when idolatry was rife in the land, there was a regular order of women who wove hangings for the Asherah, the image of Ashtoreth (2 Kings xxiii. 7) ; this was probably a prostitution of the original class to idolatrous purposes, the institution surviving the change of religion, though perverted from its object. While, then, the women of the tabernacle attended to the bodily wants and training of the child Samuel, his mental and religious culture was no less carefully regarded by Eli. If we may consider his education to have been conducted on the same principles as those which obtained in after time, we may suppose that he was early taught to read and write, was instructed in the Law, and learned the facts of Jewish history, and the great deeds of his forefathers. Many portions of the Pentateuch were by him committed to memory, and the child was encouraged to ask the meaning of the various celebrations and ordinances which he witnessed or in which he took part. The utmost reverence for even the words of the law was inculcated ; as Philo says :[1] "Looking on their laws as oracles inspired by God, and instructed in them from early childhood, the Jews carry the image of the Commandments in their very souls." This was the staple of the instruction imparted, the foundation on which religion and morality were

[1] " De Legat. ad Caium," 31. ii. p. 577, M.

reared. The soil in which this teaching was to take root had been industriously prepared by Samuel's parents. Chiefly the pious Hannah had sanctified the first dawnings of intellect in her little son, and used those early receptive years to good purpose. Who can tell the effect of a holy mother's training upon even an infant's character? The love that speaks in her eyes and controls her actions, finds its way to the child's heart ; the look and voice of the tender parent meet with responsive efforts from the little one in her arms; the education for heaven begins at the mother's knee. A ready pupil was the infant Samuel, and made no difficulty in mastering the tasks suitable to his age, while he also ministered before the Lord, performing such duties as lay in his capacity. Doubtless there were many children and youths under training at Shiloh, as, later, Samuel gathered a school at Naioth in Ramah ; and the emulation of companions, and the petty trials of a common life, helped to give a steadfastness to his purposes, and promoted the growth of forbearance, courage, and unselfishness. But young as he was he was distinguished from his comrades by his dress. Being dedicated to a life-long service in the sanctuary, he wore a linen ephod like a priest or Levite, or one who took part in a religious service.[1] The ephod consisted of two pieces of white cloth or linen hanging from the neck in front and behind, joined together by shoulder straps, and confined round the waist by a band. Besides this dress, Hannah, when she came with her husband to the annual sacrifice, brought for her boy " a little coat," a garment reaching to the feet, like that worn by the high priest under the ephod, though of less costly material and not so elaborately ornamented. It was a simple frock without sleeves and with a hole for the head to pass through, woven throughout without seams, as that for which the soldiers cast lots at the Crucifixion of our Lord Jesus Christ. Though surrendered to God's service and separated from his parents, Samuel was still an object of care to his mother, and her loving thoughts were exercised on this absent child. As she plied her busy spindle in the making of his "little coat," her heart went out to him in his distant home ; and she hailed with joy the recurrence of the yearly festival which for a short interval united the severed link in the family chain. She marked his growth, she tested his progress

---

[1] Comp. 2 Sam. vi. 14, where David is thus clad when dancing before the ark. 1 Chron. xv. 27.

SAMUEL'S YOUTH.

in learning, she watched his temper and disposition; and she could thank God that the child was preparing for his high destiny, and fitting himself to be an example as well as a leader to his people. And Eli had great hopes of this dedicated child; the remarkable manner in which he had become associated with him pointed him out as designed for some great purpose; and the old priest took the better care of him, and attended more scrupulously to his training, as he saw the evil conduct of his own sons, and recognized with sorrow that he could look for no worthy successor in either of them when he himself was called away. The conduct of these sons, Hophni and Phinehas, was indeed a scandal of the utmost magnitude. They were profane, greedy, dishonest, profligate. They showed their evil character in many ways. Their downward course was plain enough; they had lost all faith in God, and handling holy things with unholy hands, they were given over to a reprobate mind, and without a struggle gratified each wicked passion as it arose.

By the Law of Moses a certain portion of the sacrificial offerings was due to the priests in lieu of fee, the remainder of the animal being returned to the offerer to be consumed by himself, his family, and the Levites who dwelt in the neighbourhood (Deut. xii. 12). It was only fair that "they which minister about sacred things should eat of the things of the temple, and they which wait upon tne altar should have their portion with the altar" (1 Cor. ix. 13). This portion of the peace-offerings was strictly defined, and might not be altered or exceeded. The legal due, as we learn from Lev. vii., was the breast, or brisket, and the right shoulder. These were solemnly dedicated to the Lord (the former by being "waved," that is, moved repeatedly in presentation to the Saviour and Preserver on earth; the latter, by being "heaved," or once lifted up, to the Intercessor in heaven), and were then made over to the priests. But before this was done the fat had to be burned upon the altar, which was the appointed way of consecrating the whole sacrifice; and no portion could be lawfully appropriated till this rite was performed. The fat, or suet (for the rule referred only to the pure, internal fat, not to that which was mixed with the flesh), was thus offered, not simply because it was the most combustible part of the carcase, but because it was regarded as the best portion, the plain token of a perfect and well-nourished body. And as being God's share, it was never to be eaten; upon its use the same restriction was laid as upon blood (Lev. iii. 17), with this difference, that, whereas the eating of blood was forbidden under all circumstances, the interdict on the consumption of fat applied only to animals sacrificed, or to such as were capable of being sacrificed. Now the sons of Eli would not be restrained by any law in the gratification of their appetites. They not only took their allotted portion in an illegal manner, but they claimed more than their due share. Instead of waiting until the sacrifice had been solemnly dedicated by the burning of the fat upon the altar, as the Law ordained, these unscrupulous ministers sent their servants to seize the portions before the offering was made, thus robbing God and dishonouring the symbolical ceremony. Besides this, they plundered the offerer of what was indisputably his own. When he was preparing the sacrificial feast from such parts of the animal as were not otherwise appropriated, Eli's sons violently took possession of portions that were being cooked. Their servants came with the flesh-hooks, or tridents, that were used for turning the sacrifices on the fire and for collecting fragments, and struck them into the pot or pan in which the flesh was being boiled for the repast of the offerer and his friends, and all that the hook brought up they took for their masters' use. Such acts of profanation and robbery could not pass unnoticed. The requirements of the Law were well known to the people who frequented the sanctuary; and when they saw its very guardians openly disregarding the plainest directions, and setting an example of sacrilege, cupidity, and dishonesty, they were wholly scandalized, their moral susceptibilities were outraged, and they "abhorred the offering of the Lord." What hope could there be of respect being paid to piety and justice in the community, when at the very centre of the religious life of the people was displayed such gross contempt of the Law? Like priest, like people. The iniquity of the leaders was reflected in the conduct of those who looked to them for guidance. We see the depth of degradation to which the Israelites had sunk in the terrible narratives contained in the last chapters of the Book of Judges. Such harrowing incidents are the natural result of the impiety and immorality of the ministers of the sanctuary. To their other sins these priests added shameful licentiousness. They introduced into this holy place the vices of obscene heathen worship; and Shiloh saw its glades and woods defiled with the foulest exhibitions of lust and sensuality. The licensed unchastity which commonly was associated with idol worship, and which had often proved a temptation to Israel, was openly practised by these unworthy priests of the Lord, who scrupled not to lead astray the very women who were dedicated to Divine service. Their debaucheries found another opportunity for indulgence in the joyful season of the vintage, when the maidens assembled together with singing and dancing. This happy festival they darkened by their vices. Now these crimes were committed openly. There were two parties in Israel at this time. The lawless, godless part of the community followed the example of these irreclaimable youths, and emulated their license. But there were still some who feared the Lord, and clung to the good old ways of obedience and reverence. These were thoroughly scandalized at the abuses which went on unchecked in the very sanctuary. They come to Eli as the representative of law and religion; they narrate with righteous anger the evil conduct of his sons; they demand from him the condemnation of these practices and the punishment of the offenders. But their remonstrances have little effect. Always cold and apathetic, Eli in his old age is more than ever averse from action, and disposed to let things take their course without troubling himself overmuch. He satisfies himself with a few words of warning addressed to his sons, but takes no steps to repress the wickedness which was brought to his notice. "Why do ye such things?" he says, and his hoary head and trembling voice added emphasis to his words; "I hear of your evil dealings from all this people. Nay, my sons; for it is no good report that I hear: ye make the Lord's people to transgress and to cease from worshipping before His house."[1] And then he quotes an ancient proverb which might well admonish them of their danger in thus profaning holy things:

"If one man sin against another, God shall judge him;
But if a man sin against the Lord, who shall act as judge for him?"

That is, in the case of wrong between man and man, God, as arbitrator, settles the dispute through the regular judicial authorities; but when a man sins against God, what power can interpose? The dispute can be settled only by the verdict being given against the offender, followed by his punishment at the Lord's hand.[2] This remonstrance, which indeed took but low

[1] 1 Sam. ii. 24, combining the Sept. and Syr. reading with the Hebrew.
[2] The proverb is obscure, but the interpretation given as above by Keil and Dean Payne Smith seems most reasonable.

ground, and was little calculated to touch the conscience of these hardened sinners, had no effect. They had reached that terrible condition when the Holy Spirit is withdrawn, and the sinner is left to himself, and judicially blinded. "They hearkened not unto the voice of their father, because the Lord would slay them." Sin works out its own punishment by the will of God; it hardens the heart, deafens the conscience, kills faith, drags down ever to lower depths, makes repentance, except by miracle, impossible. These are its natural consequences; but they are in accordance with God's eternal purpose, in due subjection to His moral government of the world. Eli's sons had grown up in a degenerate age, and had let the evil tendencies around them influence their lives and characters, while they themselves in turn gave a fresh impulse to lawlessness and profligacy. It may have been, according to the mysterious law of *hereditariness*, that the character of some evil ancestor was reproduced in them, and had not been modified by careful training. A mother's tender guidance and sympathy had perhaps been wanting; the father's weak good nature had been unable to control these turbulent spirits; official duties may have occupied the judge's time and thoughts; he had omitted to attend duly to his domestic duties, had not watched the bent of his sons' minds, nor selected their companions, nor checked the first beginnings of evil. If this were so, what wonder that they turned out sensual, godless, and, acting as priests to a God whom they knew not, in whom they had no faith, brought discredit upon religion and ensured their own condemnation? It was indeed necessary that some serious check should be put upon this evil state of things. There was no hope of improving the material condition of Israel without a corresponding improvement in religion. Reverence had died out, the natural tendency to imitate the worship and belief of surrounding nations was strengthened, and the power of defending themselves against enemies was impaired. Such consequences resulted from the example of wickedness set in high places.

Eli himself had not been left without warning. A man of God, a prophet, had suddenly appeared soon after Samuel's dedication, and before the wickedness of Hophni and Phinehas had become inveterate and hopeless, and sternly denounced the father's weakness, and foretold the judgment of God upon himself and his house. And thus this unknown visitant spake: "Thus saith the Lord, Did I reveal Myself unto the house of thy father, Aaron, when they were in Egypt in bondage at the house of Pharaoh? And did I choose him out of all the tribes of Israel to be My priest, to go up unto My altar, to burn incense, to wear the ephod before Me? And did I give unto the house of thy father all the offerings of the children of Israel made by fire? Wherefore kick ye at My sacrifice and at My meat-offering, which I have commanded in My habitation; and honourest thy sons above Me, to fatten yourselves with the chiefest of all the offerings of Israel My people? Therefore the Lord, the God of Israel, saith, I said indeed that thy house, and the house of thy father, should walk before Me for ever; but now the Lord saith, This be far from Me! for them that honour Me I will honour, and they that despise Me shall be lightly esteemed. Behold, the days come, that I will cut off thine arm, and the arm of thy father's house, that there shall not be an old man in thine house. And thou shalt behold the affliction of My habitation [1] in all the wealth which God shall give Israel; and there shall not be an old man in thine house for ever. Yet will I not cut off every man of thine from My altar, to consume thine eyes and to grieve thy heart;[2] and the majority of thy house shall die as men in the flower of their age. And this shall be the sign unto thee, that shall come upon thy two sons, on Hophni and Phinehas: in one day they shall die both of them." Thus far the man of God had announced woe and punishment to the house of Eli; now he rises to a higher strain, and foretells the rise of a faithful priest in exchange for the present evil ministers. The terms of this prophecy are very remarkable, and have not only an immediate, but a future and final fulfilment. "I will raise Me up a faithful priest, that shall do according to that which is in My heart and in My soul; and I will build him a sure house; and he shall walk before Mine Anointed for ever. And it shall come to pass that every one

[1] So the R.V. Dr. Payne Smith translates: "narrowness of habitation," and explains this to mean distress, especially in domestic relations. Most commentators consider that the "habitation" signifies the tabernacle, the affliction of which, in the loss of the ark and the ruin of Shiloh, the priest should see, amid all the blessings which the people experienced.

[2] This is the marginal rendering of R. V., and is that adopted by Keil and Dean Smith. It implies that there shall always be some one of Eli's family serving at the altar, though in an inferior capacity.

that is left in thine house shall come and bow down to him for a piece of silver,[1] and shall say, Put me, I pray thee, into one of the priests' offices, that I may eat a morsel of bread." The primary fulfilment of this prophecy is found in the life and office of Samuel; thus early was he designated as "the faithful priest." It is true that he was not of the family of Aaron, but we find him continually discharging the sacerdotal office; and, as far as can be read in our Books, the regular priesthood seems to have been in abeyance for some fifty years after the destruction of Shiloh and its inhabitants which we shall soon have to narrate. There is no mention of an Aaronic priest from Eli's time till we come to Ahiah, his great-grandson in the days of Saul (1 Sam. xiv. 3). During this interval the regular and ordained ministrations were suspended, and Samuel, by special commission from God, supplied their place. To this extraordinary delegation of duty the prophet refers in the text. A further, but inferior, fulfilment of the prophecy is found in the substitution of the house of Zadok for that of Eli on the deposition of Abiathar (1 Kings ii. 27, 35), when Zadok became sole high-priest and transmitted the office to his descendants. For he was of the house of Eleazar, not of Ithamar, as Eli was, and arrived at the chief dignity both by force of character and by reason of the substantial service which he rendered to the State as a staunch supporter of David, and able to lead a powerful contingent to his assistance (1 Chron. xii. 26–28). He may truly be called "a faithful priest." But who does not see that a greater than Samuel or Zadok is here? The terms used are larger, the promises grander, than any earthly personage could satisfy. The mere removal of the presidency from one line to another more worthy, the narrowing of the everlasting priesthood promised to the first Phinehas (Num. xxv. 12, 13) to one eminently faithful representative, could hardly have been expressed in such glowing words. We must look further, and see, as the Jews themselves were meant to see, a grander future, a Divine Samuel, a Priest who has superseded the Aaronic dynasty, even the Messiah, who "abideth a Priest for ever."

[1] Dr. Briggs ("Messianic Prophecy," p. 122) considers the words "and a loaf of bread," found in the Massoretic text, an interpolation. They are "not in the LXX., disturb the rhythm, make the line too long, and are a premature statement of that which comes appropriately in the climax of the last line."

Here again we may note that the prophet, as Hannah in her Hymn, has in view the existence of the kingly power in Israel. The faithful priest is to walk before the Lord's Anointed for ever. If this announcement meant primarily that Samuel and his successors should preside over spiritual matters in a State governed by a consecrated monarch, without doubt it also pointed to the Messiah in whom the regal and sacerdotal offices were united.

The fulfilment of some portion of this denunciation will be narrated in the next chapter. For if, as is mostly the case, God's threatenings are conditioned by man's acceptance or rejection of them, the warning in this case was unheeded; Eli's apathy and his sons' continued iniquity brought a sure result.

> . . . "The sovereign Lord of souls
> Stores in the dungeon of His boundless realm
> Each bolt, that o'er the sinner vainly rolls,
> With gathered wrath the reprobate to whelm."[2]

---

[2] Keble, "Christian Year," Second Sunday in Lent.

CHAPTER II.

FIRST REVELATION TO SAMUEL. CAPTURE AND RESTORATION OF THE ARK.

Life of Samuel at Shiloh—The doom of Eli revealed to Samuel—Samuel accredited as Prophet; meaning of the term—Condition of Israel and need of reformation—Oppression by the Philistines—Rebellion of Israelites—Battle of Aphek—Defeat of Israelites—Capture of the Ark—Death of Eli—Tabernacle removed to Nob—Shiloh destroyed—The Ark taken to Ashdod—Dagon—Philistines plagued—Ark sent to Gath; to Ekron—Divination—Propitiatory offerings—Ark returned to Israelites at Bethshemesh; placed at Kirjath-Jearim.

WHILE the evil priests were filling up the measure of their iniquity, and the mutterings of the coming storm that was to overthrow Eli and his house were heard in the distance, the child Samuel ministered before the Lord. Like some sweet refrain in a gloomy poem, like a soft strain in some tempestuous piece of music, the notices of the early life of this holy boy break in upon the narrative of vice and weakness. In sharpest contrast stand forth pure devotion and unbridled licentiousness, the life of holiness and the life of shame. Lower and lower in degradation sank the wicked ministers; but, like the great and perfect pattern of holy childhood, "the child Samuel grew on, and was in favour both with the Lord, and also with men."[1] If he was not spared the sight of vice, the care of Eli secured him from contamination, and his own inward purity, fortified by the grace of God, repelled all evil influences. Hophni and Phineas, in their priestly robes, profaned the worship of the Lord whose ministers they professed to be; Samuel, in his little white ephod,

[1] 1 Sam. ii. 26; Luke ii. 52.

FIRST REVELATION TO SAMUEL.

served the Lord purely and reverently. The former were blindly hastening to their awful doom; the latter was preparing himself for the great career that lay before him. Familiarity with holy things bred in the one contempt of religion and practical infidelity, and in the other strengthened belief in the unseen and increased true devotion. Thus, under Eli's eye, Samuel grew up "before the Lord," living as in His presence, with the thought never forgotten of Him that dwelt between the cherubim, docile, obedient, gentle, feeling his dedication to the Lord, and ratifying it by daily life and conduct.

So passed twelve years;[1] and then, as in the life of our Blessed Lord at the same age, came a change. In the general degeneracy of the times the prophetic spirit had long been little heard. Ehud had acted as one who had a word of God to announce,[2] Deborah had celebrated her great victory with a prophetic ode, Hannah had sung of Christ, and a man of God once and again had come with a stern message of warning; but "the word of the Lord was precious in those days, there was no open vision." It was but rarely that the Lord spake by the Prophets. The prophetic utterance which had been promised as the exponent of the will of heaven[3] was restrained by the unbelief and disobedience of the people, even as it is said of Christ (Matt. xiii. 58): "He did not many mighty works there because of their unbelief." There was no special order of inspired men to promulgate the decrees of God; the sins of the community had contracted and impeded Divine revelation, and such manifestations as had been vouchsafed to Abraham and Moses and Joshua were known no longer. This long silence was now to be broken; and the recipient of the new communication was this pious child, the unstained Nazirite, Samuel. He was good and pure and holy, and his heart and conscience recognized the presence and the power of God; but of Him as a personal God, as one who reveals His will by external signs, who gives commands and warnings and directions in some other fashion than by secret influence on the mind, he as yet knew nothing. He was a fit instrument to receive further light, and to be called to a higher service. Hitherto his work had been divided between the care of the sanctuary in such offices as were in his power, and attention to the aged priest Eli, whose dim-

[1] Josephus, "Antiq." v. 10. 4. [2] Judg. iii. 20.
[3] Deut. xviii. 15 ff.

ness of sight and increasing infirmities rendered him largely
dependent upon others' help. He had, for instance, to close
and open the doors of the Tabernacle, and to light the seven-
branched candelabrum, which stood on the south side of the
Holy Place, to the left of the entrance, and opposite the table of
shewbread. The lamps in this candelabrum were lighted every
evening, and extinguished, trimmed afresh, and supplied with
pure olive oil every morning. The High Priest slept in a
chamber adjoining the Tabernacle, and Samuel had his resting-
place near at hand, so as to be within call if his infirm friend
needed anything at night. One night, as the boy lay on his
little bed, and the morning was about to break, he was awakened
by a voice which called him by name. Thinking that Eli wanted
him, he rose immediately and went to him, eager to do him
service. But the voice was not Eli's, and the old man sent him
back to his chamber. A second time the same thing happened,
with the same result. But when the circumstance occurred a
third time, and a voice, which only Samuel heard, again cried,
"Samuel," Eli saw that the matter was supernatural. He had
not lost his faith in the Lord's providential care; though he
himself was not receptive of Divine revelation, he knew that
others might be more largely blessed. No petty jealousy troubles
the good old man; he perceives that heaven is communicating
with his holy foster-child; and he bids him go and lie down
again in patient expectation, and, if the mysterious voice once
more came to his ears, to answer and say, "Speak, Lord; for
Thy servant heareth." And, as the boy waited in awe for what
was to follow, not a voice alone was heard saying, "Samuel,
Samuel," but a vision, some objective presence, offered itself;
"the Lord came and stood." This was not a dream, not something seen as by a prophet rapt in a state of ecstasy, but a sight
that was presented to his waking faculties, either the Angel of
the Presence who had appeared to the Patriarchs, or the glory
of the Lord that Moses had beheld on Sinai, and which rested
on the mercy-seat in the Tabernacle. From out of this mysterious Something proceeded the call; and when Samuel answered
humbly in the words which Eli had put into his mouth, the Lord
then announced the message which He willed to make known
through this new interpreter. What was the message? One of
woe, of ruin, to that gentle and kind master whom the boy had
loved with a son's devotion, whom he had invested with all the

qualities which were required in his high office. What astonishment and pain filled his soul as he listened to the stern denunciation uttered by the voice Divine in the silence of that memorable night! "Behold," was the word, "I do a thing in Israel, the which whosoever heareth both his ears shall tingle. In that day I will perform against Eli all that I have spoken concerning his house, from the beginning even unto the end. For I have told him that I will judge his house for ever, for the iniquity which he knew, because his sons did bring a curse upon themselves, and he restrained them not. And therefore I have sworn unto the house of Eli that the iniquity of Eli's house shall not be expiated with sacrifice nor offering for ever." Here was a terrible secret confided to an inexperienced child! Why was it entrusted to him? What should he do with it? Doubtless the revelation was an honour and a glory, but it was freighted with trouble and anxiety. The call had ended his childhood. Henceforth he was to know care, responsibility, anxious forethought. And now his holy training comes to his aid. What God does must be right. As he lay and pondered till the morning, he saw somewhat of the course that lay before him; he had a stern duty to discharge in the present, he had a mighty destiny in the future. But daily offices were not be neglected, whatever might be the momentous change in feeling and circumstance. At the usual hour, wearied though he was with the excitement and wonder of the vision, he rose, and opened the doors of the sanctuary, and ministered to his foster-father with his wonted tenderness. But he said nothing of what had happened; he feared to inflict a wound on the old man whom he loved and reverenced. He was new to the prophet's office, and could not at once bring himself to announce that which he felt would cause pain and anguish to the hearer. But Eli's conscience was uneasy. He saw that something which he ought to know was being hidden from him. Certain that the Lord had in some way made a revelation to Samuel, he had a consciousness that the revelation concerned himself, and he could not rest till it was fully communicated. "I pray thee," he entreats of the young seer, "hide it not from me. God do so to thee and more also, if thou hide anything from me of all the things that He spake unto thee." Thus adjured, Samuel told him all. And Eli listened in silence. The message that had been delivered by the man of God with its definite details of severest punishment had given opportunity of repentance, but it had been disregarded or used to little purpose. This fresh denunciation, confirming former threats by the mouth of the child-prophet, awoke no pungent regret in Eli's heart, startled him not out of his apathetic resignation to the inevitable. "It is the Lord," he said; "let Him do what seemeth Him good." In some men's mouths such words would imply the highest faith and trust; from Eli's lips they show indeed submission to the will of God, but it is the submission of one whose calm temperament takes all things easily, and is greatly moved by no appeal. In spite of this twofold warning he makes no determined effort to reform abuses; though a timely severity and resolute measures might avert the ruin of his house, he lets matters drift on in the old groove; he has not energy sufficient to cope with the dominant evil; and with a hopeless resignation he leaves all in God's hands, preparing to bear with patience whatever might befall. Hophni and Phinehas, self-willed, obstinate, overbearing, had too long remained unchecked in their evil courses, and now had gained the upper hand over their weak father whose feeble remonstrances were utterly ineffectual. A powerful party was on their side. The idle, the dissolute, the pleasure-seeking, the free-thinking were their friends and comrades. The old priest had not the courage to set himself against public opinion; he masks inaction with the garb of endurance; and powerless, as he persuades himself, to cure, winks at the iniquity in which he is involved. "Shall I not visit for these things? saith the Lord." But the judgment was not yet to fall; a respite was given, during which Samuel passes from youth to manhood, and becomes accredited as the prophet of the Lord. As the influence and reputation of Eli waned, the fame of Samuel grew. "The Lord was with him." Grown men, the regular ministers of the sanctuary, had proved unfaithful; and the Lord raised up a new prophet in a mere child, who had shown by piety, obedience, fidelity, an aptitude for higher gifts. And these were granted to him. Gradually was the knowledge of Divine things unfolded to his perception; the preparation of his early life fitted him to receive further measures of grace. From time to time the Lord revealed Himself to the youth, by visible presence, by articulate voice, by secret inspiration, in divers manners; and often he was enabled to utter words of wisdom, rebuke, and warning. In the midst of the open corruption he stood forth, pure, upright, bold, a witness, and not a silent one, against the wickedness of his age. And all that he said had weight, because all his words were fulfilled. It was not experience, or foresight, or judgment, that guided his announcements, but the inspiration of God. Israel could not but see that this holy youth was directed by a mighty hand, and soon learned to acknowledge his influence, so that from Dan to Beersheba, from north to south, it was known that he was established as a Prophet of the Lord. Even in the anarchical and divided condition of Israel the reputation of this servant of God spread abroad, and all the pious throughout the country rejoiced, as one man, to hear that God had thus visited His people.

Now in calling Samuel a Prophet the sacred historian does not necessarily connote predictive power in the person so named. The faculty of foretelling the future was often indeed, and under certain circumstances, bestowed upon the Prophet; but it was not of the essence of his office, and made but a small part of his functions. The Prophet is the mouthpiece of God; he receives certain Divine revelations, and imparts them to his countrymen and to those unto whom his commission extends. The gifts which he receives are not for his selfish exaltation or edification, but for the good of the community. His call to the office is inward, depending on the Divine choice and his own receptivity. The Spirit of Jehovah rests upon him, gives him a message, and enables him to utter it. The counsels of the Lord are so far made known to him, and he has to publish this mystery abroad, whether the people hearken or not. The full consciousness of this inner call encourages him in the execution of the commission, elevates his moral faculties, and makes him a ready and eager recipient of further revelations. No mere soothsayer or oracle-monger, but an apostle of righteousness,[1] he reproves, rebukes, and exhorts; he enforces his lessons by reference to the past, he warns and confirms his message by foreshadowing the future. The enlightenment bestowed by the Lord enables him to take a spiritual view of things present and things to come; he sees the inner side of events of which other men note only the external circumstances, and he is thus empowered to offer wise counsel and to obviate

---

[1] Ladd, "Doctr. of Script.," i. 132.

unexpected results. But these effects are not the product of human genius or prudence or experience, but the outcome of communion with heaven and a word from God. Such was the inspiration of Samuel. And his call to the prophetic office carried other functions with it. It was this special commission which authorized him in after time, amid the degeneracy of the priesthood and its practical extinction, to offer sacrifice and to maintain the worship of Jehovah. It was no intrusion into the sacerdotal office when he performed those ministerial duties; he held an extraordinary commission from the Lord, who continued at intervals to appear to him in Shiloh. How far he was conscious at this time of the great part he had to play, we cannot tell; doubtless, the certainty dawned upon him gradually. As the revelations became more frequent and impressive, there grew up in his soul the conviction that, as a thorough reformation was needed, so he was destined to be the reformer, and to guide the important movement. A great crisis was approaching. If Israel was to retain its possessions, and take its proper position among nations, it must offer a solid front to enemies, it must be one in religion, interests, policy. Of late years matters had tended only to disintegration. No one tribe had arrived at undisputed pre-eminence; the most powerful cities were practically independent, and isolation had become the rule throughout most of the country. After the death of Joshua the government of the land was not directed by any one man, but was administered by the elders, being representatives from all the tribes and assembling at some central spot, as Shechem. Here they consulted together, and hence they sent to ask the advice of the High Priest, who alone could have recourse to the oracle of the Urim and Thummim. The importance of this latter functionary was very great, and on his character and energy the morals of the nation and the conduct of public affairs greatly depended. But when the national unity was loosened, and selfish independence took the place of patriotic feeling, the power of the elders sank into insignificance, and the decadence of religion and morality marked the fall of priestly influence. In the time of the Judges there was no longer any community of sentiment in the land; the tribes were simply self-governing bodies, which held their ground as best they could, either absorbing the native populations or repressing them with the strong hand, or in turn falling themselves into subjection to the

FIRST REVELATION TO SAMUEL.

inhabitants whom they had failed to dispossess. The mutual jealousy between some of the tribes likewise tended to relax the national unity. The disintegration was further increased by the attachment felt by each family and collection of families to their own settlements, with the private aims and interests which appertained to them. Becoming an agricultural people, Israel merged the national welfare in the security of its own individual possessions, and thought more of saving stock, crops, and produce when threatened by some local incursion than of combining to resist dangers which affected the existence of the whole nation. The Judges were dictators raised up to meet some great emergency in a particular district, and their influence was confined to this locality. When the crisis was over, they returned to their old occupations; the troops which they had commanded, and which had put themselves voluntarily under their orders, went home; and neither Judge nor people gave themselves any concern about the public welfare. The Judge had no governing or administrative authority, the people attended only to their private interests. It needed some formidable combination of perilous circumstances to unite Israel into one solid community. This crisis arrived in the days of Samuel, though it is impossible to affix to it an exact date. In the East the Ammonites held rule, and now the Philistines, for a long time quiet dwellers on the sea-coast, strengthened by fresh migrations from Crete, and eager for new conquests, had proved their superiority and were preparing to make themselves masters of the whole country. The spasmodic efforts of Samson, whose activity synchronizes with the later days of Eli, had no lasting effect, and merely checked for a time and in one locality the advance of the enemy. The Philistines had won the supremacy, and now the central Israelites, oppressed and humiliated, resolved to rise and throw off the yoke.

It has seemed to some commentators that it was by Samuel's advice that this insurrection, which proved so disastrous, was made. They suppose that the opening words of the fourth chapter ("And the word of Samuel came to all Israel"), which immediately precede the account of the conflict, imply that Samuel counselled the expedition, and was the cause of this unsuccessful war. Sanguine of the result, thirsting to restore the nation to independence, and not recognizing that a moral reformation must precede the appeal to arms, Samuel, it is thought.

urged the leaders to undertake this movement, and with mistaken zeal called them to attempt the deliverance of the people. But there is no good reason for attributing this blunder to the young prophet. The words at the beginning of the fourth chapter are to be connected with the preceding chapter, as is done in the Revised Version, and must be considered as carrying on the account of God's dealings with Samuel, and as having no immediate connection with what follows.

From the wording of the narrative in the Hebrew text ("Israel went out against the Philistines to battle"), it is implied that the Israelites were the aggressors on this occasion, and rose suddenly against their oppressors. It was an ill-advised and ill-conducted effort, and was unlikely to be crowned with success. We hear nothing of the Lord being consulted before the rising took place, nothing of prayer or sacrifice being offered as a prelude to the undertaking. Exasperated by their servile condition, and seeing in the prophetic spirit of Samuel a presumption that the Lord was visiting them, perhaps animated by the news of one of Samson's raids, and trusting entirely to the arm of the flesh, they gathered their forces, and encamped near to that spot which, in memory of a victory to be hereafter recorded, is called Ebenezer, "Stone of help." The Philistines were close at hand, posted at a place named Aphek, "Fortress." As there were many places of this name, it is difficult to fix upon the exact position of this one; but it was near Ebenezer, the site of which is carefully defined (1 Sam. vii. 12) as being between Mizpah and Shen. The former which, in the First Book of Maccabees (ch. iii. 46) under the name of Maspha, is described as situated over against Jerusalem, has been identified by Dr. Robinson [1] with Neby Samwil, a most conspicuous hill some five miles north of Jerusalem. Shen, or Ha-Shen, is probably the modern Deir Yesin, in the immediate neighbourhood. Aphek may be represented by the Wady Fukin, six miles west of Bethlehem; [2] but this seems rather too much to the south. Of the details of the battle which ensued we know nothing. Its results were momentous. First of all, the Israelites suffered a heavy defeat, leaving four thousand men dead "in the field," that is, in the open country where they had fought. This was felt to be a serious blow; and on returning to the camp the chiefs held a

---
[1] "Biblical Researches," ii. 144; ed. 1841.
[2] Henderson, "Palestine," 179.

council of war to consider the cause of the calamity and the best means of remedying it. They had time for deliberation and were in no immediate danger, as their encampment was entrenched, and their communications were still open. Neither Samuel nor Eli's sons were with them, and the deliberation lay entirely in the hands of the elders. They seem to have made sure of victory, and were utterly surprised that their enemies had prevailed. They feel that this could have happened only because God had withdrawn His help from them. How were they to secure His aid in the future? Obviously any prophet of the Lord, any pious Israelite who knew what true religion demanded, would have counselled them to atone for past neglect by repentance and confession. National apostasy should have been remedied by national penitence; but no thought of this nature crossed their mind; they never attempted to gain the favour of God by this proceeding. They had lost all real piety, and in its place had learned a fetishism, a superstitious regard for holy things, which was alien from true religion, and had no effect on heart or conscience. In place of appealing to the Lord in His covenant relation, as pledged to support them when they turned to Him with all their heart, and put away the evil from among them, they thought only of employing the symbol of Jehovah's presence as a charm or talisman. "Let us," the elders say, "let us fetch the ark of the covenant of the Lord out of Shiloh unto us, that *It* may come among us, and save us out of the hand of our enemies." They remembered how the Jordan had fled before the ark, and left a way for the people to pass over dry-shod; they remembered how the walls of Jericho had fallen down as the ark was carried round them; they recalled many a triumph won in its face; and they misused the history of these wonders to delude themselves into the idea that the Lord's presence was so inseparably united to this material symbol that He would always give success to those who possessed it, and that by putting it in jeopardy they could compel Him, as it were, to come to their rescue. But if this were so, what would become of God's moral government of the world? Were they to constrain Him to side with them without regard to their fitness for His favour? Should God sanction this trust in the externals of religion where there was no conformity to His will, no turning from unrighteousness? The histories to which they referred were true enough, but they recognized not

their real bearing, had wholly forgotten their spiritual significance. From this delusion they were rudely awakened.

The people sent to Shiloh, which was not far distant, and
bade the ministers, whose duty it was, to bring to the camp "the
ark of the covenant of the Lord of hosts which dwelleth between
the cherubim." Thus they describe the holy coffer in the
message, showing the reason why they fetched it, and what they
hoped from its presence. Here was the visible seat of the King
of Israel, and He would vindicate its inviolability. Now would
be realized the full import of the old battle-hymn which rose to
heaven when the ark was moved : "Rise up, O Lord, and let
Thine enemies be scattered, and let them that hate Thee flee
from Thee" (Num. x. 35). Duly, with all outward regard to
ordained precedent, borne by the appointed Levites, and accompanied by the two priests, Hophni and Phinehas, the holy
symbol was removed from the tabernacle and brought to the
camp near Aphek. Such a sight had never been witnessed
since the Israelites had occupied Canaan. The enthusiasm of
the people was raised to the highest pitch by its appearance ;
their superstitious feeling was highly excited ; the great talisman was in their midst, and they "shouted with a great shout,
so that the earth rang again." The Philistines heard these cries
of exultation, saw the general commotion in the hostile camp,
and sent scouts to find out what was the cause of this tumult.
And when they understood that the mysterious ark had been
brought from its sanctuary, they were struck with terror, and
their hearts sank within them. This was a superstition which
appealed forcibly to them, into which they could readily enter.
These Hebrews,[1] these strangers from a distant land, had now
among them their "mighty gods" ; who could withstand them?
These are the gods that smote the Egyptians with every sort of
plague in the wilderness. Confusing the true history, and in
their vague traditions mingling the judgments in Egypt and the
miracles in the desert, the Philistines increase their apprehension by the memory of the past. The heavenly powers had
often ere now stricken the enemies of Israel; the gods whom
the Israelites worshipped were mighty, and could not be
resisted ; where these deities were, there was victory. Of one
supreme almighty God of all the earth they had no conception.

[1] 1 Sam. iv. 6, 7.

They attributed to the Israelites a plurality of divinities owning that they had proved themselves powerful to protect their votaries, and fearing for the result in their own case It was, in their eyes, a conflict between the gods of the two nations, and they had every reason to dread the issue. But, as is often the case, their very despair inspired them with courage. Whatever might be the peril, they would not yield without a blow. Their rude nature, indeed, regarding as terrific all that was secret and not understood, might tremble lest their cherished Dagon should prove inferior in power to the symbol which had wrought such wonders in former time; but with dogged courage they resolved to put the question to the proof. In language, with which St. Paul has made us familiar in his animating address to the Corinthian Church,[1] they exhort one another to do valiantly: "Be strong, and quit yourselves like men, O ye Philistines, that ye be not servants unto the Hebrews, as they have been to you; quit yourselves like men, and fight." Thus down the ages passed the tradition of these words, remembered in connection with the momentous events that followed. For fighting with the energy of despair, the Philistines gained a complete victory; they defeated the Israelites in the field, put them to ignominious flight, stormed their camp, and slew of them thirty thousand men. In vain had the Israelites made a stand round the ark, in vain had the ministers offered their lives in its defence. Hophni and Phinehas themselves were slain according to the saying of the man of God, and the sacred ark was taken by the heathen. Never had such a calamity befallen the people since they left Egypt. That holy memorial, made expressly at the Lord's command by the hands of their great prophet, Moses, which had led them through all their wanderings in the wilderness, guided them to victory, enshrined the Presence of Jehovah, was lost. What did this fact mean? It implied that God's favour was withdrawn, that the sins of priests and people had separated between them and God, that they could no longer look to Him for help whom they had wilfully forsaken and outraged. Their glory had departed; their political independence was in jeopardy; hopeless servitude was their future destiny.

[1] 1 Cor xvi. 13.

Ill news flies apace. On the very evening of the defeat intelligence of the grievous calamity reached Shiloh. A fleet runner, a Benjamite (whom an ancient but ungrounded tradition identifies with Saul), rushed into the town with his clothes rent and with earth upon his head in token of unspeakable grief. The sight was premonitory; the tale was soon told. A cry rose up from the affrighted inhabitants, the women's shrill shriek was heard throughout the streets, mingled with the noisy demonstrations of the men's grief. The fatal news fell like a word of death upon the whole community, and the passionate sorrow found expression in tears, and cries, and groans. The aged Eli sat on his throne at the entrance of the sanctuary by the side of the way that led to the watch tower. Here, surrounded by the priests and Levites, he was waiting in deep anxiety for tidings. The account of these events is minute and graphic, written doubtless by Samuel, who was still in attendance on his aged foster-father, now completely blind, and ninety-eight years old. Eli heard the noise of the tumult in the town, and asked of some bystanders what it meant? The ark had been taken from its abiding place, if not without his consent, certainly against his better judgment, and without the express command of God. He knew better than to put trust in the lifeless symbol; he was conscious that the sins of priests and people had forfeited God's favour, and he trembled to hear the result of the conflict. The messenger came up to him. The blind old man could not see the rent garment and the ashes on the head, the fixed stare of his sightless eyes was unaffected by light, but he asked to hear the woful news. The answer gave him his death-blow. "I am he," said the Benjamite, "that came out of the army, and I fled to-day out of the army." And to Eli's anxious question, "How went the matter?" he replied with a terse and startling climax: "Israel is fled before the Philistines, and there hath been also a great slaughter among the people, and thy two sons, Hophni and Phinehas, are dead, and the ark of God is taken." It was too much. The weak old man could bear to hear of the defeat of his people; he was resigned even to his own private sorrow, the blow that deprived him of the sons loved only too well: but to hear that the sacred symbol of Jehovah's presence, entrusted to his special care, was in the hands of heathens and lost to the chosen nation, broke his heart. He was sitting on his pontifical throne, a seat with out a back, and when he heard of this last crushing calamity, he fell backwards in a deadly faint or fit, and his neck brake, and he died. Nor was this all. Another horror marked this fatal day. The news of these sad events reached the wife of Phinehas, and brought on a premature delivery. But amid the pains of childbirth one fact alone makes itself heard. Not the fall of her husband, not the sudden death of her father-in-law, absorbed her grieving soul. It was anguish to her greater than her own bereavement, more intense than the labour-throes, to know that the emblem of God's presence was carried away, the covenant broken, the Lord's face turned from His people. Bystanders cheered her in her safe deliverance; they told her of a son born to comfort her in her widowhood. She finds no solace there. She answered not, neither did she regard it. A mother's natural joy was swallowed up in grief at the national calamity. For a minute she uttered no word to the attending women; and then rousing herself, as she felt that life was leaving her, she spake her last command, and this referred to the naming of the child and her own estimate of the awful crisis. "Call him," she gasped, "call him Ichabod, No-glory, for the glory is departed from Israel." No more pathetic story is told in the sacred pages, the simple narrative touches the deepest chords of the heart, and rouses responsive sympathy. And it has another and instructive aspect; it shows that amid the gross corruption of the age, there were to be found in isolated instances true and earnest piety, and a high appreciation of the covenant with the Lord. Some still were left in Israel to mourn for the national declension, and to see that the only safety was in holding fast by God. The wife of this iniquitous priest, pure amid corruption, was a type of the little band of faithful patriots who preserved unshaken their faith in the covenant Lord and endeavoured to carry out His requirements.

When the funeral obsequies of Eli and the wife of Phinehas had been performed, and the consternation had somewhat subsided, it was judged expedient to take measures for the security of the Tabernacle, and the furniture and ornaments appertaining thereto. The ark, indeed, was lost; but there were left many valuable adjuncts which were endeared by consecration, antiquity, and memorial use. Such were the hangings and curtains, the great brazen altar of sacrifice which had been made in the wilderness, the altar of incense, the laver, the table of shewbread, the golden candlestick. Besides these, there were minor articles of great price used in the service of the sanctuary; there were priests' vestments, musical instruments, and written records. It was necessary that all these things should be immediately conveyed to a place of safety before the Philistines reached Shiloh. That they would pursue their advantage seemed highly probable, and it was only wise to take proper precautions. What part the young Samuel, now about twenty years of age, played in these proceedings we know not. Too young to take the leadership, he doubtless offered his divinely-guided advice, and assisted with all his energy in executing the plan suggested. The Tabernacle, with all its fittings and the national records which were stored up there, was removed to some neighbouring spot where it would be secure from molestation. If danger threatened it was again taken away, and after various changes it was finally settled at Nob, a spot in the immediate vicinity of Jerusalem, by some[1] identified with the northern summit of Mount Olivet, by others[2] with the Mizpah in Benjamin, whither, in later times, Samuel convened an assembly of the people. Here it is found, many years later, in the days of Saul (1 Sam. xxi. 1). In losing the ark it was deprived of its chief glory, and was no longer regarded as the only locality where sacrifice could lawfully be offered. In abnormal times strict rules are relaxed; nor does God so bind men to an exact obedience of ritual ordinances that they cannot claim His promises unless they carry out impracticable directions. Other spots were holy; altars were raised in Ramah, Mizpah, Gilgal; but where the Tabernacle was pitched a certain portion of the priesthood made their abode, and maintained a mutilated worship, shorn indeed of its chief honour, yet existing as a kind of protest against profanity and forgetfulness of God. Separated from that which it was intended to enshrine, it never again attained to aught but a traditional sanctity, and the awfulness that surrounded it was rather historical than actual.

The Tabernacle was no sooner removed, and with its ministers concealed in some place of safety, than the threatened storm burst. The Philistines, elated with their unexpected success, and convinced that their gods were more powerful than those of

[1] Stanley, "Sinai and Palestine," 187.
[2] Conder, "Memoirs," iii. 151. "Palestine Quarterly Statement," 1875, p. 37.

CAPTURE AND RESTORATION OF THE ARK. 43

Israel, marched at once upon Shiloh. No defence was offered. Disheartened and dispersed the Israelites attempted no resistance. Though the sacred historian gives no particulars of the onslaught, we know from incidental references that the town was plundered and demolished, and the inhabitants, young and old, were cruelly butchered. The terrible destruction that then befell Shiloh was never forgotten, and long served to point a moral. "Go ye now," cries Jeremiah (chap. vii. 12), "unto My place which was in Shiloh, where I caused My name to dwell at the first, and see what I did to it for the wickedness of My people Israel." And the Psalmist, referring to Israel's defection and the calamities consequent thereupon, says :

> "When God heard this, He was wroth,
> And greatly abhorred Israel :
> So that He forsook the tabernacle of Shiloh,
> The tent which He pitched among men ;
> And delivered His strength into captivity,
> And His glory into the adversary's hand.
> He gave His people over also unto the sword,
> And was wroth with His inheritance.
> Fire devoured their young men ;
> And their maidens were not praised in the marriage song.
> Their priests fell by the sword,
> And their widows made no lamentation." [1]

The silence of desolation brooded over the place once vocal with the praises of Jehovah and cheerful with the hum of thronging multitudes. In those deserted streets the nuptial song was heard no more, and the funeral wail was not uplifted. The stillness of the grave was there. From its ruins it never rose again to any importance, so that it was passed over by Jeroboam when he was selecting his idolatrous sanctuaries.

Such was the fate of Shiloh ; what had become of the Ark? [2] It was the prize of the victors ; what would they do with it ? How would they treat it ? In the eyes of these idolaters there had been a trial of strength between the heavenly powers which

---

[1] Psa. lxxviii. 59 ff.

[2] According to neologian critics, who are free from reverent prejudices, and are wiser than the sacred writers, the ark was a wooden box containing a meteoric stone, which was supposed to be the symbol of Jehovah's presence.

supported either side. They had taken their gods with them to battle, and the Israelites had opposed to them their own divinities. The result had proved the superiority of the local gods, and Israel, as they believed, was deprived of heavenly protection. Now, eager to secure the fruits of their victory and to dispose of their plunder, they withdrew their forces, and with exultation and triumph they carried the ark from the battle-field of Aphek to the great city Ashdod, or Azotus, as it is called in Acts viii. 40. This was one of the five chief towns of their country. It lay on the sea coast in those days, though its modern representative, Esdud, owing to the encroachment of the sand, is now three miles from the shore, and bids fair to be entirely overwhelmed in a few years' time. It is situated on a low circular hill, a little south of west from Jerusalem, from which it is some thirty miles distant. The strength of its position is denoted by its name, which means "the mighty," and is confirmed by the resistance which it offered to Psammetichus, king of Egypt, B.C. 635, who besieged it unsuccessfully for twenty-nine years.[1] The presiding deity of this city was Dagon, who was worshipped by the Philistines as the emblem of fertility, or the generative power, as the Canaanites adored in Baal the same force. He is represented in his images as having the head and arms of a man with the body of a fish. Inscriptions, dating from 2000 B.C., containing his name, have been found at Ur. From Babylon his worship spread into other parts of Asia; in Assyria he was adored as the Fish-god, and the priests devoted to his service wore garments made of fish-skins. In one of his inscriptions Nebuchadnezzar mentions that he dedicated some ornaments for a temple of Dagon.[2] Such a divinity may have been connected with maritime enterprise, and would naturally be honoured in a maritime city as Ashdod. His wife was Atergatis or Derketo, who by some is identified with Astarte, and who had a temple at Askelon.[3] Regarding the late victory as the triumph of their tutelary deity, the Philistines desired to mark this great fact by some plain exhibition; so, to show the inferiority of Jehovah, and to make the God of the Hebrews pay homage to their god, they placed the ark in the temple of Dagon Such a custom was not unknown among the Assyrians.

---

[1] Herod. ii. 157.   [2] Rodwell, "Records of the Past," v. 117.
[3] Schrader, "Keilinsch." 85, 86; Vigouroux, "La Bible et les découv mod." iii. 427, ed. 4; 2 Macc. xii. 26.

CAPTURE AND RESTORATION OF THE ARK. 45

Thus, Tiglath-Pileser I., who reigned about this time and extended his conquests from Babylon to Lebanon and the Mediterranean, mentions in his records how he carried off as trophies from Kirhi and other districts in the north twenty-five images of the gods, which he placed in the temple of Sala, the wife of Assur. He adds: "I have dedicated them to the gods of my country, to Anu, Bir, and Istar, in my city of El-Assur."[1] Similarly, on another occasion, attributing the capture of Samson to the intervention of heaven, the Philistines brought the blind giant into Dagon's temple at Gaza to triumph over him in their idol's presence. And when Saul and his sons fell in the fatal battle of Gilboa, they sent to publish the news in the house of their idols, and put the dead king's armour in the temple of Ashtaroth.[2] In the present case matters turned out in a very different way from what the Philistines expected. They had indeed conquered Israel, but they had not vanquished Israel's Lord; and they were to have a practical proof of the nothingness of their idol; they were to suffer the greatest humiliation that could be offered. In the interests of true religion it was necessary that Jehovah should assert Himself, and that the vauntings of heathendom and its false conclusions should receive a significant check. They were to learn that Israel's Lord was above all gods; no mere local divinity, but sole monarch of heaven and earth. The sacred ark, with shouts and acclamations, is brought within the gloomy temple and placed beside the image of their god. The priests perform the customary rites, secure the doors, and leave it there for the night. On opening the doors in the morning, they behold a strange and horrifying sight. Prostrate before the ark, like a suppliant before a king, or a captive crouching at his conqueror's feet, Dagon lay. The image had fallen on its face to the earth before the holy coffer. Unwilling to accept the evil omen, and determining to see nothing supernatural in the untoward event, they endeavour to regard it as an accident. They raise Dagon from the ground, restore him to his pedestal, and secure him there. As Isaiah says (chap. xlvi. 7): "They bear him upon the shoulder, they carry him, and set him in his place, and he standeth; from his place shall he not remove: yea, one shall cry unto him, yet can he not answer, nor save him out of his

[1] Vigouroux, iii. 426.   [2] 1 Sam. xxxi. 8-10; Judg. xvi. 23, 24.

trouble." And still more appositely, Baruch (chap. vi. 27) : "They also that serve them [idols] are ashamed : for if they fall to the ground at any time, they cannot rise up again of themselves; neither, if one set them upright, can they move of themselves ; neither, if they be bowed down, can they make themselves straight." With some apprehensions which they could not disguise from themselves the priests, on the following morning, opened the doors of the temple, and beheld a new prodigy which they could no longer reckon as a mere accident. Not only was their idol again dashed to the ground before the ark, but was also horribly mutilated. The head and arms of the figure were severed from the body, and found lying on the threshold where any profane foot might tread upon them, and the only part left whole was the fish's tail with which the figure ended, as though it was meant to impress on these idolaters that their god had falsely assumed the human head, the emblem of reason, and the human hands, the emblems of activity, and now deprived of them was exhibited in his true ugliness and impotence, a mis-shapen fish.[1] How deep was the impression made by this circumstance we learn from a custom which took its rise from hence and continued to very late times. From that day forward no priest or worshipper who entered Dagon's temple would ever tread upon the door-sill, lest he should profane with his feet the place where the fragments of the god had lain.[2] Though constrained to acknowledge the discomfiture of their divinity in the presence of the superior power of Jehovah, the Philistines did not swerve from their allegiance. Dagon was their national god, and must be worshipped all the more sedulously for the misfortune that had befallen him. He, in their view, was capable of very human passions, and with petty malice might resent any slight cast upon him. The destruction of his image did not involve the abrogation of his worship or distrust in his protecting power ; what happened to his representation did not personally affect them ; they had won a great victory with his assistance ; the damage to the

---

[1] Dean Payne Smith on 1 Sam. v. 3.

[2] It is usual among commentators to refer to Zeph. i. 9 : "In that day I will punish all those that leap over the threshold," as an evidence of the permanence of the custom ; but a close consideration of the passage and its context will show that it has nothing to do with the Philistines' idolatrous practices.

CAPTURE AND RESTORATION OF THE ARK. 47

idol could easily be repaired; and if the God of Israel could do no more for His people than overthrow this image, they might rest content and satisfy themselves with their late success. Thus they reasoned in their blind and ignorant hearts. They were to have a rude awakening from their false peace, and were to feel God's power in their own persons and possessions. They removed the ark from the temple, but it carried a malign influence for them wherever it was placed. In the city the hand of the Lord was heavy upon the inhabitants, and they and their neighbours perished in great numbers. What was the plague which smote them is not clear. The word rendered "emerods" (*i.e.*, hemorrhoids) in our version means tumours or swellings, and the disease may have been ulcers or one of those loathsome skin diseases for which Egypt was notorious. Aquila translates, "cancerous sores;" Josephus, "dysentery." Herodotus recounts (i. 105) a tradition that the Scythians, having pillaged a temple of the celestial Aphrodite at Askalon, were punished by the infliction of some mysterious disease, which may possibly have been of the same nature as the one in question. The words of the Jewish historian referring to these events are these:[1] "Shortly afterwards divine Providence visited the city of Azotus and its neighbourhood with a pestilence. The people died of dysentery, a most painful disease, and one that occasioned untold agonies before they were relieved by death; for their bowels rotted, and they vomited up the victuals which they had eaten undigested and corrupted. Besides this, swarms of mice springing, as it were, out of the earth, destroyed everything that grew, sparing neither tree nor produce of any kind." The plague of mice is not distinctly mentioned here as attacking the fields of Ashdod, but the Septuagint adds the information, and the fact may be safely inferred, both from the wording of chap. v. 6, which implies that the country was made desolate by a diminution of the means of subsistence,[2] and from the expiatory offerings sent to appease the offended God of Israel, among which were included "images of the mice that mar the land." These were offered not simply as symbols of pestilence, as they are found in hieroglyphics, and are mentioned under this character by Herodotus (ii. 141), but, like the "emerods," as actually representing the plague from which the

---

[1] Josephus, "Antiq.," i. 6. 1.   [2] Keil, *in loc.*

people suffered. That this was a very serious infliction we learn from many ancient authors; modern writers also have given striking pictures of this plague. Thus, Van Lennep says:[1] "The short-tailed field-mouse, as he is called by naturalists, abounds throughout Western Asia, and must be endowed with great powers of increase, for he has many enemies. The owl is after him by night, and by day the hawk, with other birds of prey, flutters in the sky, and comes down with a swoop, and carries him off to his nest, while the indefatigable little ferret creeps into his hole, successfully encountering him, and destroying his little ones; yet he seems in nowise diminished. You see him in all the arable lands, running across the fields, industriously carrying off the grain to stow it away for the winter, chirping gaily from time to time, sitting up on his haunches to get a good sight of you as you approach, and then suddenly diving into his hole. This animal is apt so greatly to multiply as at times to cause a sensible diminution of the crops, and its ravages are more generally dreaded than those of the mole. A perfectly trustworthy friend has informed us that in 1863, being on the farm of an acquaintance in Western Asia Minor, he saw about noon the depredations committed by an immense number of these mice, which passed over the ground like an army of young locusts. Fields of standing corn and barley disappeared in an incredibly short space of time; and as for vines and mulberry trees, they were gnawed at the roots and speedily prostrated. The annual produce of a farm, of one hundred and fifty acres, which promised to be unusually large, was then utterly consumed; and the neighbouring farms suffered equally."

Connecting the calamities that had befallen them with the presence of the ark, and feeling the hand of Jehovah upon them, the Ashdodites are eager to get rid of this mysterious talisman, and thus to free themselves from its evil powers. They are emphatic in their determination. "The ark of the God of Israel shall not abide with us," they cry; "for His hand is sore upon us and upon Dagon our god." But this national trophy could not be so easily disposed of. The government of Philistia was in the hands of a federal council, composed of the head of each of the five confederate cities.

[1] "Bible Lands and Customs." 285.

CAPTURE AND RESTORATION OF THE ARK.

Nothing could be done without their sanction. The Ashdodites lay their case before these lords, at the same time expressing their decision no longer to harbour this pestiferous symbol. The lords unwilling to believe what the people suggested, and very loath to part with this significant token of victory, resolve to temporize. Either the ark was in no way connected with the present distress, or the Ashdodites were themselves for some reason especially hateful to Jehovah, or the god of that locality was weaker than the god of Israel. Under different circumstances, and in another place, these untoward events would not happen. So they sent the ark to Gath where there was no temple of Dagon. This famous city lay about twelve miles south-east of Ashdod, and therefore nearer to the confines of Israel. Its actual site is still undetermined. Dr. Thomson[1] places it at Beit Jibrin, which he considers to be the ancient Eleutheropolis, near to which are some heaps of ancient rubbish now called Khurbet Get, "ruins of Gath." Dr. Porter, followed by the Palestine Exploration "Memoirs,"[2] identifies it with the remarkable conical hill named Tell es Sâfi, which guards the entrance of the valley of Elah, and must have been a place of importance at all times. Rising in isolated grandeur from the valley, this hill forms a natural fortress, which is inaccessible on the north and west, where it presents a white precipice of many hundred feet in height, and is capable of easy defence on the other sides. To this city the ark was conveyed in the hope of breaking the spell which had seemed too potent at Ashdod. But the same disasters accompanied it still. The inhabitants were immediately afflicted with a loathsome disease, and perished in great numbers.

> "He smote His adversaries backwards;
> He put them to a perpetual reproach" (Psa. lxxviii. 66).

Still untaught by bitter experience, the Philistines pass on the ark to a third of their confederate cities, Ekron, some twelve miles north-east of Ashdod, and nine from the sea. This place, now called Akir (" barren "), is thus mentioned by Dr. Robinson :[3] Akir lies on the rise of land on the north-

[1] "Land and Book," 564.
[2] Pp 415, 416. Dr. Geikie, "Holy Land and Bible," thinks the identification with Tell es Sâfi probable, vol. i. 118.
[3] "Researches," iii. 23.

western side of the Wady Rubin, and as we drew near, the path led through well-tilled gardens and fields of the richest soil, all upon the low tract, covered with vegetables and fruits of great variety and high perfection. . . . That city was the northernmost of the five cities of the lords of the Philistines, and was situated upon the northern border of Judah ; while the other four cities lay within the territory of that tribe (Josh. xiii. 3 ; xv. 11, 47). Eusebius and Jerome describe it as a village of Jews between Azotus and Jamnia (Yebna) towards the east ; that is to say, to the eastward of a right line between those places ; and such is the actual position of Akir relative to Esdud and Yebna at the present day." Located at Ekron, the ark was more pernicious to the inhabitants than even at Ashdod and Gath. The worshippers of Baalzebub[1] fared worse than the worshippers of Dagon ; every fresh removal brought augmented penalties on the hapless natives. It was only natural that the Ekronites should protest against the presence of this fatal gift, and cry in dismay : "They have brought about the ark of the God of Israel to us, to slay us and our people." They were clamorous that it should be sent away, convinced that it was connected with or the cause of their plague. So they urged the lords to convene a council, and to consider how best to get rid of the pest, and to remit it to its own place ; " for there was deadly dismay throughout all the city ; the hand of God was very heavy there. And the men that died not were smitten with emerods ; and the cry of the city went up to heaven." Yet in spite of these adverse circumstances, the princes were very loath to lose the great trophy of their victory, and thus virtually to acknowledge the supremacy of Jehovah. This mysterious chest was theirs by right of conquest ; stored in their temple it was a perpetual token of triumph, and compensated for many a year of defeat and humiliation. But in face of the general protest they did not dare to retain it on their own responsibility, and most reluctantly they came to the conclusion that it must be returned to the Israelites. The only question that remained was in what manner the restoration was to be made. They therefore consulted the priests and diviners on this matter. It is plain that they knew very little about the religion of the Hebrews, and had conceived very false and un-

---

[1] See 2 Kings i. 2.

worthy notions of the God of Israel. The Jews were not a proselytizing nation, and had nothing of the missionary spirit of the Christian Church. The Philistines could live in their immediate neighbourhood for centuries, and yet be almost wholly unacquainted with their religious tenets and worship, and possess but a very inaccurate knowledge of their past history. Priests and diviners always play an important part in the solution of difficulties such as were perplexing the Philistine lords. Thus Pharaoh, astounded at the miracles of Moses and Aaron, called the wise men or sorcerers to his aid; Nebuchadnezzar, puzzled by his mysterious dream, summoned the magicians, the astrologers, the sorcerers, and the Chaldeans to reveal it to him. Three modes of divination are mentioned by Ezekiel (chap. xxi. 21, 22), and these seem to have been common to many Eastern nations, and in corrupt times to have been adopted by the Israelites from their neighbours. The first was what the Greeks called *belomantia*, divination by arrows. This was effected in various ways. Sometimes an arrow was shot into the air, and an omen was taken from the direction in which it fell; sometimes names were written on the arrows, which were then consigned to a quiver, and one of them was drawn forth by a person blindfolded. A third method is mentioned as common among the Arabian tribes:[1] In one vessel three arrows were placed; on one was written, "My god orders me;" on another, "My god forbids me;" the third was left without any inscription. They were shaken till one fell out; if it was the one first mentioned, the thing was to be done; if it was the second, the thing was to be avoided; but if it was the uninscribed arrow that came forth, the three were again shaken together till one of the others fell out. Another mode of divination was by Teraphim, images, which were supposed to give oracular responses. A third mode was the inspection of the entrails and liver of sacrificed animals. There were many other methods practised, by which guidance in a crisis or the knowledge of the future was sought to be obtained. But these need not here be described. The soothsayers, consulted on this occasion, gave an answer, which, while it claims supernatural authority for its commands, is careful to fall in with the popular feeling. They direct that the ark is to be restored to its

[1] "Speaker's Commentary" on Ezek. xxi. 21.

owners, and enforce this injunction by a reference to the past history of the Israelites : "Wherefore do ye harden your hearts, as the Egyptians and Pharaoh hardened their hearts? When He had wrought wonderfully among them, did they not let the people go, and they departed?" As if they meant to infer that more plagues were in store for them, unless they took warning by what had already happened. They add directions for the propitiation of the offended deity, whom now for the first time they recognize by His name Jehovah.[1] A trespass-offering was to be returned in acknowledgment of their guilt in originally removing the ark, if so be (which was still open to doubt) the calamities were connected therewith. The trespass-offering was to consist of articles corresponding in number to the cities and lords of the Philistines, viz., five golden "emerods" and five golden mice, figures in precious metals of the plagues which had affected their bodies and marred their fields. But the impression made upon the inhabitants was so deep and so general that they did more than was directed. Every little village sent its offering, lest any backwardness in making due reparation might be visited by some new chastisement, and the number of golden mice far exceeded the specified amount.[2] The peculiar nature of this offering was in some respects analogous to a custom widely spread among heathen nations, and adopted in the Christian Church, and practised unto this day. The custom was this : to dedicate in a temple an offering which represented or expressed a particular mercy received in answer to prayer. Instances of the practice are numerous. Thus sailors saved from shipwreck offered pictures or their garments ;[3] sufferers relieved from diseases dedicated likenesses of the diseased parts ; and Theodoret[4] mentions that Christians in the fourth century were wont to offer in their churches gold or silver hands, feet, eyes, in return for cures effected in these members in answer to prayer. The custom obtains to this day in Eastern countries.[5] These

[1] 1 Sam. vi. 2: "The ark of the LORD," *i.e.* Jehovah.
[2] 1 Sam. vi. 18.
[3] Horat., "Carm.", i. 5, 13 ff. Virg., "Æn.", xii. 766 f. Juven., "Sat.", x. 55. Cic., "De Nat. Deor.", iii. 37, 89.
[4] iv. 321, ed. Schulze.
[5] Burder, "Orient. Customs," i. 223. A curious Carthaginian monument of a religious character represents two rats with an open hand between them. See Vigouroux, iii. p. 434.

propitiatory presents were to be deposited in a coffer made for the purpose, and placed in a new cart beside the ark. It was a reverential feeling which led them to use in this service a vehicle which had never been employed for other or baser purposes. The cart itself was probably like one of the *arabas*, the only wheeled vehicles now known in these lands. These have solid wooden wheels, encircled by an iron tire, and fixed upon the axle-tree which revolves under the body of the cart.[1] In such a cart the ark and the offerings were placed, and to it two milch-cows were yoked with a special intention. Doubtless, like the new cart, the untrained kine were intended for a token of reverence, even as such animals were chosen for sacrifice as had never been put to servile uses; but there is a further meaning in the selection. By it they hoped to demonstrate whether the plagues which had smitten the people were accidental or supernatural. Such kine, for the first time submitted to the yoke, would naturally be restive and unruly; besides this, their calves were taken from them and shut up at home. It would be only natural that when left to themselves the cows would hurry back to their young ones. So the divines make the experiment, expecting that the event would show that the idea of the calamities being miraculous was groundless. If when let go, the animals followed their maternal instinct and turned to their stalls where their calves were shut up, then they would conclude that it was a chance that had happened to them; but if, on the contrary, the kine turned from their own home, and drew the cart quietly and directly towards the borders of Judah, then, in that very unlikely case, they must needs own that they were controlled by a Divine power, and that the plagues which had stricken them were sent by Jehovah. Thus they put the God of Israel to the test, and gave occasion for a display of His Providence.

The nearest Israelite town to Ekron was Bethshemesh, which lay at a distance of fifteen miles in a south-easterly direction. The name of this city means "House of the Sun," and it had been a famous shrine in Canaanitish times. It is not visible from Ekron, being hidden by an intervening swell near that place; but when once this is past, the road runs for miles straight towards and in full sight of the Judæan town. Its ruins are in

[1] Van Lennep, 79, 80.

the immediate vicinity of the modern village of Ain Shems, "The Well of the Sun," beautifully situated on the rounded point of a low ridge, having on the north the Wady Surar, and on the south a smaller wady.[1] The Wady Surar runs between Ekron and Bethshemesh, and, when Dr. Robinson visited it, was bordered by "well-tilled gardens and fields of the richest soil, all upon the low tract, covered with vegetables and fruits of great variety and high perfection." The cart with its sacred freight was brought outside the city; the kine were yoked to it, and then left to themselves to take their own course. Usually the driver walks in front of his cart; in the present case there is no driver at all; but in deference to the greatness of the occasion, and the important issue involved, the five lords follow the vehicle to mark whither it goes and what is the result of the experiment. The cows never hesitated for a moment; they took the most direct course to Bethshemesh. Not that they had forgotten their calves, for they lowed as they went; but by some controlling impulse they mastered their natural instincts and went whither the hand of God led them. Up the rough track in the fertile valley they bore their mysterious burden, the Philistine nobles following in awe, till they came to the near neighbourhood of the Hebrew city. It was now the month of May, and the whole population of Bethshemesh were in the fields gathering in the wheat-harvest. Suddenly they lifted up their eyes and saw this strange procession approaching. As they realized what it meant, a great joy filled their hearts, the work was stopped, and all with one accord, throwing away their implements, rushed to see this wonder which had come to pass; an universal shout arose; their lost treasure was restored; the Lord was still gracious to His land. Meantime the kine went steadily forward till they came to the field of one Joshua (a man who bore the name of the great leader who had brought the ark into Canaan), and stopped there of their own accord by a rock, which rose above the surface and long marked the spot hallowed by this circumstance. Bethshemesh was a priestly city, and in it dwelt priests and Levites who knew the requirements of the Law. These gladly received the sacred symbol; they took the rock for an altar, cut up the cart for fire-wood, and offered the kine for a burnt-offering to

[1] Porter, *ap.* Kitto, *sub voc.* Robinson, ii 18 ff. Geikie, i. 103 ff. Both names of the village recall the ancient worship of the sun.

the Lord who had dealt so mercifully with them. The Ekronites watched these proceedings at a distance, and then returned wondering to their own borders. Not satisfied with the one formal sacrifice, the Bethshemites testified their gladness by further offerings. By the ministry of the priests, and in the presence of the ark, which made of the place a sanctuary, they offered burnt sacrifices and thank-offerings, following up these with the usual sacrificial feast. The excesses engendered by this banqueting, together with the general rejoicing, led some of the people to forget the reverence due to the material representation of the Divine Presence. The priests had not covered the ark with the sacred veil, as the Law ordered (Numb. iv. 5, 19, 20), and they themselves, and others, had the profaneness to open the holy coffer, which even the Philistines had not dared to do, and to gaze upon its contents.[1] The Lord who had signally vindicated His honour among the heathen, would not suffer His own people to commit sacrilege with impunity. Whether they were led by unhallowed curiosity to raise the golden cover, and look on the time-honoured tables of the commandments and the other memorials of the sojourn in the wilderness, or whether they desired to see whether the Philistines had respected these relics—whatever the motive, it was a grievous sin thus to profane the symbol of Jehovah. Solemn restrictions had encompassed it from the first ; it was to be handled by the priests alone ; if a stranger looked upon it, he was to be put to death ; even the Levites themselves might not " see the holy things for an instant, lest they died."[2] Thus was taught the awful holiness of God. Swift retribution followed the act of irreverence of which the Bethshemites had been guilty. Seventy of the chief men were smitten of God and died.[3] If we are to trust

[1] The words in 1 Sam. vi. 19, translated in A. V. : " Because they had looked into the ark of the Lord," are also rendered " Because they had looked at the ark." Vulg. : " Eo quod vidissent Arcam." So the LXX. In this case the sin consisted in a curious and irreverent scrutiny. They ought to have received it with humility and penitence, not with feasting and riot, dishonouring the sacred symbol which had been removed for their sins.

[2] Numb. i. 50, 51 ; iv. 5, 16-30.

[3] The present Hebrew text has " seventy men fifty thousand men," with no conjunction between the numbers. It is quite contrary to Hebrew usage to place the smaller number first ; Josephus says that seventy were struck by lightning, and it is quite impossible that in a mere village fifty thousand persons could have fallen. The larger number is certainly an interpolation, arising from the Hebrew method of denoting numbers by letters.

the Greek version, they were the sons of one Jeconiah who were most conspicuous for want of sympathy and irreverence towards the holy symbol—" they rejoiced not among the men of Bethshemesh because they saw the ark," as it is expressed—which means, probably, that they feared its presence might bring a plague on them as it had on the Philistines, and were vexed that the people had received it so gladly; on them consequently fell the destruction. Whoever they were that perished, the death of so many in a little community was felt as a very serious and awful calamity. Their own sinfulness was brought painfully home to them; they were ready to cry with the widow of Zarephath in the presence of her great sorrow : " What have I to do with thee, O thou man of God? Art thou come unto me to call my sin into remembrance, and to slay my son?"[1] Or with St. Peter, astonied at Christ's miracle: " Depart from me, for I am a sinful man, O Lord."[2] So like the Gadarenes who besought Jesus to depart from their borders,[3] the people of Bethshemesh cast in their mind how to get rid of this terrifying witness, for they said : " Who is able to stand before Jehovah, this holy God? And to whom shall He go up from us? " Seeing in the ark the dwelling-place of Jehovah, they wish to pass it on to others. Now some five miles south-east of Bethshemesh, and standing conspicuously on its hill, some 1,000 feet higher than Ain Shems, was an Israelitish city which had once been a noted sanctuary of Baal before it came into Jewish hands. This city was Kirjath-Jearim, the " city of woods " (as we might call it Woodtown, or Wootton), not the modern Kuryet-el-Enab, " city of grapes," as Dr. Robinson supposed,[4] but identified with Khurbet Erma, " a ruin on a thickly covered ridge amongst copses and thickets of lentisk and hawthorn, to which the name *Erma* still applies, corresponding to the latest form Arim, which took the place of the original Yarim or Jearim (Ezra ii. 25).[5]

---

[1] 1 Kings xvii. 18.   [2] Luke v. 8.
[3] Matt. viii. 34.   [4] " Researches," ii. 335.
[5] To confirm this identification it is noted that " the three principal letters (ayın, resh, mem) of the name Jearim, or of the later abbreviated form Arım, occur in the proper order in the modern Arabic Erma (spelt with the guttural *ain*); the site is, moreover, surrounded and concealed by the thickets of lentisk, oak, hawthorn, and other shrubs, which properly represent the Hebrew word *garım*, from a root signifying to be ' tangled' or ' confused.' " (" Survey Memoirs," iii. 43 ff.)

CAPTURE AND RESTORATION OF THE ARK.

This ruin is distant only three miles from the great valley towards which it looks down. It lies close to the border of the lower hills and the high Judæan mountains, and it shows evidence of having been an ancient site."[1] Since Shiloh was no longer available as a refuge, the Bethshemites applied to the men of Kirjath-Jearim to relieve them of the ark which had proved to them so fatal a boon. The inhabitants of the latter place, possibly after consultation with Samuel, willingly acceded to the request; they went and fetched the ark by the ancient road still existing, which descends north of the present ruin, and leads to Bethshemesh direct along the banks of the Wady Ismain. The ark on its arrival was brought up to the house of one Abinadab, which was on the hill or high-place. Kirjath-Jearim was not a Levitical city, but Abinadab may have been a Levite. There was, however, no priest in the place, and as recent experience had shown the danger of profane treatment of holy things, Abinadab's son, Eleazar, was sanctified as keeper of the ark, that is, not with a view of his performing priestly acts or maintaining the sacrificial worship of Jehovah, which would have been plainly unlawful, but in order to guard the sacred treasure against sacrilege, and to see that due reverence was paid to it. A site was prepared for it on the hill, or the old high-place was utilized for the purpose. A late traveller,[2] who examined the spot with this identification in view, found that the rock had been cut away in the same fashion as at Shiloh. After mentioning "a bold spur running northwards from the southern ridge characterized by a small natural turret or platform of rock rising from a knoll above a group of olives, beneath which again the thickets clothed the mountains," he proceeds: "But the most curious feature of the site is the platform of rock, which has all the appearance of an ancient high-place or central shrine. The area is about fifty feet north and south, by thirty feet east and west; the surface, which appears to be artificially levelled, being some ten feet above the ground outside. The scarping of the sides seems mainly natural, but a foundation has been sunk on three sides, in which rudely-squared blocks of stone have been fitted at the base of the wall. On the east this wall consisted of rock to a height of three and a half feet, with a thickness of seven

---

[1] "Twenty-one Years' Work in the Holy Land," 115. Geikie, i. 144, 145.
[2] Captain Conder, "Quarterly Statement," Oct. 1881, p. 265. See also Geikie.

feet. There is an outer platform, about ten feet wide, traceable on the south and south-east; and a flight of steps three feet wide, each step being one foot high and one foot broad, leads up to this lower level at the south-east angles." Thus after seven months' exile among the heathen the ark again found a home in its own land; and here it remained undisturbed till many years afterwards King David removed it to Zion, about which joyful event the writer of the hundred and thirty-second Psalm sung, where, noting that in his journey from Zion to Kirjath-Jearim the king passed Rachel's tomb, he says:

" Lo, we heard of it in Ephratah;
We found it in the field of the wood." [1]

---

[1] This is an usual explanation of the verse. Messrs. Jenning and Lowe (following Gesenius and others) in their commentary take Ephratah to represent the tribe of Ephraim, in whose territory Shiloh lay, so that the passage would mean. "We heard that the ark had rested at Shiloh, but we found it eventually in the country near Kirjath-Jearim."

CHAPTER III.

SAMUEL JUDGE AND PROPHET.

Samuel's efforts at reformation—Samuel recognized as judge—Assembles the people at Mizpah—National repentance—Insurrection—Philistines defeated at Ebenezer—Effects of the victory—Theocratic government—Samuel's judicial circuit—He establishes "Schools of the Prophets"—Chronology of his life—Samuel's sons—The people demand a king—Samuel, by God's command, acquiesces in their request, but warns them of the consequences—The people persist in their demand.

THE destruction of the sanctuary at Shiloh marks an epoch in the history of the chosen people, even as the next era was closed by the overthrow of the Temple and the Holy City at the hands of the Babylonians, and the third period was consummated by the final devastation of Jerusalem by the legions of Rome. For twenty years after the victory at Aphek, Israel lay prostrate at the feet of its Philistine conquerors. These, indeed, had been constrained to restore the ark to its original possessors, but they retained their supremacy, and oppressed the Israelites in very grievous fashion. The high-priesthood was in abeyance; there was no longer any centre to which devout people might flock for the worship of the Lord; the holy ark was severed from its connection with the Tabernacle; there was danger of a collapse of all religion, and of despairing submission to the heathen yoke. But Samuel, of whom for a time we have lost sight, was raised up to meet this emergency. Samson might casually inflict crushing blows upon the enemy; might humiliate them by showing what one strong arm, fortified by an inward consciousness of Divine aid, could effect; but it needed something different from these fitful achievements to restore to Israel its forfeited ascendancy. Samuel saw that spasmodic efforts at revolt, breaking forth in separate localities at infrequent intervals, were useless, and would result only in increased oppression. He knew where the evil lay; he knew that, in the moral government of Israel, prosperity hung upon religion; that national repentance must precede national recovery; and he turned all the powers of his great mind to produce this change. Already, as we have seen, his fame as a prophet had spread throughout the land. Young as he was, the down-trodden Israelites were well inclined to listen to his counsels. The frequency of the revelations made to him was widely known, and the influence thus early obtained paved the way for the universal acknowledgment of his judgeship. The latter was the outgrowth of the prophetical office, and was by it guided and directed. We do not know whether he had taken any part in establishing the Tabernacle at Kirjath-Jearim; but it is plain that he himself then, and for twenty years afterwards, made his headquarters at his native place, Ramah. During this period he had married and become the father of two sons, whom he named respectively Joel and Abiah, "Jehovah is God" and "Jehovah is my Father," thus indeed showing his piety by the names which he gave them; though, as we shall see, they answered but ill to the holy appellations. But home ties could not keep him from his purpose. Levite, Nazirite, Prophet, he possessed every qualification for attracting respect and acting as teacher. A life of holiness and self-denial, consistent in every particular, well known to all Israel, carried with it an authority that could not but be acknowledged by every real Israelite. As Dean Stanley well says:[1] "Whatever else is lost by the absence of experience of evil, by the calm and even life which needs no repentance, this is gained. The especial work of guiding, moderating, softening, the jarring counsels of men, is for the most part the especial privilege of those who have grown up into natural strength from early beginnings of purity and goodness—of those who can humbly and thankfully look back through middle age, and youth, and childhood, with no sudden rent or breach in their pure and peaceful recollections."

For twenty weary years,[2] which carried him from youth to

---

[1] "Jewish Church," lect. xviii. vol i. p. 413.
[2] Concerning this section of the history, 1 Sam. vii. 2-17, Wellhausen

SAMUEL JUDGE AND PROPHET.

middle age, Samuel pursued his steadfast purpose. He had a great work before him, and he set himself resolutely to accomplish it. The evils which had led to the present calamities were impiety and idolatry. The people had forsaken the Lord, had revelled in wickedness, had utterly forgotten the Law of Moses; and retribution had overtaken them as a direct consequence of their sins. Throughout the Holy Land were found the images of the Philistine deities, who were worshipped now instead of, or in company with, Jehovah. In place of resorting to the priests of the Lord and the appointed sacrifices, the people set up shrines containing images of Baal and Astarte, and offered there the foul worship of their heathen conquerors. A false peace had fallen upon them, numbing their spiritual faculties, and persuading them to fall in with the ways of their idolatrous neighbours. The Philistines doubtless made it a test of submission that they should honour the victors' religion. The weakness of human nature, the laxity of morals, thus, as it were, sanctified by religion, the tendency to acquiesce in what seemed inevitable, the fear of worse suffering if opposition was attempted —all these things offered serious opposition to any change for the better; against them all Samuel had to contend. He was preeminently a man of prayer; his love of intercession was a marked feature of his character. His communing with God supported him throughout this woful period. At Ramah, where his influence was greatest, he raised an altar and performed the worship of Jehovah with such faithful Israelites as he could find to join him. Gradually he gathered a little circle of pupils and friends, and expounded to them his views and wishes and longings. Here was formed the nucleus of that prophetic school which, starting from small beginnings, continued to the end of the Jewish history, and had so marked an influence on national events and character. Steadily and warily he won his way into the hearts of his countrymen. With unwearied zeal he went up and down among them, from one end of the land to the other, reproving, rebuking, exhorting. He recalled to mind their ancient glory, infused into their hearts the long-forgotten ideas so familiar to their forefathers—the special Providence that watched over them, the favour bestowed, the guidance exer-

("History of Israel," pp. 248, 249) affirms that there cannot be a word of truth in the whole narrative, which is simply a fictitious insertion intended to express and enforce certain ideas of much later origin.

cised, the prosperity consequent upon obedience, the punishment that followed the infringement of Divine commands. Often in danger from the Philistines, who knew that conversion to Jehovah meant rebellion against themselves ; repelled and opposed by irreligious Israelites, who were content with their bondage, and did not wish to be aroused to assert their independence, Samuel continued to execute his mission ; during all these years he never swerved from his purpose, endeavouring to make Israel see its sinfulness, acknowledge the justice of its punishment, and make itself worthy of God's renewed protection by turning to Him heartily and entirely.

At length, after this long preparation, matters seemed to be ripe for a general change; the people had learned their lesson ; calamity and oppression had driven them to repentance ; they had discovered the source of their disasters and the only effectual remedy. Then Samuel, who had long worked in secret, unto whom they looked for counsel and support, suddenly appeared in public as a heaven-sent leader. Israel had "lamented after Jehovah," sorrowed for its past transgressions, and again sought the Lord, and could now trust in the Divine help. So no longer by private remonstrance or secret exhortation, but openly Samuel stands forth to show the way of reformation. One condition only he insists upon as a token of contrition ; they must openly renounce idolatry, and be prepared to endure the consequences of such proceeding. " If," he proclaims, " if ye do return unto the Lord with all your heart, then put away the strange gods and the Ashtaroth from among you, and prepare your hearts unto the Lord, and serve Him only ; and He will deliver you out of the hand of the Philistines." The Israelites responded to the call ; the heart of the whole people was stirred ; as by a general impulse they tore themselves free from the debasing idolatry which had held them captive; they demolished the shrines ; they brake the idols to pieces. Such conduct was equivalent to an overt act of rebellion against their Philistine oppressors. It shows what a wonderful power Samuel exercised, how deeply his passionate appeals influenced the nation, that almost unarmed and undisciplined, with no military commander to inspire them with confidence and to lead them to victory, they provoked a contest with a foe greatly superior in equipment and force, and animated by a long series of successes. But it was no vain confidence in the arm of flesh that led them to make this

SAMUEL JUDGE AND PROPHET.

venture; and to prepare them for their solemn trial Samuel summons them to repentance and prayer. From this time forward he takes the lead. Now he convenes a general assembly at Mizpah to prepare for war by the exercise of religion. Mizpah, which means *watch-tower*, is a name given to many heights in Palestine; but the place intended here is that remarkable hill, the loftiest in Central Palestine, rising some five hundred feet above the surrounding country, and nearly three thousand above the sea level, about five miles north of Jerusalem, and now known by the name of Neby Samwil. If this is the same place as Nob, it was chosen as the scene of the great assembly, not only because of its commanding position, which rendered it safe from surprise, but because the Tabernacle was settled there. It is remarkable that on the summit of this hill, as at Shiloh and Kirjath-Jearim, there is a level platform some five or six feet high cut out of the rock, whereon, doubtless, some kind of building was erected to receive the sacred tent. "The view from this place, which is usually identified with Mizpah, is extensive. It includes Mount Gerizim, and the promontory of Carmel to the north; Jaffa, Ramleh, and a wide stretch of the maritime plain to the west; Jebel Furaydis (the so-called Frank Mountain), the far-distant mountains of Jebal, the town of Kerak, Jebel Shihan (the highest point in Israel), are seen to the south and south-east; the continuation of the trans-Jordanic plateau, with slightly undulating outline, stretches to the east and north-east."[1] In atonement for the past, and in dedication for the future, under Samuel's instruction, the people performed two solemn ceremonies. First, they fasted, as the Law enjoined on the great day of atonement, confessing their sins, and afflicting their soul, and humbling themselves before Jehovah. This general fast was accompanied by another rite, not mentioned heretofore, but practised by immemorial usage at the Feast of Tabernacles. "They drew water," it is said, "and poured it out before the Lord." In later time it was the custom on each of the seven days that the feast lasted for the priests to go forth from the Temple, accompanied by the Levite choir, unto the spring of Siloah, and to bring thence water in a golden vessel to be poured out at the altar as a libation at the time of the morning sacrifice.[2] Was this ceremony so long maintained, and so often

---
[1] "Quarterly Statement," 1872, p 174; "Survey Memoirs," iii. 43 ff.
[2] Comp. Isa. xii. 3, John vii. 37, 38.

mentioned by Rabbinical writers, in memory of this great national conversion, a commemoration of the reconciliation of the estranged people? It is probable that it was at this feast, and the fast which preceded it, that Samuel assembled the people. It is noteworthy,[1] that after the return from Babylon, this Feast of Tabernacles was solemnly kept by the whole congregation (Ezra iii. 4-6); and again in Nehemiah's time, when the people assembled to hear the Law read, it was at the same feast; so that it seems that this festival was regarded as the fittest occasion for making a great national demonstration or inaugurating a national movement. The pouring out of water has been variously interpreted. As used in the Temple service it was a memorial of the water from the smitten rock, and a type of the effusion of the Holy Spirit. On the particular occasion here referred to, it has been explained in connection with the accompanying fast as denoting self-denial, as David refused to drink the water from the well of Bethlehem, but poured it out before the Lord (2 Sam. xxii. 16); others see in it a token of repentance, a total renunciation of sin, the water being, as it were, a symbol of tears; or being poured on the earth it figuratively washed the land from the stain of idolatry; or it represented their abject condition and helplessness, that they were as water spilt on the ground, which cannot be gathered up again.[2]

Samuel had collected the assembly, acting in his capacity as prophet; henceforward he was to exercise another office. The people recognized his authority; they saw in him one who was well fitted to be their ruler in things temporal, and here in full convention they by universal acclamation elected him as judge. A worthier choice could not have been made. It is true he was no warrior, no sagacious general who could lead them forth to victory having the experience of many a well-fought battle to guide him; but he was strong in prayer, strong in faith; he had the prudence of calm wisdom; he knew his countrymen thoroughly, and understood exactly how far they could be trusted, what they could be expected to effect. In his capacity as judge, he marshalled them and reduced them to discipline and order so that they might resist the attack which he foresaw. The Philistines were not slow to perceive that a formidable rebellion was preparing. The general demolition of their idols

---

[1] "Speaker's Commentary," on 1 Sam. vii. 6.
[2] Corn. a Lap. *in loc.*

and this great gathering at Mizpah were signs which they could not mistake. Prompt measures were adopted. The whole Philistine force assembled to crush the insurrection. Each city sent its contingent, and an army which seemed irresistible moved towards Mizpah. The Israelites were dismayed, but not disheartened. Samuel's confidence had inspired them with trust in the Divine protection; they remembered how at Moses' prayer Amalek had been defeated, how the Lord had fought for Israel in their fathers' times, and they determined to abide the attack, and to leave the issue to the God of armies. They fly to Samuel, they bid him, the child of prayer, the man of prayer, cry unto God to deliver them out of their enemies' hands. And Samuel at once executed his office of intercessor. He raised that piercing cry to heaven which had often been heard among them; and he took a sucking-lamb and offered it as a whole burnt-offering to the Lord. This he could do, though not of Aaron's family; for he was an extraordinary priest, specially commissioned to supply the place of the regular ministry in the present abnormal state of affairs. God appoints certain means, and men are bound to use these means in the appointed way; but He does not so inseparably restrict Himself to this appointment that He never works beyond and independently of it. It is possible, as we saw above, that the Tabernacle was at Mizpah; in which case the sacrifice would have been offered in the ordained place, though not by the regular priest; but be this as it may, the prophet was delegated to rear altars and to slay victims in other spots, and to be the medium of communication with the Most High. As the smoke of the sacrificed lamb (type of the self-dedication of the afflicted people) rose to heaven, and while the loud cry of Samuel echoed through the air, the Philistine host was seen approaching, and the Israelites from their height advanced to meet the foe. Little would their half-armed and undisciplined forces have availed against the hardy warriors opposed to them. But the Lord fought for Israel. The voice of God answered the voice of the Prophet. The historian sees a Divine interposition in that which ensued. An awful thunderstorm broke over the heathen troops, filling them with dismay, and throwing them into confusion; and Samuel, like a skilful general, seizes the moment to launch his followers against them. With impetuous courage they rush down the steep; they break through the adverse line; a panic strikes the demoralized heathen host; resistance is forgotten, and the Philistines fly in abject terror before the Israelites. Jewish tradition [1] tells of another circumstance that added to the horrors of that resistless onslaught. "God disturbed their ranks with an earthquake; the ground trembled under their feet, so that there was no place whereon to stand in safety, and they either fell helpless to the earth or into some of the chasms that opened beneath them." A very great slaughter ensued. The Philistines fled down the deep valley now filled with a torrent rushing over its rocky bed, pursued by the victorious Israelites, who found themselves furnished with arms cast away by the terrified enemy. The pursuit terminated at Beth-car, now Ain Karim, "the well of the vineyards," a fortress of the Philistines, situated in a recess half way up the eastern mountains.[2] Here the small remains of the heathen host took refuge undisturbed by further attack. Long afterwards the Jews dwelt with exultation on this victory, and the son of Sirach refers to it in eulogistic strain · Samuel "called upon the mighty Lord, when his enemies pressed upon him on every side when he offered the sucking-lamb. And the Lord thundered from heaven, and with a great noise made His voice to be heard. And he destroyed the rulers of the Tyrians, and all the princes of the Philistines." [3] In memory of this great deliverance, and in view of the necessity of Divine aid in the future, Samuel set up a great stone in the plain where the defeat had taken place, and called it Ebenezer, "Help-stone," saying, "Hitherto hath the Lord helped us." This was the same spot where twenty years before the Israelites had suffered the great defeat which culminated in the capture of the ark. It is defined by the sacred historian as lying between Mizpah and Ha-Shen ("the tooth"), a sharp-pointed rock so called. This latter is identified with Deir Yesin (which preserves the name), a place three miles west of Jerusalem, and one and a half miles north of Beth-car.[4] The public erection of this memorial shows what an important reformation Samuel had effected, and what was the principle which he had impressed upon his countrymen. For ages afterwards every pious wayfarer might read the

[1] Josephus, "Antiq.", vi. 2. 2.
[2] Robinson, "Later Researches," 158; "Palestine Quarterly," 1881, p 271.
[3] Ecclus. xlvi. 16 ff.   [4] Henderson, "Palestine," 215.

guiding motive of his actions, and the ground of all national success: "Our help is in the name of the Lord, who hath made heaven and earth."

Some immediate results followed this victory. The Philistines were for a time broken, and made no fresh attack on Israel. The national spirit of the Hebrews was thoroughly aroused; they not only guarded their frontiers, but also recovered all the cities and the surrounding territories between Ekron and Gath which had been seized by the enemy in the time of their depression. The Amorites, too, in the neighbourhood of Joppa who had taken part with the Canaanites, found it to their advantage to side with Samuel, and put themselves under the protection of the Israelites.[1] "It was no mere solitary victory, this success of Israel at Ebenezer, but was the sign of a new spirit in Israel, which animated the nation during the lifetime of Samuel, and the reigns of David and Solomon and the great Hebrew kings. The petty jealousies had disappeared, and had given place to a great national desire for unity. In the several tribal districts it was no longer the glory and prosperity of Judah, Ephraim, or Benjamin, but the glory and prosperity of Israel that was aimed at. The old idol worship of Canaan, which corrupted and degraded every nationality which practised it, was in a great measure swept away from among the chosen people, while the pure religion of the Eternal of Hosts was no longer confided solely to the care and guardianship of the tribe of Levi, which had shown itself unworthy of the mighty trust. The Levites still ministered in the sanctuary, and when the Temple took its place, alone officiated in its sacred courts; and the chosen race of Aaron, in the family first of Ithamar, then of Eleazar, alone wore the jewels and the official robe of the high priest; but in religious matters the power of the priestly tribe was never again supreme in the Land of Promise. From the days of Samuel a new order—that of the Prophets, whose exact functions with regard to the ritual of the worship of the Eternal were undefined—was acknowledged by the people as the regular medium of communication with the Jewish king of Israel."[2]

The blow thus struck at the superiority of the Philistines was felt at the moment so severely that the sacred writer could say

[1] 1 Sam. vii. 14; Ewald, ii. 199.
[2] Bishop Ellicott's "Comm." on 1 Sam. vii. 13.

that, up to the time when he wrote, a few years after the event, "the Philistines came no more unto the coast of Israel, and the hand of the Lord was against them all the days of Samuel."[1]

The years of quiet left Samuel at liberty to pursue his high vocation. Previous judges had been mere warriors and commanders; they executed their office, delivered their nation, and subsided into private life, neither effecting nor trying to effect any permanent reforms. Samuel was no general, no military leader. The occasion lately mentioned was, as far as we know, the only time when he acted as a leader in war. His was a higher call, to educate his nation to realize the theocratic government, and to live as under the eye and under the direct rule of Jehovah. He partially failed in this attempt, because he could not elevate his fallen countrymen to adopt and act upon so high a view; but he laboured hard for this end, and resigned it only at the express permission of God. We have to see how he strove to carry out his idea, the measures he took to make his influence felt, and to raise the people to a knowledge and appreciation of their great privileges. The respect in which he was held, the great services he had rendered, facilitated his task; and he brought his personal influence to bear on his countrymen generally, at least in the southern part of the land, by visiting annually some of the celebrated spots of religious veneration, and there sacrificing and exercising his office of civil judge. Starting from Ramah his home, he used first to go to the time-honoured Bethel, where the Lord had twice appeared to his great forefather Jacob, and where the encampment and altar of Abraham had stood. Thence he journeyed to Gilgal in the Jordan valley,[2] the first station of the Israelites after they

[1] This seems the most obvious way of explaining the statement in 1 Sam. vii. 13, which otherwise cannot be reconciled with the fact that the Philistines in the early days of Saul were again active oppressors of Israel. Possibly Samuel himself wrote the words of the text before the Philistines had recovered from their defeat or attempted to regain their lost supremacy. The explanation of Dean Payne Smith, that "it is the method of the Divine historians to include the ultimate results, however distant, in their account of an event," though true enough in many cases, seems hardly adequate to solve the difficulty here.

[2] That this Gilgal is the one intended in the text seems most probable, as the other on the high ground to the south-west of Shiloh (2 Kings ii. 1) was of no religious importance at this time or previously, and Samuel's circuit was confined to holy sites whither pilgrims flocked at different times of the year. See Geikie, ii. 94 ff.

had crossed the river, some three miles east of Jericho, and known now by the name of Tell Jiljulieh. This had been from time immemorial a consecrated locality. Its very name, meaning "a circle," recalls the primeval stone monuments of some forgotten religion, though Joshua conferred a new interpretation on the appellation by making it commemorate the erection of twelve stones which marked the miraculous passage of the Jordan. From Gilgal Samuel visited Mizpah, and ended at Ramah, where he doubtless had succeeded to some of his father's property. But he did not confine his judicial visits to these well-known spots; he often betook himself to other places at uncertain intervals in order to redress grievances, or to punish wrong-doing, or to offer Divine worship.[1] He established a regular service at Shiloh, but it does not appear that he removed the Tabernacle hither when he built his altar here. Possibly, the priests of the family of Ithamar claimed it as their own peculiar property, and, as a kind of Palladium, removed it from one of their own cities to another, without Samuel's approval or against his will, the sacred writer with a reverent reticence omitting to record these proceedings.[2] It was not unusual, in spite of the stringent rule of the Mosaic code which ordered all sacrifices to be offered before the ark in the appointed place,[3] for altars to be reared in other localities, as by the people at Bochim, by Gideon at Ophrah, and by Manoah at Zorah.[4] It is stated in the Mishna that before the Tabernacle was erected high-places were lawful, but after it was erected they were not allowed. After the destruction of Shiloh it became temporarily lawful to sacrifice in the high-places, and this permission continued till the establishment of the Tabernacle at Jerusalem.[5] The sacrificial acts of Samuel at Ebenezer, at Ramah, and other places, were evidently sanctioned by God; the pretext of a sacrifice at Bethlehem on the occasion of the anointing of David was especially suggested by the Lord (1 Sam. xvi. 2). Now that the tabernacle and ark were divorced from one another, and there was no regularly-appointed House of God, the Mosaic rule was temporarily suspended, and what would have been an offence at one time and after the Temple was built was at this abnormal period

---

[1] See 1 Sam. xvi. 2 ff.   [2] Hummelauer, on 1 Sam. vii. 17.
[3] Deut. xii. 5, 6, 13, 14.   [4] Judges ii. 5; vi. 24; xiii. 19.
[5] Quoted by Captain Conder, "Quarterly Statement," 1875, p. 36.

allowed and condoned. And it was also shown by the acceptance of sacrifice at Samuel's hands that the Aaronic priesthood was not of the essence of religion, and that God by special delegation allowed prophets to perform priestly acts.

At Ramah Samuel gathered a company of youths, whom he taught to read and write, instructed in the Law, in the music of Divine worship, and in the practice of "prophecy." There is some difficulty in discovering what is exactly to be understood by a school of the prophets, which he is allowed to have founded. The circumstances of the times plainly demanded some order supplementary to the priesthood which had so greatly degenerated, and was now unworthy to be the instructor of the people. External acts of religion needed to be explained and illustrated by oral teaching. Samuel saw this necessity, and to aid his own efforts at reformation and to render his work permanent, he established colleges of Prophets, which should keep up the supply of teachers and of persons competent to receive communications from heaven. Trained in the arts of poetry, music, and sacred song, living a cenobitic life, cherishing their gifts in common, these persons were often affected by the spirit of inspiration unconsciously propagated from one another, and uttered words of Divine force and significance. We hear of these "schools" in various places, as Gibeah, Bethel, Gilgal, Jericho; and they continued down to the Captivity, doing a great work, maintaining pure religion in the midst of general corruption, raising a constant protest against laxity and immorality, and acting as a counterpoise to the influence of the monarchy, which was so commonly found on the side of impiety and idolatry. It is as teachers of morality and religion that the prophets in Samuel's time are to be chiefly regarded. Other functions, doubtless, they discharged; they uttered religious songs accompanied by musical instruments; they gave audible expression to the visions of the seer in some rhythmical form, which at once fixed the attention and was easily retained by the memory;[1] they prepared psalms and music for Divine service; they composed annals of the days in which they lived; but their highest duty was to hold forth a high standard of spiritual religion, and to reveal God's will to man. At the head of this institution stood Samuel. But this did not complete the sum

---

[1] Stanley, "Jewish Church," i. 399.

of his occupations or influence. He was not like those judges who held supreme authority in some perilous time, and in days of peace were lightly regarded and forgotten. He had become necessary to his countrymen; he was their friend and adviser in every matter; they consulted him in little questions as well as in great. In any difficulty, domestic, personal, or national, they had recourse to the Seer. Some doubtless regarded him superstitiously as a "wise man" or wizard, but with most he was emphatically the man of God, who had communication with the Most High, and was illuminated with superhuman wisdom by direct inspiration from heaven. He was truly the great statesman and reformer of his age. The institutions which he founded and supervised trained the young in religion and purity and literary accomplishments, fostering high education and all good habits. His own unwearied attention to business, his easy urbanity, his humble affability, brought his influence to bear on individuals, and ensured justice to each private person; while his public measures tended to raise the spirit of piety and patriotism, and to make Israel what it was intended to be, the people of Jehovah.

In these labours of his judicial office Samuel passed the best years of his life. The dates of his birth and death are difficult to determine, as the *data* on which to found his chronology are uncertain. From the monumental records of King Shishak we gather that Solomon came to the throne B.C. 1018; thence we conclude that David reigned from B.C. 1058. Saul's reign, according to Josephus,[1] lasted twenty years, which would give the date B.C. 1078 for his first anointing. Between Eli's death and the battle of Ebenezer some twenty years elapsed; Samuel was then the recognized Judge for twelve or fifteen years, and for eighteen held co-ordinate authority with the king; and, as we gather from the Biblical narrative and the particular place where mention of the decease occurs,[2] his death preceded that of Saul only by two years, so that he died B.C. 1060. The battle of Ebenezer, which put an end to the forty years of Philistine oppression, was fought about B.C. 1095. At Eli's

---

[1] "Antiq.," vi. 14. 9, where καὶ εἴκοσι ("and twenty") is an interpolation, the genuine reading being, "Saul reigned during Samuel's life eighteen years, and after his death two." In another passage ("Antiq.," x. 8. 4) he states expressly that Saul's reign lasted only twenty years.

[2] Comp. 1 Sam. xxv. 1; xxvii. 7; xxviii. 3.

death, twenty years previously, Samuel must have been about twenty or twenty-five years old. This would bring his birth to B.C. 1140, and make his death to have happened in his eightieth year or thereabout. Some of these dates are only probable, but they are well grounded and consistent with ascertained facts and the Biblical record.

As time went on, and Samuel advanced in years, and his counsel was sought more extensively, he found himself unable to fulfil satisfactorily the increasing duties of his combined offices. Accordingly, he associated his sons with him in his judgeship, and placed them as his substitutes in the extreme south of Judæa, at Beersheba, on the Philistine border. Such an appointment shows the wide extent of his authority. Josephus [1] intimates that his influence extended also northward; for he states that one of these sons was established as judge at Bethel. It is difficult to see how this good man could have so little knowledge of the character of his sons as to appoint them to these high posts. The example of Eli might have warned him against such a mistake. But probably it was the very elevation that developed in the young men the seeds of evil which had hitherto lain dormant. The elders had complained that Samuel's increasing infirmities rendered him unable to administer justice effectively in all parts of the land; the most natural and ready means of remedying this defect was to delegate some portion of his powers to his own sons, who had grown up under his eye, and might be supposed to be capable of carrying out their father's principles and to be willing to do so. That they turned out very different from what he expected showed indeed that they had not profited by his example, but does not prove that he was wanting in prudence or judgment. Their education may have been careful, their training excellent; they had in their father a model of integrity, faith, unselfishness, rarely equalled; and yet they went wrong, walked not in Samuel's ways, were greedy and rapacious, perverted justice, and, after that very common Eastern failing, took bribes. The elders of Israel, the heads of the families, who formed a kind of popular assembly, and who had learned to admire the inexorable justice of Samuel's administration, felt aggrieved at the state of matters which now existed; they saw that a change

[1] "Antiq.," vi 3 2.

was absolutely required, if they were to continue faithful to the Lord and hold their own against their enemies. The Philistines had recovered from their defeat, and had strong garrisons in the very heart of the country; the Ammonites, who had been subdued by Jephthah years ago, were threatening the region on the east of Jordan; a strong hand was needed to unite the whole people at this crisis, and to lead the nation to victory. If the great prophet was not able to be their general, and if his sons were unworthy and unfit to command, what was their resource? They saw only one alternative. They had read the Book of the Law, they knew what was virtually promised therein; so confiding thoroughly in Samuel's justice and patriotism, and being convinced that no thought of the private interest of himself or his family would interfere with his calm judgment, they come to him at Ramah, saying: "Behold, thou art old, and thy sons walk not in thy ways: now set a king for us, to judge us like all the nations." Their words recalled and were meant to recall the expressions in Deut. xvii. 14, which seemed to expect this very crisis—"When thou art come unto the land which the Lord thy God giveth thee, and shalt possess it, and shalt dwell therein; and shalt say, I will set a king over me, like all the nations which are round about me." This was their request, and it displeased Samuel greatly, for many reasons. The least of these was the slight put upon him by such a demand; the ingratitude for his vast services, the dissatisfaction with his righteous government, affected him in a very inferior degree. He had more serious and wholly unselfish causes for displeasure. They had come of their own motion, influenced by worldly motives, without having consulted the Lord or laid the matter before Him. They should not have offered this bald request, "Make us a king," but should have entreated the prophet to find out God's will in the matter. They make no reference to the Almighty; they want to be as the neighbouring heathen, to have a monarch to rule them and fight their battles. It was their very privilege to be different from other nations, and this they lightly cast away as of no account. They did not realize the grand idea of the theocracy —"to be Jehovah's own subjects, ruled directly by Him, a republic with Jehovah for its chief, and its officers speaking at His command, and under His direct influence and control."[1]

[1] Dean Payne Smith, *ap* "Pulpit Commentary."

The principle of monarchy had never been repudiated by the law of Israel; it was only that they had to submit to a heavenly, not an earthly king. Their government was a theocracy; the Lord was their king. To exhibit and to confirm the great truth of monotheism was the chief end of all their institutions. To guard this, they were isolated from the rest of the world in the Holy Land; to teach this, they had one only appointed place of general worship; they were made to feel their entire dependence upon God; Jehovah punished their transgressions; Jehovah led them to deliverance. The one, unseen God was their only head and leader. To this idea they could not rise; it was too sublime for their grovelling minds to grasp; it needed stronger faith than they were capable of exercising. Like their forefathers in the desert, who, distrusting an invisible Deity, cried to Aaron, "Make us gods to go before us," they needed some tangible ruler and commander; they forgot how God had judged them, and fought for them, and upheld them when they were true to Him. Though they were not wrong in believing that they were some time destined to be governed by a king, as prophecy and the law and Hannah's song might have told them, yet they were misguided in asking for a king such as the heathen had. The king they needed was not a mere soldier, but a representative of Jehovah, who should act in all things under His guidance, and by himself obeying God's law and enforcing obedience on his subjects, retain the favour of the Lord. And for this they ought to have waited God's good time, and not in a sudden emergency to have fled to human means and the arm of flesh, forgetting that the Lord was their king. Very natural was it that Samuel should be grieved at this declension. But his wounded feelings did not make him unjust or unmindful of the source of comfort and wisdom. He referred the matter to Him whose servant he was. He prayed unto the Lord for guidance. Very tender to the prophet, though stern to the erring, was the answer which he received : "Hearken unto the voice of the people in all that they say unto thee ; for they have not rejected thee, but they have rejected Me, that I should not be king over them. According to all the works which they have done since the day that I brought them up out of Egypt even unto this day, in that they have forsaken Me, and served other gods, so do they also

SAMUEL JUDGE AND PROPHET.

unto thee." It had ever been so with them; they always undervalued their privileges, depreciated their own institutions, desired to be as the nations around them; and now, as they would not realize their great prerogative, God granted their request as a punishment for their offence. When He is asked for something amiss, God shows displeasure in granting, mercy in denying, the petition. So here, He gave them a king in His anger.[1] But He bade the prophet first give them warning and a time for re-consideration by pointing out the inconveniences and dangers which would attend the establishment of such a king as they desired. This Samuel proceeded to do calmly and dispassionately. And here we must pause to note the unprecedented self-abnegation of this true patriot. The ideal for which he had lived and laboured was suddenly shattered and overthrown; the theocratic government which he had believed in and righteously administered was repudiated; the subjects of Jehovah had revolted and spurned His allegiance; the people whom he had loved and saved mistrusted his government and the power of the Master whom he served; yet in spite of all he murmured not; he accepted the new situation; with rare unselfishness he thought only of what was best for his nation, and gave all his energy to regulate the transition, and make it conduce to religious and political amelioration.

"Samuel," says Ewald,[2] "is one of the few great men in history who, in critical times, by sheer force of character and invincible energy, terminate the previous form of a great existing system, at first against their own will, but afterwards, when convinced of the necessity, with all the force and eagerness of their nature; and who then initiate a better form with the happiest results, though amid much personal suffering and persecution. No new truth, stretching beyond the Mosaic first principles, impels him to action; but those principles he grasps with a reality and vividness all his own; and it was the great necessity of his time not to let such truths drop into oblivion. Those truths, rising into intense vitality in his own spirit, he has the strength and the self-devotion to embody afresh in the life of his age, and to re-constitute the whole people in conformity with them in such manner as the changed conditions of the age admit. Similarly, Luther, taking his

---

[1] Hos. xiii. 11. [2] "History of Israel," ii. 191 f. (Eng. Trans., 1867).

stand only on the fundamental principles of Christianity, from that recovered ground renovated and transformed his age, so far as seemed possible under the overpowering weight of circumstance. Being rather a man of daring and unwearied energy than of thought and reflection, Samuel at first throws himself entirely into the established system, and avails himself of all its latent powers and existing institutions, with the happiest result in strengthening and renovating his people ; giving, even up to his mature years, by the splendour and supremacy of his spirit, the last touch of perfection to all that lay within his reach. Here, against his own preconceptions and wishes, the conviction suddenly forces itself upon him that the whole existing system has become hopelessly unsound, and that the community can be saved only by a totally new organization. And at this moment, which is to decide the fate of centuries, he is the hero required, who can sacrifice his previous convictions and all the honours of his rule to give the age what it lacks ; and will take care that this gift may indeed accomplish all that can be hoped from it. Although at first a conscientious opponent of the new state of things which a higher necessity was forcing on his people, yet from the moment when he recognizes this necessity he becomes the most devoted and efficient organizer of the new age, just as Luther required to be first overpowered by the great need of the Reformation before he would dedicate his whole powers to its service. Thus Samuel stands the spiritual hero of two very different eras, equally illustrious in both, but especially happy to find the second, which he not merely lived through, but, as it were, created, an age not of fermentation only, but of progress, in which the good seed sown by him might grow and flourish. For if David's visible deeds are greater and more dazzling than Samuel's, still there can be no doubt that David's blaze of glory would have been impossible without Samuel's less conspicuous, but far more influential, career, and that all the greatness of which the following century boasts goes back to him as its real author."

Though the idea which he had fostered and delighted in received this rude check, Samuel, in his unselfish patriotism, utters no word of reproach, but simply applies himself to fulfil the commands of God, and to arrange the new constitution in the best possible manner. First, he tells the people unreservedly what the Lord had spoken to him; then he explains what may be the result of the appointment of such a king as they desired, what his rights would be, and how he might exercise them. Thus they could not help learning that a very grave responsibility lay with them, and that they might live to repent that they had thrown aside his own mild and just government, and exchanged their republican liberty for the rule of a despot. The picture which he draws embraces the usual features of the government of Eastern kings. He tells them that they must expect great changes; their quiet pastoral life would be at an end; their king would establish a splendid court, to the maintenance of which they must contribute; their sons would have to attend his state chariots as drivers and escort; war would be made on a scale to which they were wholly unaccustomed with armies duly appointed and officered; forced labour would become the rule; the young men would be compelled to cultivate the royal demesnes, and to fabricate the arms of the soldiers; the young women would be taken to make articles of luxury for the royal use, as ointments and perfumes, and to perform servile offices in the palace. No longer would each man dwell securely under his own vine and fig-tree. The king would seize the choicest of their possessions to bestow them upon his own favourites; their fields, oliveyards, and vineyards would no more be their own unalienable property. In addition to the tithes payable to the Levites, the king would exact another tenth for his own expenses, and to lavish upon the ministers of his pleasures. All the people and all their property, sheep, oxen, asses, would be absolutely at his service; no one and nothing would be free from the yoke; and they would learn too late that they had made a grievous mistake. They should cry out in that day because of the king whom they had chosen, and the Lord would not hear them.

Such a warning might well have led the people to pause in their hasty decision, and to think again ere they unreservedly committed themselves to this momentous alteration. The chiefs did indeed deliberate after they had heard Samuel's message, but their consultation only ended in a renewed adherence to their former demand. They came again to Samuel and repeated their request even more strongly: "We will have a king over us." Remonstrance was useless, and the prophet could only convey their resolution to the Lord and await His answer. This soon came, confirming again His former command : " Hearken unto their voice, and make them a king." Samuel announces this response, and sends them away, promising to attend to the matter in due time ; and the elders, quite content to leave the choice of the king and the moment of his appointment to their tried and trusted chief, returned to their homes, while Samuel waited for some communication from God to guide him in the selection of the future monarch.

CHAPTER IV.

SAUL ANOINTED KING.

Saul; his genealogy—Is advised to consult Samuel at Ramah concerning the loss of his father's asses—The high-place—Samuel warned of the coming of the destined king, receives Saul with high honour—Intimates his future lot—Privately anoints him king—Meaning of such unction—Samuel gives Saul three signs, and a premonition as a trial of faith—Saul returns home—Keeps his own counsel—Is publicly chosen king at Mizpah—Divination by lot—Saul's early policy.

SOME short time after the event narrated at the end of the preceding chapter, Samuel in some way received a communication from the Lord, that on a certain day he would meet the man who was destined to be the king of Israel. When he was engaged in his usual occupations at his own home, whither he had retired after the momentous meeting of the chiefs, the Lord had suddenly whispered[1] to him, saying, "To-morrow about this time I will send thee a man out of the land of Benjamin, and thou shalt anoint him to be prince over My people Israel, and he shall save My people out of the hands of the Philistines: for I have looked upon My people because their cry is come unto Me." The man thus pointed out was Saul, afterwards the first king of Israel. The manner of his introduction to the prophet was what men call chance, but which we know to be the working of Divine Providence,

---

[1] The Hebrew is: "the Lord had uncovered the ear of Samuel" (1 Sam. ix. 15), an expression derived from the action of pushing aside the hair or head-dress in order more conveniently to whisper something in a person's ear.

shaping and overruling the actions of men. This Saul, whose name means "asked," was the firstborn son of a Benjamite named Kish, who lived at Gibeah, a town on a hill, with a "curiously knobbed and double top," now known as Tuleil-el-Ful, and situated some six miles east of Neby Samwil.[1] The genealogy of Kish is very confused, owing partly to the Hebrew fashion of omitting links, and partly to the enormous destruction of the Benjamites recounted in Judges xx., in which probably many of the tribal records perished. A comparison of various authorities gives the following as the most probable stemma: 1. Benjamin; 2. Becher; 3. Aphiah (? Abiah); 4. Bechorath; 5. Zeror (Zur); 6. Abiel, or Jehiel; 7. Ner; 8. Kish (brother of Abner); 9. Saul. Even here some links are omitted; for in 1 Sam. x. 21, we hear of the family of Matri, or the Matrites, as being that to which Saul belonged, but the name does not occur in the existing genealogy. This Kish was a man of opulence, and his son Saul was remarkable for his stature and beauty, being now some thirty-five years old.[2] It chanced one day that the she-asses of Kish, kept for breeding purposes, and of considerable value in that primitive community, had strayed, and Saul, with one of his father's servants, was sent to seek for them. In an unenclosed and thinly populated country it was no easy task to track the wandering animals, even for these two experienced men. The servant, so called, was no slave, but a trusty and favoured dependant. If tradition is right in considering him to be Doeg, the Edomite, afterwards the ruthless executioner of Saul's cruel command concerning the slaughter of the priests of Nob,[3] he was well acquainted with the habits of cattle, and might be trusted with much confidence to find the straying asses. Leaving Gibeah, Saul and his servant first passed over the range of the mountains of Ephraim, which ran into the territory of Benjamin, then to "the land of Shalisha," or Baalshalisha, "three land," situate some fifteen miles north of Lydda, and so named because three valleys there converge in the Wady Karawa; thence they proceeded to the wild country round Tayibeh, known as Shalim,

[1] Robinson, "Palestine, ii. 118; "Further Researches," 286. Stanley, "Sinai and Palestine," 213 f. This identification, however, is not certain.
[2] This is deduced from the fact that Jonathan, his son, is mentioned as grown up some two years later.
[3] 1 Sam. xxii. 18.

SAUL ANOINTED KING.

"the haunt of jackals;" thence to the "land of Zuph," in which lay Ramah, the home of Samuel. But in all this long and weary journey, they had not found the lost asses. It was now the third day since they had started, and Saul, who had strong affections, whatever faults in his character afterwards developed themselves, began to think of his father's feelings at their long absence, and desirous of sparing him anxiety, proposed to the servant to return at once, though their expedition had been fruitless, "lest," as he said, "my father leave caring for the asses, and take thought for us." The servant, however, considered that there was still one chance left of recovering the lost animals. They might consult a wise man and ask his advice Just before them rose the hill of Ramathaim-Zophim, and the attendant opportunely remembered that in that city dwelt a man of God, highly honoured and respected, and one whose statements always proved true; he suggested that they should have recourse to him before giving up the quest as hopeless. He does not speak as if he had known Samuel by name, and Saul seems to be equally ignorant. One calls him the "man of God," and the other "the seer." The fact, if fact it were, would be most perplexing. Gibeah was not very far distant from Ramah; and that Samuel, the eminent prophet and the chief ruler of Israel, should have been unknown by name to Saul and his domestic, is quite incredible. That they had never met before is plain from what happened subsequently, when Saul speaks to him as to a stranger, and inquires the way to the seer's house (1 Sam. ix. 18); but how are we to account for this apparent ignorance? Probably, the personal name was almost forgotten in the office, and it was by this title he was generally known, the people near Ramah calling him "the seer," the Benjamites referring to him as the "man of God." Another alternative is, that the dialogue between Saul and his servant is imaginary, founded upon the facts that came afterwards into prominence, and not to be taken as literally occurring. We have a gloss in verse 9 to account for the use of the word *roëh*, "seer," as applied to Samuel, instead of the time-honoured term *nabi*, "prophet." *Roeh*, which at a later period came to include not only inspired persons, but pretenders to occult science, was used in the highest sense in Samuel's days; but as it had degenerated in meaning at the time when the editor of this book wrote, he is careful, while retaining it in the text, to explain its true meaning. The narrative exhibits the simplicity which characterizes such primæval stories. The subsequent conduct of Saul and his servant shows ignorance of Samuel and his circumstances, and the conversation attributed to them prepares the reader for what follows. It is, as a wise man, that the attendant wishes to consult Samuel, as one, who by his more than human knowledge, might direct them in their perplexity. If he and his master knew whom they were to see, and were aware of the important offices which he held, it speaks well for the kindness and affability of the great Judge, that they should have confidence to approach him, and ask advice in so trivial a matter. It would appear that it was no new thing to resort to seers for consultation in private affairs, and that it was customary to offer a present on such occasions. Whether the practice led to chicanery, and whether there was at this time a class of pretended soothsayers, cannot be decided. Saul could hardly have placed Samuel in any such category, though he is willing to appeal to him on a business which any mere soothsayer might have decided. The present case, at any rate, was divinely ordered, and the answer of the seer betrays inspiration. Having decided to consult the seer, Saul suddenly remembers that he has nothing to offer, no money with him, not even a loaf of bread. To approach a great man in the East without a present is an unheard-of proceeding; and we know from Ezekiel's contemptuous allusion to "handfuls of barley and pieces of bread,"[1] that false prophets were rewarded by the deluded people for their lying oracles. The messengers who sought Balaam took the rewards of divination in their hand; the wife of Jeroboam who went to consult the prophet Ahijah concerning the sickness of her son, took with her a present of bread and honey. We need not suppose that Samuel received payment for his counsel like a heathen soothsayer; rather it was in satisfaction of the usual etiquette that Saul was anxious to make some offering to one in his exalted position. The difficulty about the present is solved by the servant, who suddenly remembers that he has the fourth part of a shekel of silver, and this he will gladly offer

---

[1] Ezek. xiii. 19. Comp. Gen. xliii. 11; Numb. xxii. 7, 17; 1 Kings xiv. 3; Isa. lvii. 9.

SAUL ANOINTED KING. 83

for the desired information. What the exact sum was according to modern calculation, it is not possible to determine. Van Lennep considers the shekel to have been worth seventy-five cents or 2s. 7½d.[1] But silver was scarce in those days, and the value of money was considerably higher, nor was the weight arranged upon any settled system. Commentators, reasoning rather upon the statement in the text than upon any satisfactory grounds, have supposed that the coined shekel was divided into four quarters by a cross, and actually broken when needed. The piece thus separated would be somewhat larger than our sixpence, and would have been deemed a considerable fee at that time. Whatever may have been its value, the servant is ready to part with it as *bakshish* to the seer. So, relieved in mind, they went unto the city, where the man of God dwelt. The name of this city is not given, but we have good reason to suppose it to be Samuel's native-place, Ramah. There are difficulties in the identification, but these are not insurmountable. For instance, it is said that Saul, on his return home, passed Rachel's tomb, which in Gen. xxxv. 19 is placed near Bethlehem. If Gibeah were the modern Jeba, a village eight miles south-west of Bethlehem, the route would be obvious; but, identified as Gibeah of Saul is with Tuleil-el-Ful, the travellers must have made a most unnecessary circuit to return home by Jerusalem and Rachel's sepulchre. There may have been reasons that made the longer journey desirable, and now that his father's mind was set at rest concerning the lost asses, Saul may have thought a little further delay was of no consequence. There is also some doubt as to the position of Rachel's sepulchre. In Jeremiah xxxi. 15, it is spoken of in connection with Ramah : "A voice is heard in Ramah, lamentation and bitter weeping, Rachel weeping for her children." The passage is quoted to the same effect by the evangelist, Matt. ii. 18. Other difficulties have been found in the expressions used in the text, where it is not said that Samuel lived in the place, but only that he was there, accidentally as it might be.[2] But the fact is, that there is no verb at all in the Hebrew, and we may supply equally well " dwells " or " is." That it was a dwelling-place of Samuel, that it was situated on a hill, that there was an altar there, and that it was well known as the home of the

[1] P. 35.   [2] 1 Sam. ix. 6, 10.

man of God, all these facts point to Ramah as being the unnamed city.

As they approached Ramah, Saul and his servant were met by maidens coming to draw water from the spring at the foot of the hill on which the city was built, and inquired of them if the seer was there at this time. So busy a man, one so occupied with affairs of consequence, might naturally be absent from home at times, and Saul was much relieved to hear from the maidens, who, in girlish fashion, were eager to impart information to the strangers, that on that very day he had returned home, and was even now about to go up to the highplace yonder to offer sacrifice, and preside at the festival. They added that if Saul made haste, he would catch him in his own house within the city, before he ascended the hill to perform his public function. This ceremony was a feast connected with a sacrifice; it was celebrated on the Bamah, a high-place situated on the top of the hill where Samuel had erected an altar. It was Samuel's custom to say a prayer of thanksgiving, and to bless the meal before the invited guests sat down in the large room near the altar whereon the peace-offerings were offered. Grace before meat is a custom of hoar antiquity, inherited by Christians directly from Judaism. A natural instinct of gratitude led even heathens to make a libation of the wine which they were about to drink. Now Samuel had had Divine intimation, in answer to his continued prayers, that he should this day meet the man designed by God to be king of Israel. Accordingly he made all needful preparation for this momentous occasion. He arranged the sacrifice and the consequent feast, and invited thirty of the chief men of the place to assemble there, and even had a certain choice piece of meat set aside for the distinguished stranger. At the time appointed the prophet left his house in the city and walked toward the gate to ascend the hill to the high-place. Suddenly he sees before him a man of commanding presence and remarkable beauty; he doubts within himself whether or not this is the destined monarch. His hesitation is soon solved; the voice of the Lord whispers in his heart: "Behold the man of whom I spake to thee! this same shall have authority over My people." At this moment Saul comes up, and, ignorant of the person whom he is addressing, asks Samuel if he can tell him where is the seer's house. "I am he," answers Samuel: "go

SAUL ANOINTED KING. 85

up before me unto the high-place, for ye shall eat with me to-day: and in the morning I will let thee go, and will tell thee all that is in thine heart." Thus he prepares the wondering stranger for the great announcement which he has to make; and to show Saul that he might trust to his prophetic powers by which his secret thoughts were known, he adds: "And as for thy asses that were lost three days ago, set not thy mind on them; for they are found." A mysterious intimation followed that some great change was about to happen to him. The information was conveyed with much obscurity, but it evidently meant to announce that the possession of great power was destined to be his. The prophet's language, rightly paraphrased and understood, is this: "Why troublest thou thyself about a drove of she-asses or the concerns of a petty farm in Mount Ephraim? Something much higher should fill thy thoughts; for to whom does all that is desirable in Israel belong? Is it not to thee and to all thy father's house?" Here was indeed a hard saying, but coming from the lips of one so revered and high in dignity, and of unquestioned veracity, it carried with it an air of reality which awed while it amazed the listener. Such a future, thus dimly revealed, had never entered Saul's imagination; no such dream had ever disturbed the even tenour of his uneventful life; and he can scarcely credit the import of the prophet's words, or deem them more than the hyperbolical compliment of a courteous chieftain. Modestly he replies: "Am not I a Benjamite of the smallest of the tribes of Israel? and my family the least of all the families of the tribe of Benjamin? Wherefore then speakest thou to me after this manner?" The tribe of Benjamin had not yet recovered from the cruel destruction inflicted upon it some years before,[1] and the family of Kish, though rich in rustic possessions, was of no great account; how should a member of such a clan be singled out to be the recipient of those great promises? Samuel gave no answer to the stranger's question. He had awakened high thoughts, he had put grand aspirations into his mind, and he desired to let these work before he unfolded more of the Divine purpose. Meantime he conducted Saul and his servant (for the latter was thus honoured as well as his master) to the chamber where the feast was prepared and the guests were assembled.

[1] Judges xx. and xxi.

There Saul was placed in the seat of honour, not merely as being a stranger (which would not have involved any such arrangement), but on account of the eminence which his designation gave him in the seer's eyes. His servant, too, shared in this elevation as being attendant on so important a personage. The portion reserved for him, which Josephus calls "the royal portion,"[1] was then placed before him. It was the shoulder with all the fat which was not burned upon the altar. If this was the right shoulder, it was that portion which appertained to the priest, and could only have been given to a layman by the prophet's authority overruling the usual ritual observance. As such it would have been a mark of the highest distinction. The cook who brought it in speaks confidentially about the circumstance;[2] "Behold," he says, "that which hath been reserved is set before thee! eat; for it hath been kept for thee unto the appointed time of which Samuel spoke, saying, I have invited the people." When the feast was over and the company dismissed, Samuel brought Saul back with him to his house in the city, having induced him to delay taking his homeward journey till the following day, and then, for an opportunity of quiet conversation, he conducted the traveller to the flat roof of his house. These flat roofs were a favourite place of resort, not so much for privacy (for as the enjoined battlements[3] were not very high, persons assembled there were readily conspicuous), but as secure against eavesdropping and undesired companionship. Here the two communed together in peace. The prophet did not unfold his purpose fully, leaving the more complete announcement for the morrow; but he could explain to the future king his view of the state of the people and the country, and tell of his own long struggle to amend matters; he could speak sadly of the religious and political degradation, of the inability to offer any effectual resistance to enemies, of the need of a vigorous leader, obedient to the commands of the Lord and devoted to His service. He could endeavour to fill

---

[1] "Antiq." vi. 4,1.

[2] The Authorized Version of 1 Sam. ix. 24, in agreement with the Sept. and Vulg., inserts the word Samuel: "And *Samuel* said, Behold," etc. There is no "Samuel" in the Hebrew, and it is plain that the Syriac and Chaldee are correct in making the cook the speaker. So "Speak. Comm." *in loc.*

[3] Deut. xxii. 8.

SAUL ANOINTED KING.

the soul of his auditor with a holy ambition to be instrumental in aiding the great work that had to be done ; he could set before him the great principles of the Theocracy lately overlooked or neglected ; he could define the remedies which alone could meet the exigencies of the present crisis. Hitherto Saul had taken no interest in public affairs ; occupied solely in the trivial matters of his father's farm, and in his own domestic concerns, he had thought little about his country's fortunes. In his retired life he knew nothing of the religious or political movements that had taken place, and he needed awakening to higher aspirations and nobler hopes, that the fuller development of his destiny might not find him altogether unprepared. After this momentous conversation Saul had a couch prepared for his guest on the roof, and left him, full of thought and wonder, to repose. " During a large part of the year," says Dr. Thomson,[1] " the roof is the most agreeable place about the establishment, especially in the morning and evening. There multitudes sleep during the summer, in all places where malaria does not render it dangerous. This custom is very ancient. Saul, young, vigorous, but weary with his long search, would desire no better place to sleep than on the roof." Very early in the following morning he was awakened by the old man, who bade him prepare for his journey, and himself accompanied him out of the city. This was an honour that still more astonished Saul, already discomposed by the distinguished reception which he had encountered, and the obscure hints of a great future opened before him. As soon as they emerged from the town and were now alone in the open country, Samuel desired Saul to send on his servant, that he might commit to Saul's own ear the word of the Lord which he was commissioned to impart. It was a solemn moment, unto which all the previous events and actions had led. What a chain of so-called accidents conducted to this consummation ! The casual straying of some asses, the sending of Saul to track them, the servant's suggestion to consult the seer, the presence of Samuel in the city, the meeting of Saul and the

---

[1] " Land and Book," p. 39. Instead of "he communed with Saul upon the housetop," the LXX. read : "they spread a couch for Saul on the housetop, and he lay down" (1 Sam. ix. 25). In the following verse the rendering of the Authorized Version is not correct, "Samuel called Saul to the top of the house." This should be : "Samuel called to Saul upon the housetop."

prophet, the banquet to which the stranger was invited—all these occurrences, seemingly trivial and accidental, were ordained or overruled by God to effect His intended design. Without further explanation, the old prophet suddenly halted, and called on his companion to stand still before him. Then he took from his bosom a vial, one of those long, narrow-necked vessels from which the contents flowed slowly in drops. This was filled with the holy oil which was used in the inauguration of the high priest, and the prophet poured it upon Saul's head in token that he was consecrated to the service of God and represented His power and authority, and thus became the Lord's anointed. The Jews were accustomed to the idea of anointing a king even before this time, as we may gather from Jotham's parable (Judg. ix. 8), in which the trees are made to go forth to anoint a king over them. Afterwards it became customary to perform this ceremony at the introduction of a new dynasty, or where the succession was disputed. Thus we read of the anointing of David, Absalom, Solomon, Joash, Jehoahaz, and Jehu; but ordinarily sovereigns were not thus honoured, the unction of their regular predecessor being considered sufficient dedication, and the term "the Lord's anointed" applied to all legitimate monarchs, whether formally anointed with the consecrated oil or not. The ceremony was of great significance. It imported that the highest offices were centred in the person thus treated; it was his consecration and characteristic; it conferred upon him a majesty and a sanctity such as no one else in the community possessed, and which made his person inviolable, and crimes against him treason to the Lord whose vicegerent he was. Having thus designated Saul for the throne, Samuel kissed him in token of homage and allegiance, even as it is said in the Psalm (ii. 12), "Kiss the Son, lest He be angry." At the royal unction and the kiss of fealty from this venerated judge and prophet, Saul's amazement could not be restrained. His looks, if not his tongue, asked what it all meant. And Samuel answers, putting his reply in the form of a question: "Is it not that the Lord hath anointed thee to be prince over His inheritance?" "And," as the LXX. add, "thou shalt deliver His people from the hands of their enemies that are round about." Israel was the peculiar inheritance of the Lord, being especially so named in the Law and in Moses' song,[1] and there-

[1] Deut. ix. 26, 29; xxxii. 8 f.

SAUL ANOINTED KING.

fore no one could legitimately reign over it who was not directly called. We may well remark the unselfish obedience of Samuel to the Divine voice, and the humility which led him to pay these marks of respect to one so insignificant and unknown, and who was about to supersede him in his office. And now, as Saul cannot believe in his great destiny, and still looks incredulous, in order to assure him of the reality of all that happened, that the unction had been bestowed by Divine authority, and that his grand future was no dream, Samuel gives him three signs which no one uninspired could have known, which should surely come to pass directly, and which should afford to him hints for future guidance. Thus were faith and duty to be supported. The first sign was this: he should find two men "by Rachel's tomb in the border of Benjamin at Zelzah," who should tell him that the lost asses were found, and that Kish was rendered very anxious at the long absence of his son, and was sorrowing for him. The position of Rachel's tomb was well known, and is traditionally shown one mile north of Bethlehem, though if in the territory of the tribe of Benjamin it could scarcely have been in the immediate vicinity of Bethlehem, as the words of Gen. xxxv. 19 would lead one to suppose. It seems scarcely probable that so well-known a site should be defined by naming Zelzah, a place nowhere else mentioned, and the identification of which has baffled all travellers. Wilson,[1] indeed, fixes it at Beit-jala, west of Bethlehem, in the neighbourhood of the traditional Kabbet Rahil, or tomb of Rachel; but the identification is quite arbitrary and rests on no solid grounds. One would have expected not a proper name here, but an appellation; as in the case of the other signs, Samuel indicates not only the locality generally, but the very spot intended, by adding some notable object as a closer definition; thus he speaks of "the oak of Tabor," and "the monument of the Philistines." So in the present case we should expect to find mentioned not a town, but some object, as a rock or tree, to obviate all mistake about the place intended. The reading in the text is most uncertain. The LXX. give "leaping violently," *i.e.*, probably, taking part in some religious ceremony of which dancing was an accompaniment, or, as Ewald would explain the words, "in great haste," referring to the messengers bring-

[1] "Lands of the Bible," i. 141, quoted by Dean Payne Smith on 1 Sam. x. 2.

ing the news of the recovery of the asses. Klostermann would read: "from Gibeah of Benjamin," arguing that the men must have come from that place, to be able to bring the news which they reported. The Vulgate has, "in the south," or, "at midday." We may therefore regard the words "at Zelzah" as an erroneous reading, though we are unable to supply the original expression. This first sign, which duly came to pass, confirmed the information which the prophet had previously given, and led Saul to believe in the high destiny to which the prophet's words and actions had called him. Henceforward he was a new man, filled with new hopes and aims, rising to meet the lot that awaited him; as it is said very forcibly in the Hebrew text:[1] "it was so that when he had turned his back to go from Samuel, God turned to him another heart," *i.e.*, changed him and gave him another heart. He was the careless herdsman, the petty, self-interested farmer, no longer; he had become a patriot, a statesman, a hero. Such was the first sign. Its object was to free him from the cares incident to his former humble life, and thus to leave his mind open to more important interests. The second was as follows: near the oak or terebinth of Tabor (a spot now wholly unknown),[2] he should meet three men going on a pilgrimage to the ancient shrine of Bethel, hallowed by the worship of Abraham and Jacob and all their forefathers. These men would be carrying, as offerings, to the holy place, three kids, three loaves, and a bottle of wine; they would salute him, giving him the "Peace be with you" of the friendly traveller, and, stranger as he was, would present him with two loaves, intimating that he was worthy of all respect, even to the extent of sharing in the offerings destined for God's service. And he should accept these at their hands; nothing doubting that he, who had duly received the unction hitherto appropriated to the priests, was taking only his due when he admitted the homage thus paid to the Lord's anointed. Here, too, was a token that the Lord Himself would sustain him if he continued in His way. This sign also happened according to Samuel's word.

[1] 1 Sam. x. 9.
[2] Ewald and others maintain that "Tabor" is another form of Deborah, or should be so altered, and that this terebinth is the *Allon-bachuth* under which Deborah, Rebekah's nurse, was buried (Gen. xxxv. 8) Keil has given good reasons for doubting this identification, though doubtless it is a very attractive idea.

SAUL ANOINTED KING.

The third sign was to befall him close to his own home at Gibeah,[1] near a famous monument[2] of the Philistines, erected either in memory of some past victory (as Sesostris raised pillars in conquered countries),[3] or in honour of some dead hero. At this spot he should be met by a company of prophets engaged in their religious exercises, and should feel himself constrained to take part in their services. All so occurred. As he approached the place, a number of pupils from the School of the Prophets which Samuel had established there were even then coming down from the high place above the city, following a band of musicians, and chanting a psalm or hymn as they went. The musical instruments used are particularly mentioned. There was the psaltery (*nebel*), a harp without a third side, of ten strings, played by the hand, and of very deep tone: the tabret (*toph*), a tambourine; the pipe (*chalil*), a flute or a reed instrument like the clarinet; and the harp (*kinnor*) of eight or nine strings, played by a plectrum, a small piece of bone or ivory used instead of the tips of fingers. These four instruments were often employed on festive occasions, as we find them mentioned in the account of the feasts of dissolute Israelites.[4] Now when Saul met this company, and saw their enthusiasm, and heard their stirring music, his heart was strangely moved, the Spirit of God came upon him, and he, untrained as he was, joined with all his powers in the ecstatic songs and praises which issued from the prophets' lips.

---

[1] "The hill of God," 1 Sam. x. 5, ought to be rendered "The Gibeah of God," Saul's own Gibeah being thus named on account of the well-known high place near the town.

[2] The Authorized and Revised Versions give: "where was the garrison of the Philistines." So the Vulgate, "statio." The LXX. translate the word, "height," or "erection," thus also the Syriac; the Chaldee gives "leader"; the Arabic, "column." It seems improbable that the Philistines should have had a military post in Gibeah itself; and if they had, it would have been superfluous to announce the fact to Saul in order to indicate the spot where he was to meet the prophets. That indication could only be given by pointing to some definite object, *e.g.*, a pillar, a stone, a tree. The same word, *netsib*, is used, Gen. xix. 26, for "the pillar" of salt into which Lot's wife was turned. See Hummelauer on 1 Sam. x. 5. The word for "garrison" throughout chapters xiii. and xiv is different.

[3] Herod. ii. 102.   [4] Isa. v. 12.

This was indeed a new thing in the life of Saul, and astonished his fellow-townsmen and those who had known him all his life. "What is this?" they cried, "that hath happened to the son of Kish? Is Saul also among the prophets?" They were utterly amazed that one of no cultivation, a rustic with a mind hitherto occupied only in petty concerns, should vie with these highly educated youths, and take a ready part in their exercises. They did not recognize the Divine influence which had effected this sudden change. But one inhabitant, wiser than the rest, saw deeper into the matter. "Ye are surprised," said he, "that the son of Kish should be thus endowed. But what has parentage to do with prophetic gifts? Who is the father of the other scholars? Is prophecy an hereditary gift? If they received their ability from God, why may it not be so also with Saul?" Thus the spiritual transformation which the Holy Spirit was making in Saul's heart was manifested openly to all the world. This remarkable change was long remembered, and in connection with a similar experience in very different circumstances, occasioned the use of the common proverb, "Is Saul also among the prophets?"

✝ When the transitory enthusiasm had passed away, it left a certain fervour behind which could not be satisfied without further communing with God. New powers were working within him, new feelings and aspirations were excited; he wanted to be alone for quiet meditation and prayer. So before he returned to his own home, he went up to the high place, now deserted by the prophetic band, and stayed there for a time in calm retirement. Some think that a festival was being celebrated at the sanctuary, and that Saul went thither for the purpose of attending it, and there met his uncle and had the conversation with him reported below. But it is more probable that he ascended to the Bamah for a religious purpose; and we should have expected that the prophets would have been themselves going thither, rather than returning from it, if a public feast was taking place. On once more reaching his home, Saul was received with great joy by his father, who was a man of placid, sluggish temperament, and too well pleased to have his beloved son back in safety to make any very particular inquiries concerning the details of his journey. Not so, however, with another relation, who is here called his uncle, and who must have been either Ner, his father's brother, or his cousin, the subsequently celebrated Abner, most likely the latter.[1] Having heard of Saul's interview with Samuel, and the honour then paid him in the face of the assembled guests, and having also marked Saul's altered demeanour and habits, he was much more inquisitive. But Saul did not gratify his curiosity. He said no word concerning the promised kingdom. He probably knew enough of Abner's character to see that this kinsman would at once begin to scheme and plot to bring about the fulfilment of this fine promise; and this was quite contrary to the prophet's injunction, and opposed to his own modesty and humility. So he kept his own counsel, and imparted his great secret to no one. Before Samuel dismissed him after the solemn anointing, the seer had given him certain directions for his guidance, adding that in other matters he was to be governed by circumstances, and act as the spirit within prompted him. " Let it be," said Samuel, " when these signs are come unto thee, that thou do as occasion serve thee; for God is with thee." The further premonition given on this occasion referred to the time when the kingdom should have been confirmed in his hand, and he should be preparing to put in execution the purpose for which he was appointed, the deliverance of Israel from the power of the Philistines. He would naturally assemble the people at Gilgal for the commencement of the war of independence, but he was to remember that he was the servant of Jehovah, holding his authority from Him and fighting under His direction, and that therefore he must ask God's blessing on the enterprise, and inaugurate it with solemn religious services. For this purpose he was to wait seven days for Samuel's arrival, who after that interval would come to offer burnt sacrifices and peace-offerings. This was of the utmost importance, and to be a trial of his faith.[2] We shall see hereafter how he behaved under it.

[1] Comp. 1 Sam. xiv. 50, 51, and 1 Chron. viii. 33.

[2] The above seems the best explanation of the difficult passage, 1 Sam. x. 8. "And thou shalt go down before me to Gilgal; and, behold, I will come down unto thee, to offer burnt offerings, and to sacrifice sacrifices of peace-offerings; seven days shalt thou tarry, till I come unto thee, and shew thee what thou shalt do." It is plain that Samuel was not directing Saul to go at once to Gilgal, for the sequence of events was quite different; nor could he have been referring to the first meeting at Gilgal (1 Sam. xii. 14 ff.) for the renewal of the monarchy, for he himself went

And now the time was come for the public election of the future king. The private designation, and the secret unction, were to be supplemented by proceedings enacted in the sight of Israel. In a great national assembly the monarch was to be chosen by lot, which was the mode taken for ascertaining the will of the Most High, and by which assurance would be given that no private partiality had swayed Samuel in his dealings with Saul. So Samuel, as the chief authority in the country, convened all the people to Mizpah, the place where he himself had erected an altar in commemoration of his victory over the Philistines many years ago, and which was not only thus hallowed by religious observance, but revered as the spot where the erring people had been brought to repentance. Hither, to give solemnity to the occasion, and for the purpose of consultation, had been brought the mysterious Urim and Thummim, either by the High Priest himself, or, if that office was still vacant, by the priest who temporarily replaced him.[1] When all were assembled, Samuel stood forth and addressed them. He reminded them of all that the Lord had done for them in old time, how that He had saved them out of the hand of enemies and of all that oppressed them; but deliverance was always conditioned by their obedience to His requirements and acknowledgment of dependence upon Him. And now they wished to have a king who would lead and deliver them without any such condition; they were bent on trying a worldly policy; they would have a monarch and a military organization like the nations around them, and be free from any religious restriction. Thus they proved themselves unworthy of the blessings of the pure Theocracy: "ye have this day," he says with sorrowful indignation, "rejected your God, Who Himself saveth you out of all your calamities and your distresses; and ye have said unto Him, Nay, but set a king over us." They had had time to reconsider their former decision, and opportunity was offered

thither with the people, and Saul had no occasion to wait for his arrival. The second gathering is the one intended by the Prophet's words. After executing certain previous enterprises, *e.g.*, the attack on the Ammonites, Saul was to go to Gilgal, and there wait for Samuel's directions before commencing his great work of liberating his country from the yoke of the Philistines.

[1] This is the explanation of the expression "unto the Lord" (1 Sam. x. 17) given by Dean Payne Smith and Canon Spence *in loc*.

SAUL ANOINTED KING.

of repenting of their self-willed conduct, and of returning to the old order, but they never thought of availing themselves of it. They were bent on innovation, on remodelling the constitution, and establishing a monarchy. As this was their desire, God was willing to grant it, but the selection of the king must be left in His hands. The use of lots in order to obtain a Divine decision was very common among the Jews, as in other nations. It was conducted in this way: the names in question, written on tablets or some other substance, were placed in a basin or urn, which was shaken until all but one fell out; the one left in was considered as declaring the Divine choice. By this means the scapegoat was chosen, the land of Canaan was distributed, the sin of Achan was detected, and, very remarkably, in after time Matthias was elected apostle. The solemn estimation in which this mode of divination was held may be gathered from such passages in Scripture as Prov. xvi. 33: "The lot is cast into the lap, but the whole disposing thereof is of the Lord." On this occasion the people were arranged in their tribes and their families or thousands; the lot was cast, and the tribe of Benjamin was taken. Then the heads of the families of this tribe came near and drew lots, and the family of Matri or Bikri [1] was taken; this again came up by households, and the household of Kish was taken; and on the lot being cast man by man, Saul was selected. He had foreseen the result of the trial, and had concealed himself; and when search was made, he could not be found. We see here the humility and modesty of a great mind, filled with no mean ambition, and shrinking from weighty responsibilities which he felt unequal to sustain. It is true that he had become "another man," but the consciousness of unfitness for the high position to which he was called still haunted his footsteps, and led him to postpone the formidable moment as long as possible. Nor can we doubt that this was a genuine feeling. It was no affectation of reluctance which only needed a certain amount of pressure to give way. Like Athanasius, who timed his absence that he might avoid the perilous dignity of Bishop of Alexandria; like Ambrose, who fled more than once to escape

---

[1] As Matri does not appear elsewhere in the genealogies, and it is extremely unlikely that one of the heads of a chief sub-division should be omitted, Ewald has suggested that Matri is a corruption of Bikri, a descendant of Becher (1 Chron. vii. 6, 8, 2 Sam. xx. 1)

an office alien from his former manner of life; Saul thought himself unsuitable for the proffered dignity, and was slow to undertake its duties. In this dilemma recourse was had to Divine direction, and the High Priest was requested to inquire by means of the Urim and Thummim whether the man had yet come hither. The answer was that he had come, and was now hidden among the baggage. Such a vast assembly as was here gathered together in the immediate vicinity of their implacable enemies had doubtless brought with them wagons and arms and stores, and arranged the camp in military fashion, so as to be able to repel any sudden assault. Drawn at length from his hiding-place and escorted into the midst of the concourse, Saul stood forth conspicuous for his towering stature, his goodly proportions, and his manly beauty. He was taller than any of the people from the shoulders upward; "there was not among the children of Israel a goodlier person than he." So in classic times the heroes of old story are pre-eminent in stature: Ajax is fair and huge, and overtops the Argives by his head and broad shoulders; Turnus is higher by the head than all his compeers.[1] Samuel leads forth his *protégé* and presents him to the people. "See," says he in evident allusion to the direction in Deut. xvii. 15, "See ye him whom the Lord hath chosen"; and the populace, led as always by the eye, and attributing all the faculties required in a ruler to one whose bodily superiority was so evident, shouted with loud acclaim, "Let the king live," or, according to our English phrase, "God save the king," meaning to express the wish that he might pass a prosperous and blessed life. Samuel had already spoken of the way in which monarchs abused their powers and intrenched on the rights of their subjects, when he first heard of their demand for a king; he now communicates to the people the right and law of the kingdom which were to regulate the monarch's action under the Theocracy. He was no irresponsible tyrant who might act as caprice or self-interest guided, but a constitutional sovereign, whose conduct was set forth in the Mosaic Law, and checked and directed by the influence of the prophets who were the mouthpiece of Jehovah. And this was the constitution then established in due accordance with the ancient enactment (Deut. xvii. 14 ff.): "Thou shalt in any

---

[1] Homer, "Il." iii. 227. Virgil, "Æn." vii. 784.

SAUL ANOINTED KING.

wise set him king over thee, whom the Lord thy God shall choose," etc. These and similar words, which formed the Law of the kingdom, Samuel solemnly rehearsed in the ears of the people, and then, when time allowed, probably in the retirement of his own house at Ramah, drew up a formal document, containing not only the above principles and regulations, but also all the details of the election of the first king. This roll was placed among the national archives in the sanctuary, by the side of the Mosaic Law which was kept there,[1] as a guide for future sovereigns, and that future ages might know how it came about that Saul the Benjamite was appointed. Having accomplished this great work, Samuel dismissed the assembly and returned to Ramah.

Saul did not at once commence to exercise his new office; he displayed no undue haste to seize the reins of government, but quickly returned home to Gibeah, and resumed his usual habits, awaiting a favourable moment for showing himself worthy of his advancement. He returned, however, not alone The best and most valiant of those who had been present accompanied him, escorting him with all honour, and bringing him presents according to the Eastern custom. These men's hearts God had touched, and they gathered round the new king to prepare for the coming struggle and to consult for the nation's good. But if all were conscious of the necessity of this radical change in the constitution, all were not equally willing to undertake the duties and burdens necessary for its establishment and maintenance; and some were ready enough to scoff at and depreciate it if it did not at once fulfil their expectations. And further, as is generally the case where a person is suddenly elevated from the ranks to high office, there were not wanting envious people, "sons of Belial," worthless creatures, who spoke of Saul disparagingly. Perhaps they belonged to the great tribes of Judah and Ephraim, and were disgusted at the king being chosen from the meanest of all the tribes, Benjamin; they despised him, and asked sneeringly: "How shall this man save us?" But although such language and the refusal to bring presents were equivalent to rebellion, Saul with rare self-restraint paid no regard to the malcontents, and acted as though he knew nothing of the disaffection. This was consummate

---

[1] Deut. xxxi. 26. Josephus, "Antiq." vi. 4. 6.

prudence. Had he shown that he heard these murmurs, and yet took no notice of them, he would at once have been accused of pusillanimity; on the other hand, if he had punished the disaffected, he would have been considered cruel and vindictive, and would have aroused a civil war the results of which must have been most disastrous. Yet these unfriendly chieftains had no reason to doubt the warlike propensities of a Benjamite. Benjamin had always been the most martial tribe in Israel, and it retained this character to a late period.[1] It had shown its courage and endurance under the crushing treatment that befell it in the time of the Judges. We read later of its warriors being beyond all others skilled in the use of the sling and the bow; we read of many of them being as efficient with the left hand as with the right, a dexterity which must have made them formidable enemies in close encounter.[2] It was therefore mere envy and jealousy which dictated the opposition of these malcontents. An occasion soon arose for proving how mistaken they were in their estimation of Saul's abilities, giving him an opening for action undertaken cheerfully and successfully for the welfare of the state, and winning for him that deference and confidence without which it would have been vain to attempt to govern.

[1] Ewald, ii. 54. [2] Judg. iii. 15; xx. 15 f.; 1 Chron. xii. 2.

CHAPTER V.

SAUL'S FIRST VICTORY.

The Ammonites; they attack Jabesh-Gilead; offer ignominious terms to the inhabitants—Saul hears of the distress; summons all Israel; makes a forced march and relieves Jabesh-Gilead—His wise forbearance and magnanimity.

SOME portion of the country east of the Jordan was occupied by the Ammonites, a savage, marauding nation, descended from Lot and closely allied to the Moabites, though not partaking of their civilization and refinement. A hundred years before this time Jephthah had inflicted a severe defeat upon them, which had insured tranquillity in that quarter for a lengthened period; but Israel had not properly used the advantages which she possessed; she had not availed herself of her privileges to complete her conquests and to improve her moral and political strength, and the Ammonites (like other of her enemies) profited by her backsliding and supineness. They had now recovered their powers, and had attacked the trans-Jordanic tribes, treating them with barbaric cruelty. If we believe Josephus,[1] they had reduced many cities to slavery, and so distressed and weakened the inhabitants that they had no heart to revolt from the yoke which galled them. Such indeed as resisted and were subdued in battle were spared only on condition of losing their right eyes, the design being to render them incapable of engaging in war, the other eye, the left, being hidden by the shield which in fighting they held before them. The Ammonites were notorious for revolting cruelty and un-

[1] "Antiq." vi. 5. 1.

bridled rapacity. The prophet Amos many years later witnesses to their atrocious character. "For three transgressions of the children of Ammon," he says in his oracle (chap. i. 13), "yea, for four, I will not turn away the punishment thereof: because they have ripped up the women with child of Gilead, that they might enlarge their border." The king of the Ammonites at this time was Nahash, the father, probably, of the monarch of the same name of whom we hear later in David's time. He had now turned his arms against the Gileadites and attacked their chief city Jabesh-Gilead, deeming the moment a fit opportunity for revenging the ancient defeat, now that the judge Samuel was stricken in years, and as far as he knew there was no one to take his place. Jabesh, a city appertaining then to Manasseh, stands on the side of the Wady el Yabis, a ravine which winds down the side of Mount Gilead, about six miles south of Pella. Its site is marked by some ruins known by the name of Ed-Deir, "the convent," a convenient appellation often given by the Arabs to ruins of which they have no traditional explanation.[1] It had been depopulated and destroyed some years before for having neglected to join in the war against the Benjamites,[2] but by this time had recovered itself, and was again a city of some importance. It occupied a strong position, and could not be taken by sudden assault, but the inhabitants had no hope of resisting the invaders effectually for any lengthened period; they had no trust in God, and only wished to make the best possible terms before surrendering themselves to their opponent. Their isolated situation, and the lack of unity in the nation, rendered them incapable of any combined movement of defence; and this petty despot might work his will upon them. His claim to the country, a claim which had been already made by his predecessors (Judges xi. 13), they had no courage to dispute; and they came forth from their city as suppliants, humbly praying him to settle the conditions on which they should serve him. Nahash, scorning this abject people, and wishing to revenge on Israel the humiliation which his nation had previously suffered, offered the terms mentioned above: "On this condition," he says, "I will make a covenant with you, that all your right eyes be put out." A horrible alternative indeed, but one to which their

---

[1] Robinson, "Later Researches," 319. [2] Judg. xxi. 8 ff.

SAUL'S FIRST VICTORY.

impotence and pusillanimity were ready to submit; only they stipulated that they should have seven days' respite, during which they might send messengers throughout Israel to see if there were any able and willing to rescue them. This condition Nahash granted, not from any chivalrous feeling such as we might expect in a generous warrior of the Middle Ages, but because he saw little hope of reducing the city in the interval, and, knowing nothing of the recent events that had transpired across Jordan, he thought himself quite safe from any vigorous attack at the hands of the Western Israelites. He was the more willing to grant the request, as the message thus sent abroad would publish his triumph and display his contempt for his enemies. It was only a month [1] since the election of Saul, and tidings of the new state of things had not reached the Gileadites; so in sending envoys to ask for aid, they made no application to the king, but appealed to "all the borders of Israel." First, as was natural, they had recourse to Benjamin, the tribe with which they were closely connected and for whose sake they had suffered severely in past time. As they alone had refused to join in the remorseless destruction of the Benjamites, and had given them their maidens in marriage when they were in danger of utter extinction, so now they look to their gratitude to aid them in this terrible crisis. Travelling with the utmost speed, the envoys arrive at Gibeah, and in their ignorance of the new constitution lay their business before the people generally. These listened to the sad tale with sympathy and concern. But what could they do? They were not yet used to the notion of having a king and leader to whom they might have recourse in all emergencies; they had so long been in a state of disorganization and disunion, that they had not even a suggestion to offer in order to meet the crisis; but, powerless to aid, failing to realize their position as a God-defended people and already possessing a centre of unity and organization, they could only lift up their voice and weep.

Saul had shown no undue haste to assume the authority and responsibilities of his new position. Republican Israel at present little understood the duties, powers, and privileges of a king; it was only politic, especially in the face of a disaffected party, for Saul to wait for a favourable opportunity for setting

---

[1] So Sept. and Vulg. Compare 1 Sam. xii. 12.

himself prominently before the eyes of the people as their appointed ruler. Guided doubtless by Samuel's counsel, he continued to occupy only a private station, and with a wise modesty employed himself in those agricultural pursuits which had hitherto fully occupied his thoughts and time. He had collected no standing army; even the men of valour who had associated themselves with him at first had now returned home, ready to rejoin him when the voluntary recognition of his authority or other circumstances should render their services desirable. There was no hasty self-seeking in the new monarch; patiently he waited till the moment of action arrived. And the opportunity had now arisen. We are all familiar with the Roman story concerning L. Quinctius Cincinnatus, how the envoys, whom the Senate sent to summon him to save his country by assuming the office of Dictator, found him ploughing his modest farm, and how, when he had accomplished the great work which had drawn him from obscurity, he returned to his agricultural employments.[1] Saul was driving his weary oxen home from a hard day's work in the field, when he was met with a sound of lamentation and weeping, such as even now Eastern peoples raise in times of calamity, the silent suffering of more externally apathetic nations being unknown in those sunny climes. On hearing the cause of this general mourning, and being informed of the indignity offered to all Israel, Saul was fired with a righteous indignation. The Spirit of the Lord came mightily upon him; as Samuel had prophesied, God was with him (chap. x. 7), filling him with power and energy, as He had inspired the Judges in other days. Anger at the intended insult was a just and Divinely-sent feeling, animating Saul to do and dare anything to repel and punish it. Here was a burning zeal for the honour of God, which awoke new powers in the young king's mind, drew out the high qualities which were latent in him, and enabled him to adopt such measures as would prove efficacious. A hero and a king, he steps forth, takes his proper post at the head of affairs, and issues his commands with promptness and authority, as one who had the right to be obeyed. Mindful perhaps of the action of the Levite who hewed his abused concubine into twelve pieces and sent them into all the coasts of Israel,[2] Saul slays the yoke of

[1] Livy, iii. 26 ff. Pliny, "Hist. Nat." xviii. 1. Dion., x. 24.
[2] Judg. xix. 29.

oxen with which he had been ploughing, cuts them into pieces, hands over the strips of bleeding flesh to messengers, directing them to carry them throughout the land with the stern threat, "Whosoever cometh not forth after Saul and after Samuel, so shall it be done unto his oxen." He places himself first as the man to whom was committed the chief authority, and he adds the honoured name of Samuel to show that he was acting under Divine direction, and to influence those who slighted or were ignorant of the king's position, as if he had said: "Let those follow Samuel who feel no call to follow Saul. If ye came forth as one man to punish the crime of Benjamin, now arm ye, one and all, to avenge this atrocious insult offered to all Israel by your ancient enemies." The mention, too, of Samuel in this connection proves that he continued to exercise a high office, not only as prophet, but as a chief conjointly with the king, the monarchy being limited by the theocretic principle. The threat that those who disobeyed the summons should have their oxen destroyed seems a light and moderate one, suited perhaps to the limited powers of the new-made king, who could not yet presume to dispose of the lives of subjects at his own mere word. But the loss of his oxen would be ruin to a labouring man, and the fear of such a catastrophe might well have aided to swell the levy of the people. Such a war-signal as the above is not unknown in other countries. Ewald refers to the custom in Norway of sending the war-arrow from tribe to tribe to arouse the nation to arms. Walter Scott has made us familiar with the Scottish token of the fire-brand:

"While clamorous war-pipes yelled the gathering sound,
  And while the Fiery Cross glanced, like a meteor, round." [1]

The poet, in a note, explains the symbol thus: "When a chieftain designed to summon his clan upon any emergency, he slew a goat, and making a cross of any light wood, seared its extremities in the fire, and extinguished them in the blood of the animal. This was called the *Fiery Cross*, and also the *Cross of Shame*, because disobedience to the symbol inferred infamy. It was passed with incredible celerity through all the district which owed allegiance to the chief, and also among his allies and neighbours, if the danger was common to them; and at

[1] "Lady of the Lake," iii. 1.

sight of the Fiery Cross every man, from sixteen years old to sixty, was obliged instantly to repair, in his best arms and accoutrements, to the place of rendezvous. He who failed to appear suffered the extremities of fire and sword, which were emblematically denounced by the bloody and burned marks upon this warlike signal."

The terrible message carried throughout Israel made a deep impression. A dread inspired by the Lord fell on all the people alike; they shrank from disobeying the imperious summons; they recognized the hand of God in Saul's energetic action; they zealously answered the appeal, and came forth as one man. For the first time united under its king, the whole nation took the field to rescue one of its members from injury and disgrace. There was one spirit in all the land. In threatening Gilead, Nahash menaced the independence of Israel. A common danger united the isolated tribes. They thought of their duty regarding these Ammonites; it was their mission to extirpate idolatry, and they had special instructions regarding this nation and their evil allies, the Moabites. "An Ammonite or a Moabite," it was commanded,[1] shall not enter into the assembly of the Lord; even to the tenth generation shall none belonging to them enter into the assembly of the Lord for ever. Thou shalt not seek their peace nor their prosperity all thy days for ever." So the Israelites of the surrounding districts mustered in large numbers at the appointed rendezvous. This was Bezek, a place in the tribe of Manasseh, situated, according to the Onomasticon, about seventeen miles north of Nablous, on the road to Bethshean. It is now probably identified with Ibzik, which lies on the edge of the hills just opposite to Jabesh, fourteen miles north-east of Nablous. There was another town or district of the same name, the capital of Adoni-Bezek, which is represented by the modern Bezkah, six miles south-east of Lydda;[2] but this is too remote from the scene of action to be regarded as the place intended in our text. Here at a certain high place, as the LXX. notify, the people flocked together from all quarters. The number of men assembled is represented to have been 330,000, of whom 300,000 belonged to Israel, and 30,000 to Judah. If there is no mistake in the figures (and such errors are common enough),

[1] Deut. xxiii. 3 ff.   [2] Judg. i. 4, 5.

we must regard this assemblage as a levy in mass, a *landsturm*, as the Germans call it, which would include every one capable of bearing arms. The Septuagint gives 600,000 men to Israel, and 70,000 to Judah ; Josephus, retaining the same number as the Greek version for Judah, assigns 700,000 to Israel. The separate mention of Israel and Judah has led some critics to consider the clause as the addition of some late reviser who lived after the separation of the kingdom, and was inclined to favour the northern division at the expense of the southern. But the suggestion is gratuitous. The feud between the northern and southern tribes existed long before the days of David and Rehoboam, and was popularly represented by the separation of the whole nation into Israel and Judah. The final disruption was only the culmination of previous disunion, traces of which are discernible in much earlier times. The small number of Judæans who mustered at Bezek is traceable to the same cause. Certainly they may have had something to occupy their attention and to employ their forces in making head against the Philistines in their own territories ; but, as Dean Payne Smith remarks, "Judah always stood apart until there was a king who belonged to itself. Then, in David's time it first took an active interest in the national welfare, and it was its vast powers and number which made him so powerful." In those days, too, Benjamin was included in the term Judah, while at the present time it is enumerated in Israel. Asa could boast of 300,000 warriors belonging to his own tribe, and 280,000 appertaining to Benjamin; and even in the most prosperous times of the northern kingdom Israel never more than doubled Judah.[1] It was one thing, and comparatively easy, to assemble this multitude, called forth by a common enthusiasm to meet a common danger and to punish an insult levelled against the whole nation ; it was another and harder task to organize this tumultuous host into some similitude of a regular army. Of arms, probably, they had no great supply. The Philistines had taken care to remove these as soon as ever they had the power. In the present case "furor arma ministrat"; they could only take as weapons what came first to hand of the agricultural implements which they used, scythes, ox goads, stakes. Many victories have been won by such inadequate

[1] 2 Chron. xiii. 3 ; xiv. 8 ; xxv. 5, 6.

means. Saul's untried powers were developed by the great occasion. When it is said that he "numbered" the people, this implies that he arranged them by hundreds and fifties, companies and battalions, set captains over them, and acted himself as commander-in-chief. When this was done, keeping some of the Gileadite messengers with him to guide him by the shortest route, he dismissed the others with a cheerful message to their fellow-townsmen. The preparations had occupied nearly a week, but everything being now ready, he could send word by the envoys : " To-morrow by the time the sun is hot, ye shall have deliverance." Confident in the support of Divine assistance and in the justice of his cause, Saul assumes the certainty of victory for his arms ; and the messengers, seeing his assurance, and encouraged by the great muster at Bezek, on their return to Jabesh inspire the inhabitants with the same courage. They had to pass through the Ammonites' camp in order to reach their own city, using the liberty of transit which had been contemptuously given them. But they carefully kept their own counsel, and let no suspicion of what they had witnessed reach the Ammonites ; and still farther to throw their enemies off their guard, and expose them to surprise at the hands of Saul, the inhabitants sent a crafty message to the besiegers as, if they had given up all hope of rescue, and were content to submit to the hard condition offered by Nahash on the expiration of the time of reprieve. "To-morrow," said they to him, "we will come out unto you ; and ye shall do with us all that seemeth good unto you." The words were really ambiguous, and like an ancient oracle, capable of two interpretations. While the Ammonites took them in the sense of an intention to surrender, the Gileadites in their own hearts thought, "We will come out indeed, but in hostile guise, and ye shall do what ye can, not what ye desire."

The distance from Bezek to Jabesh by the most direct route was about eighteen miles. As the undisciplined host, had it tried to march in one body, would have been thrown into confusion owing to its immense numbers, Saul wisely divided it into three bands, that it might arrive by different roads at its destination, and make its attack in three different directions. Setting out that same evening by a forced march he reached the neighbourhood of Jabesh while it was still dark, the enemy being entirely unaware of his proceedings, and despising the

SAUL'S FIRST VICTORY.

Israelites too much to take any unusual precautions for the safety of their camp. Having halted a short time to refresh his men, Saul, imitating the tactics of the great judge, Gideon (Judg. vii. 16 ff.), arranged the threefold attack. It was now the morning watch, the last of the three watches into which the Jews divided the night, and probably about five or six o'clock, when the hostile enemy was buried in slumber. The king launched his overwhelming host on the sleeping enemy; the men of Jabesh "came out," and aided their friends; and a fearful slaughter ensued. Surprised, panic-stricken, disorganized, the Ammonites fled in all directions, so that not two of them were left together, and their king himself fell in the contest.[1] Till midday the carnage and the pursuit were continued, and the victors only ceased their bloody work, when, overpowered by fatigue, their wearied limbs refused to carry them further.

It was a great and timely victory which at once placed Saul in his rightful position as the head and leader of the nation. Enthusiastic in their recognition of his ability, and aggrieved that any should have been found to dispute his authority and sneer at his pretensions, the people crowd around Samuel, who had accompanied the expedition and aided the king with all his influence, and demand the punishment of those who had asked in derision, "Shall Saul reign over us?" With tumultuous violence they clamour for their immediate execution. But Saul, not even waiting for Samuel's answer to the demand, takes upon himself to reply with generosity and wisdom: "There shall not a man be put to death this day; for to-day the Lord hath wrought deliverance in Israel." It was a politic and pious answer. Had Saul acceded to the popular demand, and given way to the natural feeling of revenge, disastrous consequences would have ensued. The jealousy between the rival tribes would have been augmented and confirmed; feuds and heart-burnings would have arisen and been perpetuated, and it would always have been cast against him as a reproach that he had commenced his reign with domestic broils and bloodshed. By his prudent moderation he saved his country from such calamities, as by skilful generalship he delivered it from menacing enemies. But there is more than this in his answer. He shows here at his best. He gratefully acknowledges God's hand in

[1] Josephus, "Antiq." vi. 5. 3.

the late events, and ascribes the victory to its true source. Under the inspiration of success and the confidence begotten by the consciousness of Divine support, he rises to a high level of magnanimity and piety. Unhappily these virtues are only impulsive and transient, and have no firm basis in his heart and character. In time of temptation he falls away. But now he shows himself a wise ruler and a good man.

Thus successfully and piously did Saul inaugurate his rule. He had gained a great victory over national enemies; he had gained a greater over himself, mastering the natural desire of revenge by the consideration of God's clemency to sinning Israel, and unwilling to mar the universal thanksgiving by any act of violence. Samuel saw that this was a favourable moment for confirming the kingdom in the hand of Saul, and relinquishing his own judgeship in favour of the new king. He therefore summoned all the people to meet him at Gilgal, the famous Benjamite sanctuary in the Jordan valley, and the place in his circuit nearest to Jabesh-Gilead. What a host of memories clustered round this spot! How it would remind the people of their forefathers' entrance into the Promised Land, and of the miracles that accompanied and facilitated that entrance! Here the wanderers had passed their first night after crossing the river Jordan; here were set up the twelve stones, still distinguishable in Jerome's [1] time, to commemorate the marvellous passage; here was the rite of circumcision, for forty years disused, performed on those who had been born in the wilderness, and thus the reproach of uncircumcision was "rolled away"; and here was celebrated the first Passover in the Promised Land. As they assembled here round the altar and the high place, and looked on the venerable mementoes of past events, the Israelites could not help feeling their dependence upon supernatural aid and the very present help of Jehovah. There had been some who murmured at the first election of Saul at Mizpah and refused to own his authority; Samuel now proposed to " renew the kingdom," that is, to proclaim the monarch by the universal voice of the nation amid prayer and sacrifice and general rejoicing.

[1] "Ep. Paulæ," § 12.

CHAPTER VI.

SAMUEL ABDICATES.

Renewal of the monarchy—Samuel abrogates the office of Judge ; defends his past career ; shows that nothing in it excused the demand for a king—His words confirmed by a portent ; endorsed by acclamation—He promises to intercede for the people.

"AND all the people went to Gilgal; and there they made Saul king before the Lord in Gilgal." It is somewhat difficult to understand the bearing of these words or what was the ceremony to which they refer. The LXX., not interpreting the Hebrew, but introducing their own view of the matter, render: "And Samuel there anointed Saul to be king."[1] And some critics acquiesce in this view, appealing to the example of David, who, after he had been originally anointed by Samuel, received the unction on two other occasions, once when appointed king of Judah, and again when accepted as ruler of all Israel.[2] But this precedent is not decisive; rather it tells against the idea ; for such a ceremony, had it really taken place, would not here have escaped mention; it would have been noted with the same precision which is displayed in the case of David. We may observe, too, that the verb translated "made" does not mean consecrated ; and the action is attributed, in the Hebrew text, not to Samuel, but to the whole people. The renewal of the monarchy consisted in the unanimous confirmation of the previous election ; it was equivalent to the public coronation of a sovereign in modern times ; the people acknowledged

---

[1] So Josephus, "Antiq." vi. 5. 4.
[2] 1 Sam. xvi. 12, 13 ; 2 Sam. ii. 4 ; v. 3.

the sovereignty, and undertook to defend and obey it; the king was no longer to lead a private life, but to assume the state and duties of a sovereign. Doubtless, Samuel again rehearsed the laws of the kingdom, and king and people swore to obey them. All this was done "before the Lord," which may mean in the presence of the Ark, and the High Priest with his mystic Urim and Thummim; or simply, in due and solemn fashion, accompanied with religious services. And then, rejoicing in their new king and animated by the thought how well and quickly he had proved himself worthy of his elevation, they showed their gratitude by presenting peace-offerings and feasting together in happy fellowship.

Now that this great work was accomplished and the importunate desire of the nation was fulfilled, Samuel is ready to resign his office of Judge, and to act only as counsellor and medium of heavenly communication. But first he thinks good to defend his past career, and once more to show the people the error which they had committed in insisting on changing the form of government, and the great truth that their prosperity depended upon the behaviour of prince and subjects before the Lord. It is customary with German critics to regard this noble discourse of Samuel as the production of a much later age, and as embodying the writer's conception of the crisis obtained by a retrospective consideration of the entire history of Israel.[1] When it was composed, they say, the subject of the monarchy had been long examined in all its bearings, and the monarchy itself had shown its operation for good and ill. But this is mere conjecture supported on no solid basis. Rather, we may naturally suppose that the account of so vastly important an assembly would be accurately preserved, and the very words of the old prophet would be carefully treasured up, as a guide and a warning for future generations. The account is natural and unvarnished; it is not simply an address put into Samuel's mouth, but a narration of a dialogue between him and the people, and of the circumstances attending it. That he should show prescience of the future, and be fully alive to the dangers that threatened the monarchy, and strongly express his opinion of the only hope of safety, is just what we should expect both from his sagacity and the inspiration which opened his sight,

[1] See, *e.g.*, Ewald, ii. 26.

and from the unselfish patriotism which regarded above all consideration the good of his beloved country. And now, as he is no longer charged with the chief government of the nation, he stands forth with the king by his side, and casts a glance upon his past administration, which he truly vindicates from adverse criticism, and shows had not been such as to create the demand for a ruler of a different character and position. And he speaks in the integrity of his heart: "Behold, I have hearkened unto your voice in all that ye said unto me, and have made a king over you. And now, behold, the king walketh before you; he is here to govern and lead you in peace and war; and I am old and grayheaded, and shall soon have to render an account of my stewardship to God; and, behold, my sons are with you; they are deprived of their judicial functions and reduced to the rank of private citizens; you have not to examine their conduct, but to pass your judgment on my administration. And you know my whole life; I have walked before you from my youth unto this day. Here I am; witness against me before the Lord;" and the old man, as he spake, reverently lifted up his eyes to heaven, and, turning to Saul who stood by his side, added, "and before the king, His anointed. Whose ox have I taken? or whose ass have I taken? or whom have I defrauded? Whom have I oppressed? or of whose hand have I taken a ransom to blind mine eyes therewith and to let the guilty escape unpunished?[1] And I will restore it you." Such is his challenge. Was there any point in all his long administration which the people could attack or which justified them in demanding a new ruler? And the people with one accord testified to his perfect justice and integrity. To further confirm their testimony to his uprightness, Samuel again solemnly appeals to Jehovah and the king: "the Lord," he says, "is witness against you, and His anointed is witness this day, that ye have not found aught in my hand." In bearing this full testimony to Samuel's integrity the people condemned

---

[1] The LXX. have: "or of whose hand have I received any propitiation, even a sandal?" So the Syriac. The reading is confirmed by Ecclus xlvi. 19: "Before his long sleep he made protestations in the sight of the Lord and His anointed, I have not taken any man's goods, so much as a shoe." Comp. Amos ii. 6. The Vulgate renders the last part of the verse thus: "et contemnam illud hodie, restituamque vobis." "I will despise it (*i.e.*, the bribe) to-day, and restore it to you."

themselves; they had no ground of dissatisfaction with his government, and yet they had been impatient and eager for change. Samuel's object in defending himself from any charge of malversation was not simply a personal matter; he desired to vindicate the justice of God's government, and to demonstrate the unreasonableness of the people's demand. "Yes," he says, "Jehovah is witness against you, even that Lord who has done such mighty works in your behalf in old time." And then he recalls to mind some prominent facts in their history. It was Jehovah who made Moses and Aaron what they were, advanced them to their high offices, and, acting as Israel's king, inaugurated their national life by leading them out of Egypt. He shows how often, when for their sins they were punished by oppression at the hands of powerful enemies, the Lord had listened to their repentant cry and raised up heroes to deliver them from calamity; never had He failed to protect and govern them; never had He given them occasion to want any other ruler; He had always been true to His promise, as their records proved. The series of these "righteous acts" began with the great proof of love in the Exodus from Egypt and the settlement in Canaan. And when they were settled in the Promised Land, and for their sin of idolatry, which was rebellion against the invisible King, were given over to their foes, always on their repentance did the Lord interpose in their behalf. At one time they were grievously oppressed by the Canaanites under Sisera, captain of the army of Hazor; but when they turned unto the Lord, He sent Barak[1] to deliver them, and Sisera perished miserably by a woman's hand. At another time Eglon, king of Moab, fought against them; at another, the Philistines had them in subjection. All this happened to punish them for serving other gods, worshipping the Baals and Astartes which were reckoned tutelar deities by the neighbouring heathens. But when, learning obedience by the things which they suffered, they renounced idolatry and turned to their own King, Jehovah, He had mercy upon them,

---

[1] Instead of "Barak" the present Hebrew text gives "Bedan," a name which occurs only in 1 Chron. vii. 17, where the person so called is utterly unknown to history. The LXX., the Syriac and Arabic Versions have Barak. In the Epistle to the Hebrews (chap. xi. 32), Gideon, Barak, Samson and Jephthah are mentioned together. The present word is probably a misreading, as Barak and Bedan in Hebrew might be easily mistaken.

SAMUEL ABDICATES.

and raised up deliverers—Gideon, Jephthah, and Samuel.[1] Yes, they must have forgotten that under Samuel himself they had gained a great victory over the Philistines, and deliverance from their long tyranny; and then when they were threatened by Nahash the Ammonite, they did not turn to the judge whom they had among them, but clamoured for a change; and though the Lord was their King, their ungrateful word was: "Nay, but a king, an earthly king, shall reign over us." Well, they had insisted on having a king; and now their desire was fulfilled. Jehovah had Himself chosen a monarch for them, to be His representative. Henceforward their future welfare depended wholly upon their piety and obedience; they were still under moral government; because they had chosen an earthly ruler, they were not released from the duty of fealty to their heavenly King. Samuel here makes a solemn appeal, ending in an aposiopesis (which is more expressive than any verbal apodosis), like that of Moses (Exod. xxxii. 32): "Yet now, if Thou wilt forgive their sin — if not," &c. Then he continues: "If ye will fear the Lord, and serve Him, and hearken unto His voice, and not rebel against the commandment of the Lord, and if both ye and also the king that reigneth over you follow after the Lord your God" (it shall be well); "but if ye will not hearken unto the voice of the Lord, but rebel against the commandment of the Lord, then shall the hand of the Lord be against you as it was against your fathers."[2] They had in some vague way connected past troubles with the form of government under which they had lived, and had thought that in the presence of their king all evils would vanish, all calamities would be repelled; the Prophet gives them a wiser lesson, and warns them that their prosperity is still, as heretofore, conditioned by their conduct. Their restlessness and discontent had arisen from distrust of God's care; they cried aloud for change of constitution, when they ought to have given diligence to improve their life and actions; no external arrangement of

---

[1] The Syriac Version reads "Samson" here, the alteration being made doubtless to obviate the difficulty of the speaker introducing his own name. One Greek Version, of no great authority, also reads Samson; but there is no sufficient ground for changing the reading of the Hebrew and all the versions.

[2] The Hebrew runs: "against you and your fathers"; but the conjunction is used in a comparative sense, and the English rendering is correct. The LXX. read: "against you and against your king."

government could secure prosperity without conformity to the will and law of God. Do they need proof of the truth of what he has said unto them, and that his words were authorized by God Himself? let them come near and range themselves in solemn order, and see how the Lord would confirm His servant's warning. It was now the time of wheat-harvest, lasting from the middle of May till the middle of June, when rain is almost unknown in Palestine. But now, to show the people their sin in doubting the overruling providence of God, and to teach that His judgments were always ready to fall upon the ungodly, Samuel stands and calls upon the Lord, and the Lord hearkens to his invocation, and a heavy storm of thunder and rain ensues. The Israelites were ever prone to see signs and omens in such untimely occurrences. In the present case they had good cause for terror. For this unusual storm had happened in answer to Samuel's prayer, and their conscience assured them that they deserved God's wrath. A wholesome fear filled their breasts, and trembling at the voice of heaven, and fearing for their life as well as their property, they came suppliant to Samuel, acknowledged their great fault in demanding a king, and prayed him to execute his intercessory office in their behalf. " Pray for thy servants," they cry, as the loud thunder peals, and the floods of rain descend, " Pray for thy servants unto the Lord thy God, that we die not." They speak of "*thy* God" as though conscious that they had virtually rejected Jehovah, and were no longer worthy to be called His peculiar people. It was a true confession, a sincere acknowledgment of guilt, and was accepted as such. Softened by their appeal, the stern Prophet relents. " Fear not," he says; " ye have indeed done all this evil; yet despair not; press on now and henceforward in the right way; turn not aside from following the Lord, but serve Him with all your heart. Yea, turn not aside to vain idols [1] which cannot profit or deliver; and the Lord will defend you." The seer's confidence in this last statement is based on the assurance of the election of Israel. Although the weal or woe of individuals depended upon their

---

[1] The Angl. Version, " For then should ye go after vain things," is probably incorrect (1 Sam. xii 21). The particle "for" is omitted in all the versions, and seems to have accidentally slipped into the Hebrew text. The LXX. read, "And turn not aside after those that are nothing." The "vain things" are idols. Comp. Isa. xliv. 9; 1 Cor. viii. 4.

conduct, and the nation might bring upon itself severe calamities by disobedience and rebellion, yet, as it had been chosen to be God's inheritance not for any merit of its own, but to carry forward His purpose for the redemption of mankind, so it must continue to act its part in this Divine plan, and would not be finally rejected, so as to make God's promises of none effect. This stupendous truth, inscrutable by human reason, was firmly impressed on Samuel's mind; and he could rest calmly on the covenant whereon it was based, and from it preach a lesson of confidence and hope. In answer to the people's request that he would intercede for them, he expressed his firm determination to do this in spite of their backsliding and ingratitude. "God forbid," he says, "that I should sin against the Lord in ceasing to pray for you." He had abrogated his office as judge; his services in that capacity were no more required; but two modes of benefiting his people were left; two duties remained for the aged man to perform. The first of these was intercession. He held it to be a grievous sin to neglect this imperative duty. Here was a weapon which he could ply as long as life should last, whose force he well knew, of whose efficacy he had had sure experience from his earliest days. For this special practice he was celebrated among the saints of Jewish history. Thus in the ninety-ninth Psalm we read:

"Moses and Aaron among His priests,
And Samuel among them that call upon His name—
These called upon the Lord, and He answered them."

And in the Book of the Prophet Jeremiah (chap. xv. 1) Moses and Samuel are named as having wonderful influence with the Almighty because they prayed for enemies. This duty he exercised with all the earnestness of desire for Israel's welfare and faith in God. The other way in which he could continue to act as the benefactor of his countrymen was by teaching them "the good and the right way." Though he was ruler no longer, he was still prophet, the inspired instructor and guide of king and subjects. The prophetic function he never surrendered. In the change to an earthly monarchy the theocracy was not lost, but the earthly monarch was controlled and instructed by the counsel of the prophet, who was the mouthpiece of Jehovah. This office he not only discharged himself with unfailing devotion and disinterestedness, but, as we have seen above, made provision for a due supply of such counsellors and teachers by establishing the schools of the prophets. "Only a Samuel," says Ewald,[1] summing up the effect of these proceedings at Gilgal, "could thus quit office, proudly challenging all to convict him of one single injustice in his past career, and by the act of resignation gaining, not losing, greatness. No longer Judge and Ruler, but simply Prophet, he is able now to discourse with the greater freedom of the monarchy about to be introduced; and he seizes the moment to cast a more distant glance into all the past and future of the community. That the recent conduct of the nation had displayed ingratitude towards Jahveh, its true King, could not be denied; and only by more faithful service of Jahveh in future, on the part alike of king and people, can the ruin they have deserved be averted." He concludes his grave address by appealing not only to the wonder just wrought in the tempest that came at his prayer (a miracle which no vain idolater could work),[2] but also to the mighty acts of Jehovah done of old in their behalf; and he leaves them with the dread warning ringing in their ears: "If ye shall still do wickedly, ye shall be consumed, both ye and your king."

[1] "Hist.," ii. 28.   [2] Comp. Jer. xiv. 22.

CHAPTER VII.

SAUL'S FIRST REJECTION.

Chronology of Saul's reign—Saul chooses a body-guard—Michmash—Jonathan destroys the column at Geba—Philistines prepare for war with overwhelming force—Saul retreats to Gilgal—Israelites disheartened—Trial of Saul's faith—His failure and disobedience—His sin explained—He is punished by rejection—A successor is announced—Samuel leaves Saul.

THE history of the reign of Saul commences with the solemn ceremony at Gilgal narrated in the last chapter. The age of Saul at this time is a disputed point. One would naturally have expected that the writer of these annals would have here given the age of the king at his accession and the number of the years of his reign, as is usual in such documents.[1] But the numbers have been altered in, or have fallen out of, the present Hebrew text,[2] which can only be translated: "Saul was the son of a year (*i.e.*, a year old), when he began to reign; and he reigned two years over Israel." The Chaldee Paraphrast explains: "Saul was innocent as a one year-old child when he began to reign." The Latin Vulgate translates the Hebrew literally as above; the Septuagint omits the verse altogether, though there is a gloss in the Hexapla which makes him thirty years old at this time. The authorised version, which partly agrees with the Syriac, implies that he had reigned one year when the inauguration at Gilgal took place, and that when he had reigned two years he

---

[1] Comp. 2 Sam. ii. 10; v. 4; 1 Kings xiv. 21; xxii. 42; 2 Kings viii. 17, 26; xi. 21, &c.
[2] 1 Sam. xiii. 1.

did what is next recorded. This interpretation was unknown to Josephus, and cannot be deduced from our existing text, where the error has arisen, doubtless, from the practice of denoting numbers by letters. The gaps or omissions in the present text are best expressed, as in the "Speaker's Commentary," and Klostermann's edition, thus: "Saul was . . . years old when he began to reign, and he reigned . . . and two years over Israel." It is possible that the writer originally left spaces in his manuscript, intending to insert the numbers after an inspection of records, and that this was never done. The first gap might be filled up by replacing "thirty-five," or, "forty;" for as immediately afterwards Jonathan, his son, is spoken of as commanding a portion of the army, Saul must have been about that age at his accession, and Jonathan could not have been less than twenty when occupying that responsible position. His son, Mephibosheth, was five years old at his father's death (2 Sam. iv. 4). The length of Saul's reign cannot be determined with absolute certainty. St. Paul in his sermon at Antioch gives the traditional view that he reigned forty years.[1] This is supposed to be supported by the statement (2 Sam. ii. 10) that Ishbosheth, Saul's son, was forty years old when he succeeded his father; for as he is not mentioned among Saul's children in the list given in 1 Sam. xiv. 49, it is argued that he must have been born after his father's accession. But this is most uncertain; the Ishui of that list being perhaps identical with Eshbaal of 2 Chron. viii. 34, and the same as Ishbosheth, and therefore we can found no argument on the connection of his birth with the length of Saul's reign. There is really nothing to rest upon but the statement of St. Paul, which is not necessarily, and is not designed to be, definite and historical, and is probably determined by the desire to make the duration of the first monarch's reign equal to those of David and Solomon. Josephus, in one place, calculates the forty years by assigning eighteen years to him during Samuel's life, and twenty-two after the prophet's death. But, as we have seen above (p. 71), the "twenty" is probably an interpolation, and the correct reading is "two." Others have considered that the traditional view includes the time during which Samuel was judge with him and before him; and that

[1] Acts xiii. 21; Josephus, "Antiq." vi. 14. 9.

SAUL'S FIRST REJECTION.

Samuel judged Israel for twenty-two years by himself, and sixteen in conjunction with Saul as king, and that Saul survived Samuel two years.[1] We are justified, from considerations already mentioned, in attributing twenty years to his occupancy of the throne.

It was in the early part of his reign that Saul began to form the nucleus of a standing army. There had been at this time a cessation of hostilities between Israel and the Philistines; and while the latter occupied many posts in Jewish territory, they did not actively molest their opponents. Saul saw that his untrained countrymen could not at once hope to attack with success a powerful enemy. He was fully determined, and the counsels of Samuel had urged him, to free the nation from the heathen yoke; but, like a wise general, he proceeded with due precaution. Profiting by the great assembling of the tribes at Gilgal, and their unanimous acceptance of him as king, he proceeded to select a band of valiant and skilful warriors, who might not only act as a body-guard to himself, now that he had assumed kingly state, but might form the framework of a military system, and train the whole nation to arms. At this moment, dismissing the rest of the people, he contented himself with oganizing a picked body of three thousand men, keeping two thousand under his own eye, and placing one thousand under the command of his son Jonathan. This is the first mention of that gallant and ill-fated prince, the friendship between whom and David is one of the most touching circumstances in Scripture history. Comely in person, brave to rashness, expert in the use of weapons of war, swift of foot as the gazelle,[2] upright, faithful, affectionate, Jonathan has well been called the perfect type of a Jewish warrior. The trust reposed in him by giving this, his first command, was abundantly satisfied, and he handled his little army very skilfully, with happy daring seconding his father's plans. The position chosen for the two companies showed no mean knowledge of strategy. A brief description of the locality will best explain Saul's tactics.[3]

---

[1] So Wordsworth.
[2] See marginal rendering in 2 Sam. i. 17, R. V.
[3] The description in the text is derived mainly from Lieutenant Conder's "Tent Work" (ii. 110 ff.), and the "Memoirs" of the Palestine Explora-

A great valley, some twelve miles in length, has its head west of Ai (the modern Haiyan, a ruin close to the village of Deir Diwan and still showing the huge cairn raised over it by Joshua), and curving round eastward it runs down to Jericho. The road is wonderfully smooth considering the mountainous district which it traverses, passing over a kind of undulating plateau, and falling more than 2,000 feet ere it debouches on the Dead Sea. A similar plateau leads eastward to Bethel. The valley is now called the Wady Suweinit, *i.e.*, the "Valley of the Little Thorn Tree" (which recalls the name of the crag Seneh, "thorn," mentioned below), and was in old times the main road from the East to the hill country of central Palestine. About two miles from its head the valley becomes a narrow gorge, with vertical precipices some eight hundred feet high. Approached from the south this great fissure is at first quite invisible; but following the path down the steep slopes you come to a sort of promontory, from whence you see, what it had previously shut out from view, the true pass looking very grand with precipitous rock on either side. On the south side of this chasm stands Geba of Benjamin on a rocky knoll, with caverns beneath the houses and arable land on the east. Looking across the valley, the stony hills and white chalky slopes present a desolate appearance; and on the opposite, or north side, considerably lower than Geba, is the little village of Michmash (Muckhmas), situated on a sort of saddle, backed by an open and fertile corn-valley. About a mile to the west of the village the crag is crowned by a sort of plateau sloping backwards into a round-topped hill. Bethel lies four miles to the north, and the interval is filled up by a range of hills which is called in our narrative "Mount Bethel" (1 Sam. xii. 2). In Michmash, which is situated less than a mile due north from where the valley begins to contract, and on some other heights in the neighbourhood, Saul posted his two thousand choice warriors, with the object of watching the movements of the Philistines should they venture to push southwards. Jonathan with his troops was stationed at Gibeah, the old home of his father,

---

tion Fund. I have also, by the kindness of Mr. W. Robertson Smith, the courteous Librarian of the Cambridge University Library, been permitted to use some extracts from his Diary made on the spot during his travels in 1879. Dr. Geikie's "The Holy Land and the Bible" has also greatly helped me.

SAUL'S FIRST REJECTION.

where he would have the support of his family and friends, and, possibly, the assistance of an able counsellor and leader, Abner, his near kinsman. Thus, for some time, the two parties stood closely observing each other, but abstaining from active operations. At length the impetuous Jonathan, tired of inaction, and inwardly vexed at the daily sight of the great Philistine pillar which reared itself on the hill-side as a token of the heathen supremacy, could not restrain the impulse to do an act which would at once animate his countrymen and show the enemy that the Israelites were capable of asserting their independence. With his father's full connivance, he suddenly demolished the monument [1] whatever it was, and prepared to abide the consequences. These were serious, though not altogether unexpected. The Philistines heard of what had happened, and saw that the proceeding meant revolt. Saul, too, had thrown down the gauntlet, and followed up the action by rousing his people to immediate preparation. The trumpet of alarm was sounded throughout the country, and the exploit of Jonathan was proclaimed everywhere by a formal announcement commencing with the old formula: "Let the Hebrews hear." Thus with the blast of the trumpet Ehud had summoned the Ephraimites, and Gideon the men of Abiezer, even as in earlier days the assembling and the movements of the host in the wilderness were regulated by the sound of the silver trumpets.[2]

The news of this event roused the Philistines to fury. They had viewed with grave suspicion the election of an Israelite king; the subsequent victory over the Ammonites, and the fame thereby acquired by Saul, warned them of danger, which was rendered more imminent by the fact that he had gathered around him a body of trained soldiers. So they made immediate and extensive preparations for war; and Saul, lest he

---

[1] The Authorized Version (1 Sam. xiii. 3) is, "Jonathan smote the garrison of the Philistines that was in Geba." For this, we should translate: "destroyed the pillar that was on the hill." We have seen above that the word *netsib* is to be rendered "monument" not "garrison;" and it is most unlikely that if the Philistines occupied Geba, thus threatening Benjamin and Judah, Saul should have posted himself on their north and thus left his own territory undefended. Ewald considers that the word should be rendered "officer," and that the person meant was placed by the Philistines in Gibeah for the collection of tribute remaining due after former levies ("Hist. of Israel," iii. 30) This is an assumption incapable of proof.

[2] Judges iii. 27 ; vi. 14 ; Numb. x. 2 ff.

should be overwhelmed by the numbers opposed to him, withdrew down the Wady Suweinit, which, as we have seen, opened a ready road to the plain of the Jordan. He posted himself at Gilgal, the old headquarters of Joshua's army, and the most sacred spot in all the land, and summoned the people to join him there. His call was not quickly or zealously responded to. Either from pusillanimity, or from some unexplained want of confidence in their leader, they did not flock in large numbers to his standard. And long before he had collected any adequate force, the Philistines had taken the field with an immense army which he was entirely unable to resist. It is true that the numbers given in our present text are quite untrustworthy; but with every deduction, they are such as to show that Israel was no match for her enemies at this conjuncture. The Philistines are said to have had "30,000 chariots and 6,000 horsemen," and, as the writer adds, quoting the exaggerated account which the frightened messengers gave, "people as the sand which is on the seashore in multitude." Evidently they had made a great effort, had enlisted foreign support,[1] and marched forth, determined at one blow to crush the rebellion and exterminate these interlopers. But the numbers are palpably erroneous. The proportion between the chariots and horsemen is absurd. In all the rolls of armies which have reached us, the number of the former is always very much smaller than that of the latter; and such an amount of war-chariots is unheard of. Jabin had only 900; Pharaoh pursued the Israelites with 600; and Solomon at the height of his power possessed only 1,400.[2] Three hundred[3] would have been sufficient for all purposes, and even these would have been of little efficacy in the rocky country where they were used. But the cavalry and infantry were indeed formidable. As Saul retired from Michmash and Bethel, the Philistines occupied these posts, and holding the passes, prevented reinforcements from reaching the king from that side. The northern portion of the district, which would

---

[1] Josephus, "Antiq.," vi. 6. 2.
[2] Exod. xiv. 7; Judges iv. 3; 1 Kings x. 26. Comp. 1 Chron. xviii. 4; 2 Chron. xii. 3; 2 Macc. xiii. 2.
[3] As Dean Payne Smith notes, the Hebrew letter *shin*, the numeral for 300, has been read with two dots, which makes its value 3000.

comprise the territory of Ephraim, was completely overrun by them without opposition. The Israelites were so thoroughly disheartened that many hid themselves in the caves with which the limestone hills abounded, and in the dry tanks wherein during the rainy season water was stored ; some retreated to the fastnesses in the mountains where they could not be easily followed ; and some took refuge beyond Jordan in the country of Gilead, now after the late defeat of the Ammonites rendered a secure asylum. Even those who had collected round Saul at Gilgal were far from being confident; they "followed him trembling." They were in despair as they compared their own puny force with the mighty host arrayed against them; a cowardly terror replaced their late patriotic ardour ; they had no heart for the contest which awaited them, and fell away from their king's side at the moment of peril.

A few years before this time, when Saul was first consecrated to his office, Samuel had solemnly warned the young king that a great crisis in his life was to happen at Gilgal. There the war of freedom was to commence, and to be inaugurated with sacrifices and offerings, which the prophet himself was to offer ; and there he was to receive Samuel's final directions, and, remembering that he was the servant of Jehovah, to act on the counsel communicated to him by the Lord's minister. From the time that he arrived at Gilgal, he was ordered to wait seven days for the prophet's appearance, and to undertake nothing till the religious service was celebrated, and the seer had explained to him how he should act. The command was plain and emphatic. Doubtless, during the time that had elapsed since the order was first delivered, Samuel had reminded the king of his duty, and enjoined strict obedience. Now the time of trial had arrived. Here he was at Gilgal ; a momentous crisis was before him ; he had but to trust in Jehovah and calmly obey His servant, and all would be well. And Saul failed utterly. He waited with increasing impatience for Samuel's promised arrival. Day by day his position at Gilgal appeared more untenable ; his camp on the open plain could not resist an attack ; at any time his retreat to the mountains might be cut off ; continually news was brought of the progress of the Philistines ; continually the weak-hearted people slunk away ; even the greater part of his own choice soldiers left him in this emergency. Perplexed and distracted by what seemed to be opposing duties, Saul knew not what to do. Should he wait in inaction in obedience to Samuel's unreasonable command, and see his troops fall away, and his hope of engaging the enemy successfully ruined ; or should he think only of his business as king and general, and do that which became a prudent commander? He left the decision to the last moment; but when the seventh day dawned, and still the prophet came not, his determination was taken ; he hesitated no longer ; he saw that the people would not fight unless God's favour had first been secured by the offering of sacrifice ; so he called for the burnt-offering and peace-offerings which had been prepared for Samuel's ministration, and by the hand of Ahiah, the priest who was present at Gilgal,[1] he offered the burnt-offering. Scarcely was the first part of the ceremony ended ; the smoke from the altar still was rising to the heaven, and the peace-offerings had not yet been presented, when Samuel came on the scene. Either he had been delayed by the difficulty of making his way through the enemies' lines, or he had been divinely directed thus to try the faith and patience of Saul. It was towards the close of the seventh day that he suddenly appeared in the sight of the impatient king. Always filled with reverence for the great prophet to whom he owed so much, and eager to do him public honour, Saul goes forth to meet him with humble salutation. Samuel looks around, sees the smoking altar and the remains of the victims, and asks in stern displeasure : "What hast thou done?" Saul does not simply own his fault and plead for forgiveness ; he tries to excuse his action. "Because I saw," he says, urging three pleas, "that the people were scattered from me, and that thou camest not within the days appointed, and that the Philistines assembled themselves together at Michmash ; therefore said I, Now will the Philistines come down upon me to Gilgal, and I have not entreated the favour of the Lord : I forced myself, therefore, and offered the burnt-offering." What was the reply of Samuel? Was the excuse valid in his eyes ! Nay, it but aggravated the guilt, showed that the culprit knew what he was doing and sinned wilfully. "Thou hast done foolishly"—as there is no folly greater than disobedience—"thou hast not kept the commandment of the Lord thy God which He com-

[1] See 1 Sam. xiv. 3.

SAUL'S FIRST REJECTION.

manded thee." It has often been asked, what special command Saul had broken? and what was the sin which brought upon him the punishment denounced? Many have thought that his error consisted in the usurpation of the priest's office, in offering with his own hand the oblations which appertained to the sacerdotal function. But there is no reason to suppose that he did this. We find that he has a priest with him immediately after this transaction, and kings are often said to offer sacrifice when we know that they did so by the hands of the lawful minister.[1] Neither does Samuel accuse him of intrusion into the priest's office. In the present abeyance of discipline, and the severance of the ark and the tabernacle, it is doubtful whether the offering of a sacrifice by an anointed king would have been considered a crime such as that of Uzziah in later days and under different circumstances.[2] At any rate there is no mention of any such charge in Saul's case. The command which he broke was that given three years before, viz., to wait for the prophet's blessing and the prophet's directions before taking any steps in deliverance of his people from heathen thraldom. This command included much. It was really a test whereby should be proved whether the king was a theocratic ruler or a self-willed despot, whether he would take his directions from the co-ordinate authority of the inspired prophet, or be guided solely by his own will and caprice. The working of the two independent powers, the regal and the prophetic, was tried by the order in question. It had been virtually repeated at the renewal of the kingdom at Gilgal, when the seer had bidden him to fear the Lord and to serve Him in truth with all the heart, and had added the warning that, if he did wickedly, he and his people should be consumed.[3] This command, confirmed originally by the exact fulfilment of the three appointed signs, and enjoined in many other words since then, Saul deliberately broke. The filial fear and dependence which were required, he rejected. Whereas his appointment and continuance in office were conditioned by unquestioning obedience, he had failed on the first great occasion of its being called into exercise. Doubtless he had ere now shown symptoms of the same independence and self-will, but the present is recorded by the historian as a typical instance,

[1] 2 Sam. xxiv. 25; 1 Kings iii. 4; viii. 63. [2] 2 Chron. xxvi. 16.
[3] 1 Sam. xii. 24 ff.

and as that which led to serious and lasting consequences. At the bottom of all his error lay distrust in Divine help, and overweening confidence in human prudence and sagacity. True, he offered sacrifice in imprecation of the favour of Jehovah ; but this he did not from any really devout feeling, but chiefly for the effect which it might have upon the people. It was rather in satisfaction of popular prejudice, than with any desire of pleasing God, that he called for the arranged sacrifice. The externals of religion were all that he cared for ; he had fallen into that spirit, so often and so strongly denounced by the later prophets, the spirit which regarded the outward act as everything, and which deemed that ceremonial observances would be accepted where reverence, faith, and moral obedience were wanting. What did such a man think of the stories which told of deliverances granted in earlier times, of the victories of Joshua, of battles gained against overwhelming odds, when the Lord fought for His people ? Did he think that the Lord's arm was shortened, that nothing of the kind was to be expected now-a-days, that the earthly king had no dependence upon the heavenly King whose vicegerent he was, and needed no supernatural assistance ? If so—and his action proved that this was the case —he had altogether misconceived the position of Israel and its ruler. The prosperity and existence of the people depended wholly upon obedience to theocratic government ; with the help and favour of their invisible King they were strong and successful, without them they were powerless and humiliated. How could one who despised or ignored this primary principle be fit to govern Israel ? Could the government be rightly entrusted to one who showed such a dangerous disposition ? This open violation of the first condition of national life could not be passed over unnoticed. The king's example might lead to a general repudiation of dependence upon Jehovah, terminating in apostasy and infidelity ; the childlike faith which, while simply obeying, waits for deliverance in God's good time, which is content to stand still and see the salvation of the Lord, would have received a severe check ; and men would have been tempted to trust to national sagacity and the arm of flesh rather than to the commands of God and the counsels of His ministers. And as Saul was, so would his posterity be. Therefore to continue the monarchy in his line would only perpetuate the evil. The prolongation of the succession in the same family was a boon desired by all occupants of a throne. The prayer, "Grant the king a long life, may his years be as many generations," [1] was the natural outpouring of the wish for the preservation of a dynasty. But this duration was to be refused to Saul. It had indeed never been promised; but he had now shown himself unworthy of it And then the prophet pronounces his doom, not his final rejection (for he might by repentance have regained the Lord's favour), but a punishment which should affect his posterity. Had he proved himself a humble and obedient servant of Jehovah, his kingdom would have been "established upon Israel for ever," in his family. "But now," the prophet announces, "thy kingdom shall not continue." He was to remain king himself; nothing is as yet said of his personal rejection; that was to follow on the occasion of another and more aggravated disobedience. It is the kingdom, not the king, that is here denounced. No son should succeed to his honours; a successor had already in God's counsels been provided. "The Lord hath sought Him a man after His own heart, and the Lord hath commanded him to be prince over His people." It was many years afterwards that David, the future king, was appointed; as he was only thirty years old at the time of Saul's death, [2] he must have been at this moment in his early youth. But with God the future is present; in His foreknowledge things to come are accomplished facts, and His purposes are completed deeds. So the prophet speaks of the choice as already made, and the selected person as of a certain high character, though for fear of awakening Saul's jealousy he does not mention his name and family, if he knew them as yet. This new monarch was not to supersede Saul, or to reign while Saul lived, but to take that place which the family of the present king would have assumed had he been found worthy. And now for a time the old prophet sorrowfully leaves the wilful king, not without hope that he may yet see his error, and by timely repentance avert the threatened doom. For Samuel well knew that God's judgments, as well as His promises, are conditional, not over-riding man's free will, but depending for their fulfilment on human conduct. So, sadly, he turns homeward to his house at Ramah, stopping for awhile on his way at Gibeah to encourage the people and the little band

---

[1] Psa. lxi. 6.   [2] 2 Sam. v. 4.

128   SAMUEL AND SAUL.

of soldiers there, and to convey the king's injunctions to his son
Jonathan. These orders were to take the earliest opportunity
of uniting his forces with his father's, that together they might
make a stand against the invaders.[1] Meantime, Saul's troops
had dwindled away ; he had gained nothing by his disobedience ;
the very object of his self-willed sacrifice had not been fulfilled ;
the dispersion of the people had not been prevented, and when,
before moving from Gilgal, he numbered his troops, he found
that only six hundred remained with him.

[1] The Septuagint, with the intention of filling a supposed gap between
the two portions of 1 Sam. xiii. 15, has introduced a gloss which is somewhat
unintelligible : " and Samuel arose and went from Gilgal (on his way, Alex.);
and the rest of the people went up after Israel to meet the people of war.
And when they had come from Gilgal unto Gibeah of Benjamin, then Saul
inspected the people," &c. One wants to know whence came these
" people of war," and how, in spite of these reinforcements, Saul could
muster only 600 men.

CHAPTER VIII.

BATTLE OF MICHMASH.

Saul at Geba—The Philistines devastate the land—Jonathan and his armour-bearer attack their garrison—The Philistines, panic-stricken, fly—Saul joins in the pursuit—Great slaughter of the Philistines—Saul's rash vow; broken unwittingly by Jonathan—The violater discovered by lot—Jonathan rescued from death by the people.

MARCHING from Gilgal with his diminished force, Saul posted himself in a strong position at Geba,[1] a village, as we have seen, on the south side of the Wady Suweinit, about two miles east of Ramah, whence he could observe the tactics of the enemy opposite to him at Michmash, and check, or at any rate harass, their troops if they attempted to enter further into the territory of Benjamin. Here he was joined by Jonathan with his small company of picked warriors.[2] It was a prudent movement, and showed the skill of an intelligent commander. We do not know why the Philistines had not crushed his little army on the plain of Jordan, where their cavalry and chariots would have had free scope for their operations, and the Israelites could have offered no opposition. Why again they permitted their enemies to retreat unmolested to the fastness of Geba and intrench themselves there, is equally unintelligible to a military view. Probably, conscious of their own immense superiority, the Philistines utterly despised their antagonists, and feeling able to overwhelm

---

[1] The Authorized Version reads (1 Sam. xiii. 16) wrongly: "Gibeah of Benjamin"; the Revised gives "Geba."

[2] The LXX. to the clause (1 Sam. xiii. 16): "abode in Gibeah of Benjamin," add: "and wept," which reminds one of Chap. xi. 4, but is not very suitable to the character of Saul and Jonathan.

them at any moment, did not take the trouble to interfere with
their movements till the time came for striking a final blow.
Meanwhile they turned their attention to devastating the land
that lay open to their troops. Retaining the camp at Michmash
as their central station, they despatched companies of marauders
in various directions. No opposition could be offered, and
terrible suffering ensued. The historian carefully notes the
course of these plundering expeditions. The south alone was
barred by the presence of Saul's forces ; the rest of the
country was at their mercy. So one company of these
light-armed forayers turned northward to Ophrah, [1] a town
near Ai, five miles north-east of Bethel, thirteen from Jerusalem, and now represented by the village of Tayibeh, which
stands on a conspicuous eminence. From it a wady, afterwards
occupied by a Roman road, runs down to the Jordan valley.
A second company turned westward towards Beth-Horon, now
Beit Ur, the place renowned for Joshua's victory over the
Amorite king (Josh. x.), and situated on the main approach from
Philistia to the interior of the country. A third band extended
its ravages to the Jordan valley on the south-east, which is
here called the "Valley of Zeboim." In such raids a considerable
time was spent. Probably we have here the summary of events
that occupied a year or two. By the end of that time the
condition of the Israelites was sufficiently miserable. It had
always been the policy of the Philistines to deprive the conquered
of their arms. It is noted that the Judge Shamgar, who is said
to have delivered Israel, slew the Philistines with an ox goad ; [2]
and in the history of Samson's achievements there is no mention
of sword or spear being used by him or those around him. The
Israelites had indeed obtained a supply of arms from their
enemies after the successful battle of Ebenezer, but of these they
had been deprived directly the Philistines recovered their
supremacy. The same fate had befallen the spoil won from the
defeated Ammonites. It seems to have been the custom of the
Philistines at stated times to make a visitation of the conquered
territories, levying tribute, collecting arms, plundering villages,
and erecting trophies of their successes in various places. At

---

[1] This is described (ch xiii 17) as being in "the land of Shual," *i.e.*,
"of jackals," a local name, not identified, but perhaps the same as "Shalim"
(ch ix 4).

[2] Judges i.i. 31.

BATTLE OF MICHMASH.

the present time they had not only deprived the Israelites of all means of offence, but carried off all the smiths and armourers from the district, so that the writer, speaking of his own days, and of the territories of Benjamin and Judah with which he was most familiar, could truthfully say : " There was no smith found throughout all the land of Israel ; for the Philistines said, Lest the Hebrews make them swords or spears." [1] Even to sharpen their agricultural implements, their ploughshares, sickles, axes, and mattocks, they had to apply to the nearest Philistine settlement, and this was found to be so troublesome and degrading that many let their tools rust and become useless, rather than submit to the terms imposed.[2] Very few of the Israelites therefore were efficiently armed, being quite unable to meet on equal terms their enemies, who were clad in defensive mail and fully equipped with sword and spear. It is most probable that the Hebrews were possessed of bows and arrows, to the use of which they were well trained ; and the skill of the Benjamites with the sling was notorious. But their " artillery " [3] was of little avail against soldiers protected by breast-plate, helmet, and shield of metal ; so that they had little hope of successfully attacking their opponents, and were compelled to stand on the defensive only, and to see their homesteads plundered and their land desolated without making any attempt at rescue.

The Philistines now pushed forward a post from their camp at Michmash to an eminence somewhat nearer to Geba, that they might be more ready to intercept the Israelites, should they attempt any onward movement. The camp of the Philistines is described by Josephus,[4] who must have been familiar with the

---

[1] 1 Sam. xiii. 19. See Hummel. *in loc.*

[2] The Hebrew here (ch. xiii. 20, 21) is very confused, and is variously translated. The explanation given above is adapted from Bunsen. The word translated "file" is now considered to mean "bluntness," and the whole passage is thus rendered by Dean Payne Smith : " But all the Israelites went down to the Philistines to sharpen his sickle, and his plough-share, and his axe, and his mattock, whenever the edges of the mattocks, and the plough-shares, and the forks, and the axes were blunt, and also to set the goads." The LXX. represent ver. 21 by the following : " Now the harvest was ready to reap. And the tools were (sharpened) at three shekels for a tooth (*i.e.* for each tool), and for the axe and the sickle there was the same rate."

[3] 1 Sam. xx. 40. Comp. xvii. 5 f.

[4] "Antiq." vi. 6. 2.

locality, as being situated on a very steep hill with three tops, ending in a long, sharp tongue, and protected by cliffs which almost surrounded the tents. "Exactly such a natural fortress," says Lieutenant Conder,[1] "is found east of Michmash, and it is still called 'the Fort' by the peasantry." It is described as "a ridge rising in three rounded knolls above a perpendicular crag, ending in a narrow tongue to the east with cliffs below, and having an open valley behind it, and a saddle towards the West on which Michmash itself is situate. Opposite this fortress, on the south, there is a crag of equal height and seemingly impassable;" as the sacred writer says (1 Sam. xiv. 4), "there is a sharp rock on one side, and a sharp rock on the other." The southern cliff is called Seneh, the northern Bozez, "shining." The valley, of which Lieutenant Conder gives a drawing, runs nearly due east, and thus the south side is almost entirely in shade during the day. "The contrast is surprising and picturesque between the dark cool colour of the south side and the ruddy or tawny tints of the northern cliff, crowned with the gleaming white of the upper chalky strata."

While such was the position of the Philistine camp, Saul occupied the northern extremity of the hill of Geba,[2] having set up his spear, the emblem of command, under a pomegranate tree,[3] facing Migron, "the precipice."[4] Here he watched and

---

[1] "Tent Work," ii. 112 ff.

[2] I have no doubt that the Gibeah of Ch. xiv. 2 is not Saul's city, but Geba. There is continual confusion between the Gibeah of Benjamin, Gibeah of Saul, and Geba. The LXX. in the present passage translate: "at the extremity of the hill," taking the word as an appellative. They evidently have no thought of Saul's own city being meant. It is not at all likely that the king should have left Jonathan, where we find him, at Geba, while he himself with the bulk of his forces withdrew to Gibeah; nor is Michmash visible from the latter place, while it is separated from Geba only by the width of the valley, and everything done there could be plainly seen from the Israelites' position. The distance from Gibeah to Michmash which places are separated by many little rugged valleys) is too great for Saul to have been able to arrive in time to give any effective help to Jonathan in his rash enterprise.

[3] The Hebrew word for "pomegranate" is *rimmon*, and many have thought that the Rimmon of Judges xx. 45, where the defeated Benjamites took refuge, is here meant. But this is a mistake.

[4] See Isa. x. 28, describing Sennacherib's march, and Cheyne's note there in the last edition of his commentary.

waited, fretting at inaction, yet too weak to make any offensive movement. But there was one fiery spirit in his army who bore this quiescence with an impatience which increased every day. Jonathan could ill brook the sight of the insolent enemy close before him and exulting in his superiority; and inspired by a Divine impulse, like that which seized on Gideon, and Othniel, and Samson, he determined to strike one desperate blow or perish in the attempt. He told not his father of his intention; he asked no counsel of the High Priest Ahiah, the great-grandson of Eli, who was present there with the Urim and Thummim, but trusting to the help of the Most High and his own strength and courage, he undertook one of the strangest enterprises which any hero of old time ever attempted. Looking upon the Israelites as an undisciplined, unarmed rabble from whom no danger was to be expected, the Philistines kept but slight watch, and were ill prepared to resist any sudden attack. Jonathan saw this from the higher ground at Geba, and determined to take advantage of it. He communicated his intention to his armour-bearer, a youth animated with the same courage and inspired by the same faith in Divine protection as himself. He makes no great matter of the proposition. "Come," he says, "let us go over to the garrison of these uncircumcised; it may be that the Lord will work for us; for there is no restraint to the Lord to save by many or by few."[1] The armour-bearer readily agreed to accompany him, and to share the danger whatever it might be. Before, however, actually setting out, Jonathan, according to the custom of his age and country, wished to ascertain whether he might look for God's blessing on his enterprise against these enemies of the Lord, his hatred of whom is expressed by the term of contempt applied to them, "these uncircumcised." Like Abraham's servant, Eliezer of Damascus, when sent on his mission to Rebekah (Gen. xxiv.), or like Gideon, wishing to be certified that God would save Israel by his hand (Judg. vi.), Jonathan, in his full trust in Providence, wished for some sign to determine his purpose. This was not done in blind superstition, nor was it an irreligious tempting of God. It sprung from a strong persuasion that Israel was the Lord's people, and that endeavouring to fight the Lord's battles a devout man might rightly look for some token from heaven to

---

[1] Comp. 2 Chron. xiv. 11.   1 Macc. iii. 18; iv. 30.

guide his actions. The sign which he chose was this: he and his companion were to pass over to the Philistine side of the valley, and when discovered were to observe the first words spoken to them. If the enemy said, "Tarry till we come to you," they were to give up the enterprise; but if they were invited to come on, they were to consider this as a token that their undertaking would be successful, and that the Lord had delivered the foe into their hands. So like a gallant knight and squire of mediæval time, Jonathan and his armour-bearer set forth on their perilous enterprise. The situation has already been described. Passing down the long slippery ledges of the cliff Seneh, they arrived in the valley, and crossing this began to make towards the opposite crag Bozez. And now the sign was to be tested. It was well chosen. If the Philistines bade them wait till they came, it would show that they were cautious and on the alert and might not be attacked with impunity; but if they asked them to come up to their camp, it would be a proof that they were careless and despised the Hebrews too much to take any precaution against surprise. It was early morning, and the Philistines at length discovered these two solitary figures who had crossed the ravine and were directing their way towards the outpost. Probably they had already gotten some distance up the precipice, which is some sixty feet high, before they were discovered "Ho," cried the Philistines, "Hebrews are coming forth out of the holes where they had hidden themselves." And they called to them, "Come up to us and we will shew you a thing." They spoke in raillery, deriding the adventurous approach of these two youths, and perhaps thinking that they could never make their way up the face of the precipice. But in the words Jonathan saw the sign which he desired. "Come up after me," he cried with exultation to his comrade; "for the Lord hath delivered them into the hand of Israel." The Philistines might easily have hurled them to the bottom by rolling stones upon them from above; but they treated them only with good-humoured contempt and let them do as they liked. So the two rapidly clambered up the rock on hands and feet, and suddenly appeared at the parapet with their deadly bows bent. According to the account of Josephus,[1] as soon as he received the answer of the enemy Jonathan and his friend

[1] "Antiq" vi. 6. 2.

crept out of sight and got round to the side of the rock which was left unguarded. Clambering up this, they entered the camp on the further side, and surprised the Philistines sleeping in fancied security. However this may be, no sooner had they surmounted the difficulties of the ascent than they commenced the attack, as the Septuagint says, with darts and slings and stones of the field. The armour-bearer ably seconded his master; the Philistines surprised at the suddenness of the assault made but little resistance, and in a few minutes twenty corpses attested the vigour of the attack and the prowess of the Israelites.[1] A panic seized the unbelievers; they could not believe that two men would dare to attack the garrison; they thought that those whom they saw were only the precursors of a large storming party, and offering no further resistance they fled in confusion towards the main camp, spreading terror as they ran. The panic was even communicated to the parties of marauders whom they met in their flight. The confusion was augmented by the admixture of foreigners in the Philistines' army; for in the sudden supernatural terror that seized them they ceased to distinguish friend from foe, and fell in numbers by mutual slaughter.[2] The watchmen of Saul at Geba could plainly see what was going on at Michmash, and in that clear air even hear the cries of the combatants across the valley. With the utmost surprise they beheld the signs of combat in the camps of the enemy, the gleam of arms, the rushing of excited multitudes hither and thither; and they hurried to tell Saul of the astonishing occurrence. At once suspecting that some of his own warriors were concerned in the matter, the king ordered the muster roll of his troops to be called, and the absence of Jonathan and his armour-bearer was

---

[1] There is some difficulty in explaining the last clause of 1 Sam xiv. 14 The R V. gives: "within as it were half a furrow's length in an acre of land (marg · half an acre of land)" Ewald interprets thus: "at the very beginning he thus strikes down twenty men at once, 'as if a yoke of land were in course of being ploughed,' which must beware of offering opposition to the sharp ploughshare in the middle of its work." Klostermann gives "half in the camp and half in the open field." One might have expected some measure of time instead of space.

[2] "And the earth quaked, so there was an exceeding great trembling" (ch. xiv. 15). This has been taken to imply that there was an earthquake at this moment, but the Hebrew does not necessarily denote such an event, and it is well not to introduce supernatural interpositions into texts which do not plainly express them.

quickly discovered. The crisis called for some action on his
part. Having, therefore, Ahiah at Geba with the sacred garment containing the Urim and Thummim,[1] Saul desires the
High Priest to ask counsel of God. Our present Hebrew text
makes Saul say: "Bring hither the ark of God"; adding:
"for the ark of God was there at that time with the children of
Israel." But the ark was last heard of at Kirjath-jearim (ch.
VII. 2), where it was found in David's time, nor is it at all likely
to have been moved in these troublous days to Geba. The
term rendered "bring hither" is never used for the ark, but only
for the ephod;[2] nor was the ark ever employed in any way to
obtain an oracular reply. The Greek version has doubtless
then preserved the true rendering: "Bring hither the ephod;
for he bore the ephod in that day before Israel." While Saul
was speaking to Ahiah, the uproar in the enemies' camp increased tenfold, and it was evident that now was the time to
strike a decisive blow. Saul can wait no longer; his instinct
as a commander told him that delay might be fatal. This was
the time for action, not for prayer. He saw what was to be
done and needed no Divine counsel. "Withdraw thy hand,"
he cries to the priest. Impatient at one moment for the heavenly
oracle, he is at the next too impatient to wait for it. As in all
his conduct, he set too little store by Divine guidance. Had he
listened to the word of God, he would have escaped the errors
which marred the completeness of his victory. Now filled with
ardour he called upon his men to follow him, and they, raising
the familiar battle-cry, put themselves under his guidance, and
hurried down the hill eagerly to the battle. There was but
little fighting to be done. When they arrived upon the scene
they found the enemy doing their work for them. Every
man's sword was against his neighbour; Philistines and their
alien confederates were involved in inextricable confusion,
fighting one with the other; and the Israelites coming fresh in
the field with their compact, well-trained little troop, had
merely to slay and to glut their vengeance on their once scornful
foes. Aid, too, appeared from unexpected quarters. Probably
some of the auxiliaries who were serving unwillingly took this
opportunity of turning their arms against their employers; and
it is certain that the Hebrews, who had been taken from con-

[1] 1 Sam. xiv. 18.   [2] Comp. 1 Sam. xxiii. 9, xxx. 7.

BATTLE OF MICHMASH.

quered districts and compelled to act as servants and camp-followers for the Philistines, openly sided with their countrymen, and seizing the first weapons that came to hand, added greatly to the confusion and the slaughter. The flight became general. Tidings of the event flew quickly around. The villagers who had deserted their homes on the approach of the Philistines and betaken themselves for refuge to the caves and hills of that wild country, came forth from their hiding-places and fastnesses, and joined in the pursuit. In headlong course the heathen fled down the valley past Bethaven, the bleak desert on the east of Bethel; they made no stand there, but turned westward first to Upper Bethhoron, then down the steep descent to Lower Bethhoron, in order to gain their own country by the valley of Aijalon. This is a broad and beautiful valley running west-by-north through the tract of hills and then bending south-west through the great western plain. Aijalon itself, now represented by the village of Yalo, stands on the side of a long hill which skirts the valley on the south. By this wady, the remnant of the Philistines, utterly broken in spirit, wounded, and wearied with a flight over some twenty miles of rugged ground, reached their own territories with the loss of arms and treasure and equipments. Thus as the Lord delivered Israel at the Red Sea, so He this day saved them from the hands of their enemies, and gave them a great victory, sixty thousand of the Philistines having perished.[1] But circumstances had occurred to make the victory less complete than it might have been. The troops of the Israelites had increased by the influx of the country-people and of the Hebrews in the Philistine camp to ten thousand men; and Saul, wishing to take advantage of this powerful force, and desiring that nothing might hinder the pursuit, had foolishly made the people swear to eat no food until the evening. So intent was he upon the one object of avenging the long insults offered to him and his royal power, that he forgot humanity to his soldiers and the limits of human endurance, and made them agree to devote to death any one who as long as daylight lasted should cease from the work of slaughter in order to take rest or refreshment. The consequences of this inconsiderate vow showed themselves in the faintness and lassitude of his followers, who from sheer exhaus-

[1] Josephus, "Antiq." vi. 6. 6.

tion were unable to continue the pursuit with the necessary persistence. Their course led them through a wood where honey lay in abundance on the ground; for the wild bees build their nests in rocks and hollow trees, and oftentimes the combs bursting with the weight or liquefying under the influence of the heat let the honey ooze out and fall to the earth. Canaan, we know, was a land flowing with milk and honey, and travellers tell of the vast quantity of bees found therein to this day.[1] The Jews were naturally very fond of honey, and used it largely for food; but on this occasion no man dared taste any for fear of the oath which they had taken. Jonathan, however, had not been present when his father had exacted the vow, and had heard nothing about it; so when he came to this wood and saw means of refreshment at his very feet, he picked up a piece of honeycomb with the point of the staff which he carried and conveyed it to his mouth. The effect even of this slight nourishment on his exhausted frame was notable. The dimness of sight caused by extreme fatigue and hunger passed away; "his eyes were enlightened," and he was able to continue the pursuit with renewed vigour. One of his comrades, seeing what he had done, and shocked at what he thought to be an infringement of a grave obligation, repeated to him the oath which Saul had made the soldiers take, adding, what was indeed the fact, that for want of food the people were faint and worn out. Jonathan inveighed strongly and perhaps somewhat disrespectfully against the impolitic measure, which had rendered the splendid victory incomplete. "My father," he says in high displeasure, "hath troubled the land: see, I pray you, how mine eyes have been enlightened, because I tasted a little of this honey. How much more, if haply the people had eaten freely to-day of the spoil of their enemies which they found. For had there not been now a much greater slaughter among the Philistines?"

The pursuit had now continued the whole day, passing from city to city, and, as we have seen, had reached the valley of Ajalon many miles from Michmash. Latterly indeed the weariness of the troops had prevented them from overtaking the flying Philistines, but the latter had cast away everything that could impede their flight, and had left behind them stores of provisions and cattle. And as the sun sunk in the west and the

---

[1] Thus Tristram, 'Natural History of the Bible.'

continuance of the vow was no longer of obligation, the people, faint with hunger, flew greedily upon the spoil, the sheep and oxen and calves, and without attending to the requirements of the Law, ravenously satisfied their appetites with animal food not duly prepared. The blood being regarded as the life and mysteriously connected with atonement, the Law gave very strict directions concerning the slaughtering of animals for food. Every such animal was regarded as a kind of Peace-offering, and the taking its life was a solemn sacrificial act. It was to be slain as expeditiously as possible by cutting the throat with a sharp knife without tearing the flesh; the blood was by no means to be eaten, but to be let flow on the ground and then covered with earth [1] In their ravenous hunger the people sinned in more ways than one. They did not wait for the carcase to be entirely drained of blood before eating it; and they let the slaughtered animal lie in its blood on the ground, and used the flesh thus soaked in blood. Whereas the Law said: " Whosoever it be that eateth any blood, that soul shall be cut off from his people." Some have thought that they did not wait even to cook the meat, but ate it raw. At any rate they violated another very remarkable enactment, intended to foster tenderness of feeling and to teach the sacredness of the relation of parent and offspring. In contradiction of the rule which forbade the dam and her young one to be killed on the same day (Lev. xxii. 28), they slaughtered the calves with the cows in their pitiless voracity. These infringements of the Law could not pass unnoticed. Some of the Levites who had accompanied the expedition came and told Saul what was being done, and he, though he had himself occasioned the transgression by the prohibition which he had issued, is quick to acknowledge the people's sin; and though himself ready to reject the counsel of God's ministers, he is at the same time determined that the letter of the Law should be obeyed. " Ye have dealt treacherously," he cries; " ye have not kept the covenant between yourselves and Jehovah." And he ordered a great stone to be brought to him, and setting it firmly in its place, he bade all the people to bring their beasts there and kill them upon it, that the blood might be properly drained away from the carcasses and that this important law might not again be violated. With the

---

[1] Lev. iii. 17; vii. 26; xvii. 10 ff. Deut. xii. 16, 23.

same unquestioning obedience which they had always showed the soldiers submitted to this new command, and it was far in the night ere the slaughter ceased and their appetites were satisfied. While this was going on, Saul built an altar as a thank-offering to God for his victory, and had sacrifices offered thereon. This was the first public acknowledgment made by him of his obligations to the God of the armies of Israel. Other victories he had won, but he had not thought of attributing his success to heavenly powers. In his gratitude for the present unexpected blessing he commences that practice, which monarchs followed in after time, of raising altars to Jehovah in memory of great national successes.[1]

And now to make the most of his victory he proposes to complete the work by attacking the conquered enemy at once on this very night. He was conscious that his own inconsiderate vow had greatly interfered with the execution of his purpose, and he now wished to repair his error by making a new and unexpected onslaught. The people refreshed by their rough repast, and ready to follow wherever he should lead them, willingly agreed to the proposal. They rose from the ground whereon they lay around the glowing camp fires, took up their weapons, and prepared to resume the weary march. But the High Priest interposed. He was not carried away by the king's unreflecting impetuosity, and with the courage that comes from the consciousness of a righteous cause, he urges him not to take a new enterprise in hand without first ascertaining God's pleasure. "Let us draw near hither," he says, "unto the altar just built and ask the Lord's will." Saul could not deny the reasonableness of this proposal, and proceeded, through the priest's means by the Urim and Thummim, to propound two questions: Shall I go down after the Philistines? and, Wilt Thou deliver them into the hand of Israel? No answer was given; the oracle was dumb; Ahiah was not directed by any Divine impulse to resolve the king's doubt. Then he explained

---

[1] See 2 Sam. xxiv. 25. The literal translation of the passage on which our account is formed (1 Sam. xiv. 35) is: "the same he began to build as an altar unto Jehovah." From this some have thought that Saul began to build with characteristic impetuosity, and left off before the erection was completed. But the Sept. and Vulg. confirm the rendering of the Authorized and Revised Versions, which is also quite in accordance with the idiom of the Hebrew language.

BATTLE OF MICHMASH.

to Saul that the failure to obtain a reply was occasioned by some offence committed in the army and as yet unatoned. God's name had been invoked in the oath which Saul had made the army take, and therefore its observation became a matter of religious obligation. The violation of this vow involved Israel in guilt, and until this was expiated, God regarded not their application. Where the guilt lay, was another question, whether on him who unwittingly transgressed, or on him who without authority from God issued the command which led to the transgression. Atonement had to be made for the profanation of the Divine name, and this duty was pointed out by the inability of the High Priest to obtain the required answer. Incensed at this untimely delay, the king summoned around him the officers and leaders, "the corner stones" [1] of Israel, and bade them help him to discover where the transgression lay; "for," he cries with a profane oath, "as the Lord liveth, who saveth Israel, though it be in Jonathan my son, he shall surely die." He spoke thus not as having any idea that Jonathan was the guilty person, but desiring to impress upon his hearers that no favour should be shown, but that the offender, be he who he may, should pay the penalty of death. Thus without inquiring what the crime was, with no premeditation, a second time in this one day he takes a rash oath, and despotically dooms to death an unknown and unconvicted criminal. Horror-stricken, and cowed by the king's violence, the people answered him never a word, though many of them knew at whom his menace pointed. God had refused to answer his former question, so Saul determined to discover the culprit by casting lots. The fault must be either in himself and his son, or in some soldier of the army. Satisfied of his own and Jonathan's innocence, he made the people stand on one side, while he and his son took up a position on the other. When their freedom from guilt was established he would be free to make an example of the offender. Then he prayed to the Lord, the God of Israel, and said: "Shew the right." [2] This

---

[1] So called in the Hebrew, 1 Sam. xiv. 38.

[2] The Authorized Version has: "Give a perfect *lot*," supplying the word "lot" which is not in the Hebrew. The expression is really equivalent to "Shew the truth." The LXX., with whom the Vulgate partly agrees, have a long paraphrase here: "And Saul said, O Lord God of Israel, Why is it that thou didst not answer Thy servant to-day? Is the iniquity in me or in Jonathan my son? O Lord God of Israel, give light (Urim); and if he shall

was not by the means of Urim and Thummim, through which no answer was now to be obtained, but by lot. The lot was cast; Saul and his son were designated, but the people escaped. One more trial was made, and Jonathan at length was pointed out as the offender. Sternly does Saul inquire what sin he has committed that God has turned His face away. Jonathan, who meantime had learned the connection between his breach of the vow and the silence of the Divine oracle, confesses what he has done. " I did certainly taste a little honey with the end of the rod that was in mine hand ; and lo, I must die." The Syriac puts the last words in an interrogative form: " must I die for this?" as though Jonathan complained of his hard fate. But the phrase really implies resignation to his lot. Though his fault was originally one of ignorance, he never dreams of escaping the penalty. He is quite convinced that his father's vow, however rash and disastrous, must be kept. Josephus, who always tries to exalt his heroes in the eyes of his Roman friends, puts a speech into Jonathan's mouth which expresses entire resignation: " I ask thee not to spare me, O my father. Sweet it is to me to suffer death to satisfy thy oath and after so glorious a victory. For it is my greatest comfort to know that I leave the Hebrews conquerors of the Philistines." [1] Saul gives him no hope of escape. However grieved at the consequences of his hasty vow, and however bitterly he must have felt the loss of such a son, Saul is influenced more by formalism and pride, than by piety and natural affection, and adheres immoveably to his decision. Though Jonathan's error, being committed in ignorance, might have been sufficiently expiated by a trespass offering, Saul, like Jephthah, considered himself irretrievably bound by his vow. "God do so and more also," he says austerely ; " for thou shalt surely die, Jonathan." But it was not so to be; that young and

say this, give to Thy people Israel, give holiness (? Thummim); and Jonathan is chosen, and Saul and the people went forth. And Saul said, Cast lots between me and Jonathan my son; whomsoever the Lord shall choose, let him die. And the people said to Saul, This is not thy word. And Saul prevailed over the people, and they cast lots between him and Jonathan his son, and Jonathan is chosen." For the obscure clause in the above version Wellhausen and others read: "if the iniquity be in me or in Jonathan my son, O Lord God of Israel, give Urim ; and if it be in Thy people Israel, give, I pray Thee, Thummim."

[1] "Antiq." vi. 6. 5.

glorious life was not to be thus prematurely cut off. God had other work for him to do, before the sad end came. The people hitherto had acquiesced with sullen silence in Saul's despotic proceedings; but their complaisance had its limits; they could not unmoved permit this last outrage. As one man they raised an indignant protest against the threatened doom of their idolized hero. What, should he who had wrought this great salvation in Israel be mercilessly put to death? Far be it! The Lord had shown that He had inspired and aided Jonathan in his heroic deed, and should they condemn one whom He had approved? " As the Lord liveth," they firmly exclaim, '· there shall not one hair of his head fall to the ground ; for he hath wrought with God this day." Saul, not unwillingly perhaps, was constrained to forego his purpose, and Jonathan was saved from the penal consequences of his error. The king recognized that the fault was really his own; he acquiesced in Ahiah's counsel, and discontinued his pursuit of the Philistines, returning to his headquarters at Gibeah, and leaving the enemy discomfited indeed, and for the time disheartened, but by no means broken or annihilated. Thus did self-will and impatience mar the completeness of a great triumph.

CHAPTER IX.

SAUL'S FINAL REJECTION.

The family of Saul—He gathers a chosen band of warriors—His successful wars—The Amalekites—Saul ordered to destroy them utterly—A trial of obedience—The Ban—Great destruction of the Amalekites—Saul spares Agag and the best of the spoil—Samuel warned of Saul's disobedience, taxes him with his sin; pronounces his final rejection—Slays Agag—Abandons Saul finally.

WE may here fitly introduce a few words concerning Saul's family. He was, as we have seen, the son of Kish. The father of Kish, Abiel, had also another son named Ner, who was the father of the masterly general and high-principled man, Abner. Thus this latter was Saul's first cousin, and it was doubtless owing to his energy and military skill that the many wars of this reign were conducted with such great success. Saul was not so uxorious as David, and he appears to have had only one wife and one concubine. His wife's name was Ahinoam, the daughter of one Ahimaaz. David had a wife of the same name, who is distinguished as "the Jezreelitess." [1] The word means "brother of grace," and from the predilection for names beginning with *Ah* shown by Eli's family, it has been argued that she was of that lineage. But the question cannot be decided, and is indeed of no importance. The concubine was Rizpah, the daughter of Aiah, famous afterwards for her devoted love to her unfortunate children doomed to death for their father's fault (2 Sam. xxi. 8 ff.). The sons of Saul by Ahinoam whose names have reached us were four in number, viz., Jonathan,

[1] 1 Sam. xxv. 43.

SAUL'S FINAL REJECTION.

Ishui or Abinadab,[1] and Melchishua, all three of whom perished with their father in the battle of Gilboa, and a fourth who survived him, Ethbaal or Ishbosheth.[2] The daughters were Merab and Michal, who are heard of again in connection with David.

The reign of Saul was wholly occupied with wars. As soon as the defeat of the Philistines and their retreat to their own territories left him king of his own dominions, and the people emerging from their hiding-places flocked around him or reoccupied their abandoned homes, he at once began to establish a regular army, and to turn all his attention to the safety and consolidation of his government. In those days when personal courage and dexterity in the use of arms were the chief elements of success in military engagements, and tactics and strategy were of the most elementary character, it became of supreme importance to have around the king a body of practical warriors whom he could trust to carry out his plans with energy and skill. For such men Saul was always seeking; and whenever he met with any one of merit, either from bodily superiority or approved valour, or unusual adroitness with spear and bow, he enrolled him in his service. By this means he gathered the nucleus of a strong army, and laid the foundation of that military power which enabled Israel not only to hold her own, but in later days, like one of the great Eastern empires, to extend her conquests far beyond her own borders.

The position of Saul at this time was one of considerable difficulty. Enemies were on every side. Feeling that the new monarch was an able general, and likely, if unchecked, to make his people into a powerful nation, the neighbouring tribes attacked him, and used their utmost endeavours to overthrow or weaken his government. By the late victory the Philistines were only checked and dispirited for a time. Their strength was still very formidable, and they were only one out of nume-

---

[1] Ishui is not mentioned elsewhere among the sons of Saul. His place is occupied by Abinadab in 1 Sam. xxxi. 2, and 1 Chron. viii 33; ix. 39; and doubtless the two names belong to the same person.

[2] The compound with *Baal* was altered into *besheth* or *bosheth*, "shameful," which rather concealed the allusion, or cast discredit upon it. Thus Jonathan's son Meribbaal (1 Chron. viii. 34) is called Mephibosheth, and Jerubbaal becomes Jerubbesheth in 2 Sam. xi. 21. Compare the names Beelzeboul and Beelzebub.

rous foes against whom he had to contend. That "wherever he turned he conquered" was owing to his prudence and energy and skill. The narrator has given no details of many of those wars which occupied his whole public life. From the brief summary which he does afford, we see that Saul was engaged with all the countries that bordered the Holy Land. The Moabites and Ammonites vexed him on the east; the Edomites, always the implacable enemies of Israel, on the south; in that quarter, too, the Amalekites were found, the war with whom is recorded in fuller detail for the grave consequences involved therein. The west now as ever was threatened and harassed by the Philistines; and at the northeast the kings of Zobah, a country extending from Damascus towards the Euphrates, endeavoured to push their conquests into the northern parts of Palestine. All these opponents were successfully resisted; the freedom once gained was never lost; Israel crouched no more beneath a heathen yoke, and, secure in its allotted territories, had time and opportunity for internal development under Samuel and the schools of the prophets.

The historian turns from this prosperous time to a darker scene; he leaves the detailed account of wars and battles to secular writers, and concerns himself with incidents which reveal character and have a moral importance. So consigning to oblivion Saul's heroic feats of arms and the great doings of his mighty men, he narrates at some length only the wars with Amalek and the Philistines. The former led to the final rejection of the king and the irremediable rupture between him and Samuel; it is therefore of great and melancholy importance.

The Amalekites occupied the Negeb, or country south of Palestine, roaming through the wilderness of Sinai and pasturing their flocks and herds in the green wadys of the Peninsula. We hear of them disputing with the Israelites the entrance into this region immediately after the Exodus, and being defeated with great slaughter[1] For this conduct they had been threatened by God with extermination. When the battle was ended, we are told,[2] Moses built an altar to commemorate the victory, and called its name Jehovah-nissi, "The Lord is my banner"; adding, "The Lord hath sworn, the

---
[1] See Prof. Rawlinson, "Moses: his Life and Times," pp. 136 ff.
[2] Exod. xvii. 15 f.; Deut. xxv. 19.

SAUL'S FINAL REJECTION.

Lord will have war with Amalek from generation to generation." And it had been expressly ordered that, when the Israelites were securely established in the Promised Land, they should not forget to "blot out the remembrance of Amalek from under heaven." The time for exacting this long delayed vengeance was now come. They deserved their chastisement. They were a fierce nomad race, continually making inroads on their neighbours; and lately, seeing the Israelites fully engaged in war with the Philistines, they had, under the leadership of their relentless king, who appears under the generic name of Agag, made destructive and sanguinary raids on the southern districts of Canaan. A considerable time had elapsed since the events narrated in the last chapter, and Saul's resources had so largely increased, and his military power was so firmly established, that he was quite capable of executing a perilous enterprise, and carrying it to a prosperous issue. Now he is ordered to smite Amalek with utter destruction. Will he do the Lord's bidding? He had failed once in the earlier part of his reign, and had been punished by the exclusion of his posterity from the throne. A second trial is now vouchsafed. His character has developed itself, he has had experience of God's directing hand, he knows his own power and weakness; will he now unhesitatingly and thoroughly obey the Divine command, and prove his fitness to be a theocratic king? Samuel comes to him, and prefacing his message by reminding Saul that he was not self-appointed, but had been anointed by Jehovah to be the king of the Lord's people, and had therefore special duties towards Him and towards them, he bids him give good heed to the order which he was commissioned to announce. The precept was conceived in these uncompromising terms: "Now go and smite Amalek, and utterly destroy all that they have, and spare them not; but slay both man and woman, infant and suckling, ox and sheep, camel and ass." The word translated "utterly destroy" is that expression of terrible import which means "to put under the ban," "to devote to God or destruction." It is used continually in the Book of Joshua to denote his treatment of the heathen cities which he conquered. Any thing thus devoted might not be redeemed; it must be destroyed; and when a country was thus denounced, it was regarded as accursed, no spoil could be taken save of the precious metals, all living creatures were to be slain, all other things were to be burned. It was an awful sentence.

If modern humanity revolts from such wholesale slaughter and devastation, the people of that age regarded it in quite a different light, and needed this formidable lesson. The Amalekites themselves were hopelessly and utterly corrupt; their prolonged existence as a nation would only have worked further mischief; they deserved demolition. And the Israelites were God's instruments in inflicting chastisement. Like the pestilence or the famine or the storm, they did God's bidding. In executing His mandate they had to lay aside all tenderness and pity, and regarding themselves as the executors of the Divine sentence, they imbrued their hands in blood without repugnance or remorse. The age, too, was not as careful of human life as men are now-a-days; people then were not scrupulous about shedding their own or other's blood in a proper cause; and when the command came from the invisible King of Israel, there was no squeamishness felt in executing it, even in its most cruel and sanguinary details. Thus were they taught God's hatred of sin. In a moral government enforced by temporal rewards and punishments such severe lessons that all could observe were needed; and more especially would such be felt, when the people themselves who were to profit by them were made with their own hands to inflict the ordained vengeance. Nor was this general destruction of a tribe or a nation an atrocity unheard of: it was common enough; the mind was accustomed to the notion, and felt no special repugnance to the proceeding. As an earthly king in ordering such a measure would be acting only in the usual way, so Israel's King when He enjoined the annihilation of the Amalekites was only vindicating His righteousness as it behoved Him to do. The age was rough, and required a rough lesson, accommodated to its existing moral state. More delicate measures would have failed in producing the intended effect. Saul was not loath to obey the Divine behest thus conveyed to him. He had long been harassed by these roving pillagers; he was not unacquainted with the malediction pronounced upon them in the days of his forefathers, and he was glad to take an opportunity of checking once and for ever their further advances. It was, however, no easy matter to destroy a nomad people who would be little likely to offer a chance of a pitched battle, and whose movements were more rapid and unexpected than those of regular armies. Saul made large preparations for the expedition. He summoned all

SAUL'S FINAL REJECTION.

his forces to meet at Telaim, a place called Telem in Josh. xv. 24, situated on the south-eastern border of Judah and possibly identified with Dhullam, the headquarters of the Dhullaim Arabs.[1] The numbers that responded to his call were ten thousand men of Judah, which was the tribe chiefly threatened by the marauders, and two hundred thousand from the rest of Israel. The separate mustering of the two bodies repeats the hint of the jealousy between the northern and southern tribes of which we have had previous intimation. The army, great even in modern estimation, was none too large for the work which it had to perform. The Amalekites were not builders of towns; it was rare for them to have any settled abode, and their architecture never rose above fortifying a camp with a circular wall. Remains of this nature are still found in the districts where they are known to have lived.[2] Saul, we are told, came in the course of his march to the city of Amalek, perhaps named Ir-Amalek, as we have Ar-Moab, Ir-Shemesh, Ir-Nahash.[3] Here he laid an ambush in a dry wady, and finding that some Kenites were settled there, he warned them to depart lest they should share the doom destined for the Amalekites. The Kenites, who were descended from Abraham and connected with Moses through his wife Zipporah, had always been friendly to the Hebrews. They were a peaceful, pastoral people, and gladly hearkening to the warning, removed for a time to some other spot secure from the encounter of hostile armies. The account gives no details of the war, but the success of the expedition was perfect. Victory everywhere attended the arms of the Israelites; the enemy fled before them, and left enormous spoils to the conquerors. They were smitten "from Havilah to Shur," an expression which denotes the wide extent of the raid. It is used in Gen. xxv. 18 to denote the limits of the Israelites' territories. Havilah was some place, not yet identified, on the south of Judæa in the wilderness, and Shur, which means "wall," is either the wall which was built by the

---

[1] Tristram. It is evidently a place that is meant, and not some open spot where lambs (*telaim*) where collected, which would have been too vague for a rendezvous Comp. xi. 8. The LXX. and Josephus ("Antiq." vi. 7. 2) make the place of meeting to be Gilgal, and the numbers respectively 400,000 and 30,000

[2] "Our Work in Palestine," 276.

[3] Num xxi. 28   Josh xix 41   1 Chron. iv. 12.

Egyptians to defend their north-east frontier from the incursions of the desert tribes, and which ran from Pelusium past Migdol to Heroopolis, or else that wall-like cliff of limestone which extends southward from Suez, called by the Arabs from its remarkable appearance Jebel er Rahah ("mountain of the palm of the hand"). Thus the devastations of the Israelite army extended from the south border of Judah to the close vicinity of Egypt, including the seizure of numerous stationary camps and the collection of an immense quantity of booty and captives. Now according to the terms of the ban, universal destruction was to be dealt to all that was taken from this accursed nation. This penalty Saul inflicted without reserve on all the Amalekites that fell into his hands, and on the less valuable of the cattle. Doubtless of these hardy dwellers in the wilderness a large number escaped, both owing to the difficulty of overtaking them, and because the pursuit flagged when the Israelites laid their hands on the cattle. But the awful interdict was not carried out in all its strictness. Saul himself spared the Amalekite king, either in the hope of receiving a rich ransom for him, or to grace his triumph by the exhibition of so illustrious a captive. The king is called Agag, but this is probably only the official or generic name of the Amalekite monarch, as Pharaoh was that of the Egyptian rulers, since Balaam in his prophecy (Num. xxiv. 7), speaking of Israel, says:

> "His king shall be higher than Agag,
> And his kingdom shall be exalted."

In other particulars the stern command was infringed. The soldiers in their covetousness could not endure to part with so rich a prize as that which had fallen into their hands. To a pastoral people the temptation to appropriate the cattle which they had seized was irresistible; so with Saul's connivance they spared the best of the sheep, oxen and fatlings, and the lambs, silencing any scruples with the idea that the ban was sufficiently executed by the destruction of the human creatures and of all that was worthless among the flocks and herds. They were soon undeceived. To save aught of that which was devoted to destruction was to fail in a sacred duty, and to rob God of His due. The backsliding of Saul was revealed to Samuel in his house at Ramah. The word of God reaches his inward ear in the dead of night, telling that Saul had turned back from follow-

SAUL'S FINAL REJECTION.

ing the Lord, that he wished to be independent of Divine control, and had acted and intended to act as absolute master of Israel. And God says, "It repenteth Me that I have set up Saul to be king." This was a very bitter announcement to the old prophet. He was not only grieved at this failure on the part of one whom he dearly loved, he was indignant [1] that his unselfish promotion of the people's desire, and his willing self-abnegation should have this lamentable issue. Here was one who had been elected under his auspices, solemnly and publicly anointed by him acting on God's behalf, who might be said to be the choice of the Lord, deliberately breaking a plain and positive command, and showing himself neither religious nor obedient as he had hoped that he would prove. Was there not fear that hereby occasion would be given to the enemies of the Lord to blaspheme? Would not dishonour be done to the name of God, when His vicegerent thus insulted Him and received the punishment which he deserved? Well might the prophet be angered at this poor result of all his labours and the seeming frustration of Jehovah's purpose. But this feeling did not lead the man of intercession to forget his duty. All night long till morning dawned he cried unto the Lord for the erring king, praying for his repentance and the restoration of the favour which he had wilfully cast away. In vain. There was no thought of repentance in Saul's breast; prosperity and power had hardened his heart and augmented his proud independence; so for him there was no forgiveness; his final doom was imparted to Samuel, and he was ordered to deliver it. Saul had by this time returned from the expedition, bringing his booty with him. On inquiry, Samuel found that he had come to Carmel (now *Kurmul*), a place on a rich plateau about seven miles south of Hebron, had there erected a trophy of victory, and was now gone on to Gilgal in the Jordan valley, to offer sacrifices and thank-offerings at that holy place. The monument of victory is called in Hebrew *Yad,* "a hand." The same term is used in a similar way on two other occasions. Thus Absalom, having no sons, raised a pillar near Jerusalem to perpetuate his memory, which was known by the name of "Absalom's hand" (2 Sam. xviii. 18). And Isaiah (ch. lvi. 5) says: "Unto them will I

---

[1] This is the meaning of the word translated "grieved" in 1 Sam. xv. 11. (Comp. Num. xi. 10.)

give in mine house and within my walls a *hand* and a **name.**"
The monument doubtless was a pillar, either shaped like a
hand or with an open hand engraved upon it, containing the
record of the victory over the Amalekites.[1] The kind of
memorial then set up has been familiarized to our minds by
the discovery of the famous Moabite stone, erected at Dibon
by Mesha, king of Moab, in memory of his successful revolt
against Israel.[2] Similar memorials are found in Egypt. Samuel
immediately followed Saul to Gilgal, which was some fifteen
miles from Ramah; and on his coming being notified to the king,
the latter went to meet him, saluting him in the usual respectful
way: "Blessed be thou of the Lord!" Then, either to pre-
clude objections to his late breach of the command, or so blinded
by self-will as not to see his fault, he continues complacently,
and as though he expected congratulations on the prophet's
part, "I have performed the commandment of the Lord." This
was true in part, but only in part. He had obeyed just so far
as was agreeable to himself, and had failed to carry out the
order thoroughly and to the letter. To his assertion the voices
of the animals preserved in spite of the ban gives the lie. With
a sad irony the prophet asks: "If thou hast performed the
Lord's commandment, what meaneth this bleating of the sheep
in mine ears, and the lowing of the oxen which I hear?" Saul
cannot escape this dilemma; the animals were brought from
the Amalekites, and formed part of the spoil devoted to destruction; he must allow this, but he throws the blame upon the
people. It was they who insisted upon sparing the finest of
the sheep and oxen; but they did this with the best of motives,
to sacrifice to that Lord ("the Lord thy God") whom Samuel
so fervently adored, and who, he hints, is too exacting in His
requirements. He had done all that could reasonably be demanded: "the rest," he says, "we have utterly destroyed." In
all this the hypocrisy and low tone of morality were very evident. Such a defence marked a sad declension in the Lord's
anointed. The people had always obeyed him unresistingly.
How easily might he have exerted his authority to repress their
wish to evade the stern command! To throw the blame of his

[1] Vigouroux, "La Bible," &c., iii. 447 ff.

[2] A popular account of this important monument, with an engraving of
the stone, will be found in Professor Sayce's "Fresh Light from the
Monuments," pp. 76 ff.

own covetousness and disobedience on his subjects was an action unworthy of a king, mean and mendacious. Samuel will listen no longer. He has a sentence to deliver; that sentence which he had prayed all night long might be withheld; and these feigned excuses show him painfully how necessary the severe verdict had become. "Stay," he cries, as Saul would fain have said more, or, perhaps, was turning away desiring to end the interview; "stay, and I will tell thee what the Lord hath said to me this night." He begins by reminding Saul how from low estate God had exalted him to be king of His people Israel; there was a time when he had thought himself utterly unworthy of so high a position; but in spite of this the Lord had specially chosen him, and by the solemn unction had engaged him to obey his Divine head. And God had sent him on a mission to destroy the sinners the Amalekites, whose iniquity was now filled up. "Wherefore then," continues the prophet, "didst thou not obey the voice of the Lord, but, in thy greed and self-will, didst fly upon the spoil, and do that which was evil in the sight of the Lord?" But even now Saul will not admit his fault; either he knew little about the details of the law which he had violated, or he wished to intimate that as king he had no superior, and would carry on his affairs without dictation. He reiterates his former excuses, evidently caring nothing for the verdict which the Reader of men's hearts might pass on his conduct, and desiring only to justify himself before Samuel. "I have obeyed the voice of the Lord," he repeats. "It is true that the people spared the chief of the devoted things.[1] But why? To pay public honour to the Lord whose prophet you profess to be, they selected the very best of the spoil which would otherwise have been wasted. And in proof of my victory and of the extermination of the Amalekites, see, I have saved none of them but their king, who stands here before you." Samuel will listen no longer. He stops this justification of the infringement of a plain command on a pretence of religion by enunciating that grand principle which later prophets so constantly taught and enforced, and which our Blessed Lord Himself endorsed,[2] viz., that external ceremonies

[1] The Authorized Version (1 Sam. xv. 21) gives a wrong impression by rendering: "the chief of the things which should have been utterly destroyed." This reads rather like an ironical parenthesis (Payne Smith).
[2] Ps. l. 8. Isa. i.; ii. Jer. vi. 20. Hos. vi. 6. Mic. vi. 6 ff. Matt. ix 13.

and ritual conformity are nothing worth without the obedience of the heart. Then the seer in rhythmical measure, as uttering a Divine oracle for all ages to remember and to profit by, proceeds to pronounce the awful sentence with which he is charged :

> "Hath the Lord as great delight in burnt offerings and sacrifices
> As in obeying the voice of the Lord?
> Behold, to obey is better than sacrifice,
> And to hearken than the fat of rams.
> For rebellion is as the sin of witchcraft,
> And stubbornness is as idolatry and teraphim.[1]
> Because thou hast rejected the word of the Lord,
> He hath also rejected thee from being king."

The solemn sentence struck Saul with terror. What, should he be ranked with idolaters and dealers in witchcraft? Had he to whom such offences were really abominable laid himself open to such a charge? And was the authority to which he had learned to cling with such satisfaction to be torn from his grasp? Sunk as he was, he cannot contemplate the sentence unshrinking. He trembles at the prophet's word. "I have sinned," he cries ; "for I have transgressed the commandment of the Lord, and thy word." There was repentance in the language ; there was no real repentance in the heart. He was vexed at the turn things had taken, annoyed that the only authority to which he felt inclined to bow should view his conduct so harshly ; and even while acknowledging his fault he endeavours to minimize it by insinuating that he was not a free agent, and by ascribing it to a laudable desire to gratify his subjects' wishes. The excuse only exhibited more clearly his unfitness for his position. He should have used his power to check these unlawful desires ; he should have set forth before the people the Law of God, and his intention to uphold it at all costs. How was he suited for the post of theocratic king who set popularity above duty? He still felt no sorrow for the sin itself ; he grieved only for its consequences, present and future. He saw that this public rupture between himself and the great and honoured prophet would diminish his authority and do him

---

[1] The *teraphim* were the household gods of the Israelites, like the Lares of the Romans. They were probably images of ancestors, and if not actually worshipped, were used in unlawful magical rites.

irreparable mischief; so he begged Samuel not to desert him at this crisis. Seeming to fear the minister of Jehovah more than Jehovah Himself, he made another appeal: " I pray thee," he says to Samuel, "pardon my sin, and turn again with me, that I may worship the Lord." Samuel at first was deaf to the entreaty, and repeated the message of doom: " I will not return with thee; for thou hast rejected the word of the Lord, and the Lord hath rejected thee from being king over Israel." But as Samuel turned to leave him, the king, in despair, seized the border of his upper-robe, holding him by its collar in order to detain him. With such violence did he do this that it tore under his grasp. The prophet takes this as an omen of the future. "The Lord," he announces, "hath rent the kingdom of Israel from thee this day, and hath given it to a neighbour of thine, that is better than thou." Saul had already deprived his posterity of any share in the kingdom, and now he has ruined his own prospects. Samuel does not yet know who is the person intended by his prophetic announcement, and therefore he uses the vague term " neighbour," which may mean any man; but he will be one who will be more obedient than Saul. And he confirms his words by adding, " He who is the changeless glory of Israel will not lie nor repent; for He is not a man that He should repent." God's purpose stands immutable. Saul's election to and continuance in the kingdom had been conditional; his rejection is absolute and final. Yet certain as this now was, Samuel at length yielded to Saul's renewed entreaty, and consented to hide the rupture from the people's eyes by assisting at the public sacrifices and worship now about to be offered. It was no part of Samuel's mission to create anarchy and confusion by withdrawing all countenance from the king *de facto* before a successor was appointed. In his cooler moments he saw that to decline Saul's request and to slight the monarch in this open manner might give a new impulse to any disaffection that existed, opponents supporting their antagonism by the authority of the prophet's great name. So he turned and joined Saul in his religious acts. But he had one more duty to perform ere he left the assembly. He must show that he did not sanction the violation of the Divine command, and do this by an act which would prove that he was terribly in earnest. Agag, the wicked king of a wicked nation, had been devoted to death. Saul, by an ill-advised clemency, had saved him alive;

but he could not be permitted to live; the ban must be carried out. Samuel had heard of his preservation, and now orders him to be brought forward. Agag comes, fettered hand and foot;[1] and when he is in the presence of the king and the austere prophet, though he knows that at such a great national festival held in honour of victory it was only natural that his life should be sacrificed, he will not abandon all hope of escape, and says, with an implied doubt amid the seeming confidence of his words: " Surely the bitterness of death is past."[2] Samuel immediately disabuses him of the notion that he will escape death. Sternly he pronounces the doom: " As thy sword hath made women childless, so shall thy mother be childless among women." And with his own hand he executes the sentence. There before the altar of Jehovah, as a righteous act of retribution done for the glory of God, he hews Agag in pieces. This act seems so repugnant to modern ideas and to a superficial estimate of the prophet's duty and character, that many assume that Samuel merely gave the order for the execution, and left it to be carried out by others. Certainly there is nothing in the language of the narrative to confirm this notion; and we have no right to introduce into the sacred record interpretations solely suggested by our idea of the fitness of things. From what is written we gather that Samuel, roused to high excitement by the present circumstances, and for the moment gifted with unusual vigour, did in his official capacity slay the *devoted* Agag. Thus he carried out the ban, did that which the king had failed to do, and removed from the nation the guilt of a broken oath. Thus he gave an example needed in, and suited to, that rough age, of uncompromising obedience to God's commands, and left to all time the lesson that God's work must be

---

[1] This is the rendering adopted by Dean Payne Smith and Klostermann. The Authorized Version gives "delicately"; the LXX. "trembling"; Vulg, "very fat and trembling"; Aquila, "with daintiness"; Symmachus, "delicate." The Syriac omits it altogether. Most modern commentators take the word to mean "cheerfully"; but Agag's observation next recorded scarcely bears out this interpretation. The word occurs in Job. xxxviii. 31, where it is rightly rendered "bands."

[2] Ewald's idea that Agag's words imply a cheerful acquiescence in the sentence pronounced upon him, is surely most unreasonable. What could lead this cruel, luxurious heathen to come to his death not "unwilling and struggling, but rather, as if suddenly transformed by a loftier impulse, with delight and joy"? ("Hist. of Israel," iii 39).

SAUL'S FINAL REJECTION.

done thoroughly, no thought of self being allowed to influence the due execution of His directions.

Having thus vindicated the rights of Jehovah, Samuel parted from Saul and returned to his home at Ramah, leaving affairs of state, and devoting himself to the training of younger prophets and citizens, thus laying the foundations of national welfare on safer grounds than popular favour or royal caprice.[1] The old relations between himself and the monarch were entirely broken off. Saul was no longer the theocratic king to whom the prophet communicated the word of the Lord, and who went in and out under his guidance. He was *de facto* king; but his kingdom was altogether of this world: he had sunk away from God by little and little, and now communion with God was his no longer. Samuel's reproachful words at Gilgal had been very unwelcome to him; he had never cordially sought his counsel from that time; he engaged at Michmash without asking his advice; he had not invited his presence at the solemn thanksgiving for victory over the Amalekites. But Samuel hitherto had clung to the king in spite of manifold discouragements. Now at length he is forced to give him up. Never more did he come to see him as long as he lived. Once indeed, they met at one of the schools of the prophets, but this was inadvertently, and nothing passed between them. Yet Samuel could not forget Saul. He had loved him for his early promise, for his high and noble qualities, for his brave services, and he mourned his fall, as a father sorrows over a beloved son's degradation and ruin. Perhaps, too, he saw in his suspiciousness and unrestrained self-will signs of that terrible malady which darkened the later years of Saul's life; and the good old prophet grieved, not only for the king who had thrown away his great opportunities, but also for the man whose future was clouded with a dreadful apprehension.

[1] Ewald, iii. 47.

CHAPTER X.

A SUCCESSOR ANOINTED.

Samuel sent to Bethlehem—Anoints David—Condition of Saul—David summoned to soothe him with music—Philistines invade Judah—Valley of Elah—Goliath challenges the Israelites—David accepts the challenge; kills the giant—Defeat and slaughter of the Philistines—Saul takes David into his service—Friendship of David and Jonathan.

SAMUEL was unable all at once to reconcile himself to the repudiation of Saul. He mourned for the wreck of the high hopes which he had entertained, and for the seeming frustration of the purpose of God in allowing the election of a king. He knew not as yet how the vacancy in the theocratic throne was to be filled up, and he feared that the rejection of the present king might lead to the loosening of all authority in the state and a return to that disunion and political weakness from which Saul had raised the nation. And the cry of intercession ceased not to rise from the hill of Ramah; it may be that in answer to that mighty supplication immediate vengeance was suspended. The voice of God roused the old seer from his sorrowful inaction, and bade him go and anoint a successor to the rejected Saul. He was to take a vessel filled with the sacred oil kept with the ark, and to go to Bethlehem, and there anoint one of the sons of Jesse, a well-known inhabitant of that village. David,[1] the one to be selected, is not specially named at this stage of the transaction. Samuel will be guided in his choice

---

[1] The history of David is very briefly handled in the present work, as it is fully narrated in another book of this series, "David: his Life and Times."

in such a manner that all may see that the election is of God, and that no private feeling interferes to control its freedom. Bethlehem, which was some twelve miles south of Ramah, was not one of the places visited by Samuel in his judicial circuit, and the families who dwelt there were probably unknown to him. Certainly he had no acquaintance with David when this intimation reached him. The mission was a perilous one. Samuel was not one to show fear or hesitation when a duty was set before him, yet even he is in dread. "How can I go?" he asks. "If Saul hear it, he will kill me." That jealousy and suspicion which dominated Saul's later life had already begun to display themselves, and since his rejection had made rapid progress. Besides, being still actually king, he would naturally consider the anointing of another in his stead as an act of treason, which, in his view, might justly be punished by death; and though probably he had too much respect for the old prophet to deal with him thus violently, still he might have restricted his liberty, or banished him from the land, or taken a bloody revenge upon Jesse and his household. This fear, therefore, was not unreasonable, and Samuel is instructed how he may escape the danger and yet perform his mission successfully. He had long been accustomed to visit various localities for the purpose of offering sacrifice, which, in the abnormal condition of religious matters, when the ark was separated from the tabernacle, it was lawful for him to do as the commissioned prophet of the Lord. He is now directed to use this custom in order to cloak his design from the jealous eye of Saul. He was to take a heifer and to go to Bethlehem, and to announce that he was come to offer a sacrifice to the Lord. He was further to invite Jesse and his sons to the sacrificial feast that followed, and then God would show him how to act in the matter of the unction The object of Samuel's visit to Bethlehem was, as far as his public actions were concerned, to offer accustomed sacrifices. If he had a further purpose, in which the people generally were not interested, he was under no moral obligation to disclose it. Samuel, guarding well the secret commission, went, as he was directed, to Bethlehem. It was an unusual visit Never before had he come to this place, and the elders were alarmed at the solemn entry of the dreaded prophet with the heifer and the long horn of sacred oil in his hand. Had he come to hold an inquisition on them for some dereliction of duty? or was this unexpected arrival connected with the breach between him and the king of which they had lately heard? Why was their secluded little village thus singled out? Samuel quickly reassured them, and announcing that he came to sacrifice, bade them sanctify themselves and get ready to attend the ceremony and the banquet that followed. The invitation was especially offered to Jesse, the chief or sheikh of the town, and his sons. When the sacrifice was offered, before the invited guests sat down to the feast, which would not take place for some hours, Samuel went to Jesse's house, and had his sons presented to him, waiting for the Lord to point out the one whom he was to anoint. He seems to have told Jesse little or nothing of the design of this ceremony, and to have acted throughout in a mysterious manner, calculated rather to court than to satisfy inquiry. When he beheld Eliab, the eldest son, a stately man, with a fine and noble countenance, he said to himself that this must be the Lord's anointed, but was taught that he was mistaken in thinking that physical advantages necessarily imply high moral qualities. Six other sons passed in review before him, but none of them were selected, though all were gallant, strong, and beautiful. Perplexed and uncertain how to act in this dilemma, Samuel asks Jesse if these seven are all the sons he has, and is informed that there is one more, the youngest, who was in the fields keeping sheep. He is sent for, and comes before the old prophet, very different in appearance from his dark stalwart brothers, fair in complexion, with reddish hair and beautiful eyes, and withal of small and delicate frame. As Samuel gazes on this youth, the voice Divine bids him arise and anoint him, for this was the chosen son. Samuel took the oil, and without further words or explanation anointed David in the midst of his brethren. What the spectators thought of the transaction we are not told. Certainly neither David nor they saw in it any immediate delegation to the kingdom; the high destiny to which this youth was called was not mentioned, and he returned to his usual occupations afterwards as if nothing uncommon had happened. The anointing seemed to the brethren to be merely a mode of designating the boy as assistant at the sacrificial ceremony, or enrolling him as pupil in the prophetic school. But it had an inward effect on David himself; "the spirit of the Lord came mightily upon him;" his character developed itself in many ways, and the Divine influence was shown in the high and noble qualities which he exhibited.

His mission completed, Samuel returned to Ramah. How fared it with the rejected, though not deposed, Saul? His state is described in awful words: "the spirit of the Lord had departed from Saul, and an evil spirit from the Lord terrified him." Whether Saul's was a case of demoniacal possession, or merely of morbid mental disease, cannot be determined. An unscientific age ascribed madness, epilepsy, and some other diseases, to the direct action of the devil; and doubtless such inflictions were sometimes rightly so designated, God allowing the evil spirit to exercise a certain influence on the bodies and minds of wicked men. Saul's state was regarded as a Divine judgment upon him. Reasoning from all the circumstances known to us, we may come to the following conclusion: the denunciations of Samuel, the withdrawal of the kingdom from himself and his descendants, a feeling of being ill-treated, a proud self-will which would not submit to rebuke, and an uneasy expectation of the sudden appearance of some competitor to the throne, rendered him gloomy, suspicious, irascible. To these feelings he gave himself over; fits of despondency became more frequent as he less and less resisted them; discontented with himself, he made no effort at reformation; every year, every day, increased the evil, till his mind gave way, and he became to some extent actually insane.

As these fits of frenzy grew more violent, Saul's attendants became alarmed, and considered how best to alleviate them. The influence of music in such cases was well established. Æsculapius used it in the treatment of insane patients, and throughout the East it was regarded as one of the best agents for allaying troubled spirits. So they recommended Saul to seek for some cunning player on the harp who might soothe his mind by his sweet strains, and restore to him peace and comfort. According to one historian, this suggestion led to David's introduction to the king; according to another and more reliable tradition, the combat with Goliath first brought him to Saul's notice, and his attendance at the court as minstrel commenced subsequently to that event. Our present Hebrew text does not give the accounts of these matters in strict chronological order, as they are derived from different authorities, and inserted with no attempt at reconciliation. The writer of the history of Saul finishes his record (1 Sam. xvi.) by telling generally how David was anointed and made known to the public. In chap. xvii. the history of David is commenced from the beginning, some details already mentioned being given, and many new ones added. If we adopt the commonly received (but, as I think, erroneous) sequence of events, the story will run as follows. Saul consenting to try the proposed remedy for his malady, one of his attendants, himself probably trained in the school at Naioth and familiar with those who had enjoyed the same education, mentioned David as just the person to suit his requirements. "I have seen," he said, " a son of Jesse the Bethlehemite, that is cunning in playing, and a mighty man of valour, and a man of war, and prudent in speech, and a comely person, and the Lord is with him." From this description of David we gather that from the time of his unction he had exhibited wonderful energy and courage, his natural gifts, his qualities both of body and soul, were enhanced by Divine influence; he had taken part in resisting some inroad of the Philistines, and was well known as a good soldier and a brave defender of his father's flocks against human marauders and against wild beasts. If this conversation is, as I believe, to be referred to a later period, the allusion to David's valour will naturally be explained of his combat with the giant, after which he had returned to his homely calling till summoned to court in order to use his musical skill in Saul's service. He must have been now about eighteen years old. The king was greatly pleased with what he heard. He was always looking out for any promising youth who might make an useful soldier, and it gratified him to think that in David he might find one who was not only a skilful musician, but might in a very short time be added to his roll of mighty men. So Saul dispatched an imperative message to Jesse at Bethlehem bidding him to send David at once to court. Jesse could not disobey this order ; and as a great man was not to be approached without a present, and compliance with a superior's commands was usually thus accompanied, Jesse sent with his son an ass laden with some produce of his farm as an offering to the king. The present was simple enough, and suited to an unsophisticated state of society ; it consisted of bread, a leathern bottle of wine, and a fine kid. Thus introduced, the youthful shepherd stood before the monarch, and, when the latter suffered from an attack of his

A SUCCESSOR ANOINTED.

malady, played upon his harp and soothed the frenzied patient into calmness. These fits of insanity were at present of infrequent occurrence; and as David's presence was required only at intervals, he returned continually to his home, and resumed his pastoral occupations or received instruction at the mouth of Samuel. It is very possible that Saul in his sane moments saw but little of the young musician, and when some time elapsed without his services being called in requisition, he almost forgot his person, and thought no more about him. A year or two later, after Saul had reigned some twelve years, his attention was fixed on David by a very remarkable circumstance which the sacred historian relates at some length.[1]

The restless Philistines at this time again endeavoured to reduce the Israelites under their yoke. We are ignorant of the circumstances which inspired them to undertake this new attack, but it was made with a large force and displayed considerable skill. They had entered the territory of Judah, and massed their forces between Socoh and Azekah, in Ephes-dammim. These places have been satisfactorily identified. Socoh, now Shuweikeh, lies on a kind of natural terrace about half a mile above the valley of Elah, "the Terebinth," in the hill country some sixteen miles south-west of Jerusalem. Azekah, now Deir el Aspek, is in the more open country below the Wady Surar, eight miles north of Socoh, on the main road from the valley of Elah. About a mile to the south occurs Beit Fased, "House of

---

[1] The Vatican MS of the Septuagint, after verse 11 of chapter xvii. ("When Saul and all Israel heard those words of the Philistine, they were dismayed, and greatly afraid") goes at once to ver. 32: "And David said to Saul, Let no man's heart fail," &c., thus omitting the unnecessary recapitulation, ver. 12, "Now David was the son of that Ephrathite," &c., and the episode of David's brethren. The Greek narrates the flight, and the death of the giant, but omits from ver. 55 of this chapter to ver. 5 of chap xviii.; that is, after saying that David put the giant's armour in his tent, it proceeds with the account of the women meeting the returning army with songs, &c. We thus get rid of the difficulty of Saul's question to Abner. It is perhaps hardly justifiable to correct the Hebrew text from the Greek version, but it is plain that our present text is put together unskilfully, and that attempts were early made to eliminate supposed discrepancies. The Alexandrian MS translates the Hebrew text as we now have it, but it is evidently the work of a different hand from that which rendered the rest of the passage. Josephus seems to have had in his copy xvii. 12–31, but not xvii. 55 to xviii. 5, and he always uses the Septuagint version in his histories.

bleeding," which represents the site of the Philistine encampment, that place of ill-omened name, Ephes-dammim, "the boundary of blood," so called from the frequent and sanguinary encounters of which it was the scene. Saul took up his position on the side of the valley of Elah, the Wady Sunt, on one of the low rocky hills, covered with lentisk bushes, which there abound. Between the two hosts lay the broad open valley, rich and fertile, but divided lengthwise in its midst by a remarkable ravine, the presence of which sufficiently accounts for the opposing armies being unable to bring matters to a decisive issue by engaging in a pitched battle. Captain Conder[1] describes it as a deep trench, formed by a mountain torrent which runs with great violence in the winter, though dry in summer. This *gai*, or channel, is some twenty feet wide, with steep vertical sides, ten or twelve feet deep, and quite impassable except in certain places. The sides of this trench are strewn with rounded, water-worn pebbles, each fitted for use in the sling.

While the two armies thus lay facing one another, the Philistines sent forth a well-known champion of theirs, Goliath of Gath, the city of the Anakim (Josh. xi. 22), to challenge any of the Israelites to single combat, and to leave the issue of the war to be decided by this encounter. He was a very formidable foe. The account of his size and equipment is such as to make one marvel. His height is said to have been "six cubits and a span," some eight feet and a half at the lowest estimate; others give him almost an additional foot. The arms of this monster were suited to his dimensions. The mediæval knights in their thick plate armour were useless when dismounted or overthrown; and Goliath must have been thoroughly unwieldly and slow in movement under the excessive weight of his armour and weapons. An active adversary would have had every advantage against him in spite of his size and strength. But his appearance was what he and his friends relied upon to inspire the foe with terror. They put him forth in the vacant space between the two armies to insult the Israelites, and to offer a challenge which they presumed would never be accepted. Like Homer's heroes, he stands and boasts of his prowess and laughs to scorn his puny opponents. "Choose you

---

[1] "Tent Work," ii. 160 "Quarterly Statement," 1875, 1876.

A SUCCESSOR ANOINTED.

a man for you," he cries, "and let him come down to me. If he be able to fight with me, and to kill me, then will we be your servants; but if I prevail against him, and kill him, then shall ye be our servants, and serve us. I defy the armies of Israel this day." Thus standing on his own side of the ravine, the giant flung his challenge at Israel. Saul and his followers looked on and listened in dismay, but no one dared accept the offered combat. The issues were too momentous to be entrusted to common hands, and yet there was no one of sufficient courage and skill among the chiefs to uphold the cause of God's people. The king himself was withheld by his dignity from answering the challenge; Jonathan's life was considered too valuable to be endangered in such an unequal fight. In this dilemma they asked no counsel of God or His priest, but for forty days endured these grievous taunts, not knowing how to repress them. Saul, it is true, had made lavish offers to any one who should slay the insolent Philistine, promising to enrich him with untold wealth, to give him his daughter in marriage, and to bestow privileges and immunities upon all his family; but no one came forward to compete for these prizes at the price of what seemed certain death. Among the warriors in Saul's army were the three eldest sons of Jesse; and it was the custom of their father to send David to them with provisions during the campaign. One of these occasions happened at the end of the forty days just mentioned. David, who had not before heard of the huge champion and his insolent challenge, arrived at the waggon rampart of the camp just as Goliath stalked forward and uttered his daily boast. He was utterly amazed to see that this uncircumcised Philistine was thus allowed to insult the army of Jehovah; and having heard of the king's terms, he was moved by the spirit within him to offer himself as the champion of Israel. Brought before Saul he expressed his desire to accept the giant's challenge, and declining the offer of Saul's armour, declared that he would go as he was to the combat, and had no doubt at all concerning the issue. His ready confidence inspired Saul and Abner with like trust, and they let him have his way. But Saul's interest was keenly aroused; and wishing to know more of one who might some day become his son-in-law, he inquired of Abner whose son the stripling was; but Abner could give him no information. Meantime David, in his simple shepherd's dress, and unarmed save for

his shepherd's staff and the goat's-hair sling, in the use of which
the pastoral Israelites were well skilled, left the camp, and
crossing the plain, approached the gully that had so long proved
an impassable barrier to the operations of the hostile armies.
Sliding down the bank into the dry watercourse, he chose out
five smooth pebbles from those that lay at his feet, put them
into his wallet, and climbing up the other side, stood in the
presence of his gigantic adversary. Goliath despised his youthful opponent, and vaunted his certain victory, cursing David by
his God and defying Jehovah to save him from death. The
young champion retorted by expressing his sure trust in the
God of Israel, and his confidence that He was with him, and
would give victory into his hand. Then ere the giant could come
to close combat, he slung one stone with so true an aim, that it
struck the Philistine on the forehead beneath the helmet, there
being no visor to protect the face, and he fell stunned, if not
dead, prone on the ground. To make all sure, David, on seeing
his enemy fall, ran up with all speed, and taking the giant's
sword, slew him therewith, and cut off his head. The combat
had been watched with the keenest interest by the two armies,
and when the champion was overthrown dire consternation
filled the breasts of the Philistines, while the Israelites were
animated with the wildest exultation. They rushed down the
hill into the valley, crossed the ravine without opposition, and
formed on the other side unchecked. The Philistines, utterly
demoralized by the unexpected death of their great warrior,
turned and fled without striking a blow. It was not a battle,
but a pursuit and a slaughter, that ensued. The fugitives fled
down the valley of Elah in wild disorder till they came to its
mouth, where they separated, some taking refuge in Gath, a
frontier fortress standing on its lofty chalk cliff above the road that
led to the highlands, others turned north to Ekron, and hardly
made their escape good, being followed to the very gates by
their pursuers.[1] The camp fell into the hands of the Israelites,
and enriched them with great spoils and a goodly supply of

---

[1] "By the way to Shaaraim," in the English and Latin versions; but "in
the way of the gates" in the Sept.; and this seems most correct. There
was a town of this name belonging to Judah (Josh. xv. 36) in the
Shephelah, identified with Sakariya, three miles north-west of Socoh, and
five miles south-east of Azekah.

arms. The carnage was very great; according to Josephus,[1] thirty thousand Philistines were slain, and twice that number wounded. We are not to suppose that all this was the work of one day, as the wording of the account seems to suggest; rather it probably occupied some months, and was followed by many other expeditions, the final results being such as the history states. On returning from the fight, David was brought before Saul, carrying in his hand the gory head of Goliath, the grim trophy of his victory. And the king, naturally anxious to know more about the young hero, and of what family was the man to whom he had virtually promised his daughter in marriage, asked him whose son he was. David told him that his father was Jesse the Bethlehemite. Saul was favourably struck with the young hero; his beauty of countenance, his gallant bearing, greatly affected the impressionable monarch; he felt kindly towards him, and engaged his services from that day forward, appointing him an armour-bearer or aide-de-camp. The spoils of the slain giant were at David's disposal. The arms he took to his own home at Bethlehem, afterwards depositing them as trophies in the tabernacle at Nob, where we hear of the sword at a later crisis. The head he reserved till he could place it where it might be a permanent memorial of the power of faith in Jehovah. Such an asylum was found for it in Jerusalem when the citadel was taken, and the tabernacle erected there.[2]

At this interview between Saul and David there was one present who was fully capable of appreciating the noble character of the young warrior, and rejoicing in his success. This was Jonathan, the brave, generous, steadfast son of Saul. As David answered the king's questions, and displayed his modesty, courage, sublime faith, and wisdom, a feeling of intense affection for this youth arose in Jonathan's breast; as the sacred writer expresses it, "the soul of Jonathan was knit with the soul of David, and Jonathan loved him as his own soul." The friendship then begun never wavered, was never darkened for a moment; it continued unimpaired by envy or jealousy till the last.

[1] "Antiq." vi. 9. 5.

[2] 1 Sam. xvii. 54 is proleptical, the writer desiring to complete the history of the giant's spoils before proceeding to other matters. Some commentators think that the head was deposited with the sword at Nob, which is loosely called "Jerusalem" as being in the immediate neighbourhood.

CHAPTER XI.

SAUL'S JEALOUSY AND MANIA.

Saul is jealous of David—Progress of his malady—Saul threatens David's life—Employs him on military expeditions—Gives him his daughter in marriage on condition of his slaying one hundred Philistines—Plots against his life—Relents for a while at Jonathan's intercession—Soon resumes his evil purpose—Tries to kill David—David saved by Michal—Flees to Samuel at Ramah—Saul sends to arrest him—Naioth—The messengers prophesy—Saul goes himself to Ramah and prophesies.

THE war with the Philistines was not ended by the defeat that followed the death of Goliath. Military operations were continued for some months, during all which time David waxed higher and higher in favour with Saul and the people ; so wisely and successfully did he treat all matters committed to his care, that Saul gave him a position of trust as one of the commanders of his army. But a circumstance soon occurred to rouse the king's jealousy, which was never afterwards set at rest, but was always ready to burst out into open violence, especially when he was suffering from attacks of his malady. At the conclusion of the campaign, Saul with David and the army returned home in triumph, having for the time quite restored the supremacy of Israel. To this unparalleled success David had chiefly contributed by his military skill and personal prowess proved on many different occasions. The people were not slow to recognize this. It was not alone as the conqueror of the giant Goliath that they received him.[1] He had won

[1] Our version of 1 Sam. xviii. 6 gives: "when David returned from the slaughter of the Philistine"; but we should read "Philistines," or take the singular in a generic sense ; as it is clear from the sequence of events

SAUL'S JEALOUSY AND MANIA.

highest praise in many an engagement since then, and his reputation had risen rapidly as time went on, so that he soon bade fair to eclipse the fame of the king himself. On the final return of the expedition, the women came forth from the cities to meet them with singing and dancing, and other signs of rejoicing. They bore cymbals and triangles, and as they performed the usual solemn dance, they sang antiphonally a song of victory, of which the refrain was:

> "Saul hath slain his thousands,
> And David his ten thousands."

Saul could not listen to this unmoved. He had not forgotten his deposition from the kingdom announced by the mouth of Samuel, and the substitution in his place of one worthier than he. He had often thought over this prospect with gloomy discontent, and looked out for signs that might announce his supplanter or successor. The years that had passed since that fatal intimation was given had not lessened his dread of the future, This foreboded dethronement preyed heavily upon his mind, and increased his distemper. What if this shepherd hero were the king destined by Jehovah to take the place which he had forfeited? This darling of the people might well be the rival who was to eject him and his race from the throne. This David had stood forth as champion for Israel when all the mighty men of the army crouched in terror; this stripling had prospered in every fight, and won the hearts of all with whom he served; so exalted was his fame in the country, that the people in their ode of victory reckoned him at ten times the worth of his king and superior. "And," asked Saul in jealous indignation, "what can he have more but the kingdom?" Henceforward he regarded David with mixed feelings of hatred and love. The old magnanimity which he had showed towards enemies in his early days had been ruined by years of brooding and discontent, and the evil temper to which he had given way at times utterly displaced the old affection for the gallant friend and soothing minstrel, and left nothing in its place but a feeling of rancorous envy and jealousy. As the writer impressively says,

that the fall of Goliath is not intended, but the great success that had attended David's military expeditions against the Philistines while occupying a chief position in the army of Saul.

alluding to the supposed effect of an evil eye, " Saul eyed David from that day and forward." Giving himself up to this wicked passion, when he saw himself, as he thought, put in slighting comparison with his servant, he is said to have been mightily troubled with an evil spirit from the Lord. This was a messenger of God, allowed to hold sway over him and execute the Divine judgment upon his soul. He was left to his own wilfulness, and evil had undisputed control in his diseased mind. His intellect gave way under the working of this morbid passion, and a new phase of frenzy developed itself. No longer merely brooding, moody, melancholy, he has become violent and murderous; his thoughts were of homicidal tendency; his utterances incoherent. Acting like a man possessed by an influence stronger than his own will, " he prophesied "; inspired, as it were, but by no good spirit, he spake words of which he knew not the meaning, and which seemed to the bystanders the ravings of a maniac. Hurriedly they called for David that he might, as aforetimes, soothe the king's troubled spirit. And David played with his accustomed skill, but not with the usual effect. The evil spirit in Saul was too potent, had been too freely welcomed, to be exorcised by such gentle means. Music had lost its power, but the minstrel would not easily desert his post, while there was hope of benefiting the raving monarch. Frenzied beyond control, Saul brandished his javelin, which he carried as a symbol of his regal authority, threatening to hurl it at David, as he struck his harp. Twice he aimed the deadly weapon at the musician, and twice he withheld his murderous hand, or David escaped in time from his presence, or the attendants restrained the furious king. But this impunity, added to the high repute of David, only augmented the king's malady. He saw in all this the Lord's hand; but this conviction, instead of leading him to acquiesce in the present circumstances, and to recognize the inexpediency of attempting to remove the youth who had served him so well and faithfully, only made him hate him more, and even fear him greatly. David did not withdraw himself from the court; he counted the animosity exhibited as a sign of the king's diseased state of mind, and did not resent it. Saul, however, even in his saner moments could not endure the continual presence of one whom he considered a rival, and whom he felt himself powerless to injure, while he could not but acknowledge the high qualities which had gained the affection of the whole army; he therefore freed himself from this constant source of irritation by giving David a command of a thousand men, and employing him on military expeditions. In this capacity the latter conducted himself so well that everything prospered in his hands; Israel and Judah, the northern and southern tribes alike, gladly put themselves under his leadership, and loved him universally. His promotion could not be prevented, but it was gall and wormwood to Saul to consent to his advancement. What he was forced to do he did ungraciously, slighting David's claims as far as he dared. The king had promised to give his daughter in marriage to the warrior who should overcome the Philistine champion Goliath; he felt constrained to acknowledge this obligation, hoping thereby to find some means of destroying him by using his zeal against the enemies of his country. So he now offered David his eldest daughter Merab, on condition that he fought valiantly in the wars of Jehovah, thinking all the time that he might thus be emboldened to enter upon rash adventures at the risk of his life. But Saul did not keep his promise. Either he hoped that David would have fallen a victim to his warlike zeal before the nuptials could be completed, or with the inconstancy of a tyrant simply changed his mind; at any rate he gave Merab in marriage, not to David, but to Adriel, of Abel-Meholah, who perhaps had offered a large dower in return for the honour. The five sons who were the offspring of this marriage were given over to the vengeance of the Gibeonites in requital of Saul's unrighteous attack upon them.[1] Merab had never loved David; but Michal, the second daughter, conceived a violent affection for him, and showed her preference plainly. Saul was pleased when he heard of this. It offered a means of keeping his promise and of atoning for his mean conduct in the former case, while the condition which he thought of imposing afforded good hope of ridding himself of his enemy. But he was not at all sure that David would now accept the position offered. The latter had experienced the king's fickleness and duplicity, and might not be willing to fall into the snare the second time. Saul saw at once a way to secure his evil purpose. He told his servants to let David know that he required no dower at his hands, but

[1] 2 Sam. xxi. 8, where the name Michal instead of Merab has crept into the text

only proof that he had slain a hundred of his enemies, the Philistines. This condition fell in well with David's warlike spirit. He never stopped to consider what might be Saul's insidious purpose in this demand, but at once proceeded to execute it. There may have been war going on at this moment with the Philistines; but in that age no excuse was needed for sudden attacks upon enemies. Power and opportunity were the only factors considered; the cruelty and injustice of such an action were never regarded. David set out with his men, made a sudden incursion into the Philistine territories, and ere the time fixed for the delivery of the dowry had expired he returned victorious, bringing with him proofs of the slaughter of more than the stipulated number, which "they gave in full tale to the king."[1] Saul, the condition being satisfied, and his malicious intention having failed, could no longer delay the marriage with Michal, and David became his son-in-law. But this new tie between them only increased Saul's unreasonable hatred. He could not doubt that the Lord was with David, and protected him in all dangers; or, if he recognized not God's hand in his deliverance, he looked on David as one of those lucky persons who were always successful, and against whom it was useless to plot. The close relationship with the king had added to David's influence, and made it impossible to punish him openly. Besides this, the consciousness that Michal loved her husband, and would use every exertion to screen him from her father's machinations, embittered his feelings and turned his home affection into poison. How different might events have turned out if the unhappy king had only accepted the situation and recognized the hand of Providence in the guidance of affairs! Here was the man destined to occupy his place admitted to his family; the change of dynasty was nothing; his daughter's husband might naturally be chosen as his successor; thus he would conciliate the good will of the people, satisfy the affection of his son and daughter, and bind David to himself by the ties of gratitude and love. But no, he persisted in his rancorous animosity, and David's continued success added fuel to the flame that consumed him.

Saul was now completely mastered by passion. His jealous

[1] Vulg.: "Et percussit ex Philistiim ducentos viros, et attulit eorum præputia, et annumeravit ea regi." Josephus ("Antiq." vi. 10, 3) makes David return with six hundred heads of Philistines.

hatred burst all control; he even dared openly to speak to Jonathan and his attendants of his intention to kill David at the first favourable opportunity.[1] He expatiated on the presumption of this young man, on his dangerous popularity with the army, on his traitorous intention of setting up a claim to the throne, and supplanting the present dynasty. He tried to deceive himself and his hearers by showing that his death was an absolute necessity, a measure of precaution which, however painful, must be taken for state reasons. He had silenced all better feelings, overridden misgivings, familiarized himself with the thought of crime, so that nothing could any longer check his murderous impulse. But David had a friend at court who saw his danger and warned him of it. Jonathan, the gallant, the upright son of a perverse father, knew that there was many an unscrupulous courtier, who, after such an avowal on their sovereign's part, would be only too ready to help him get rid of this obnoxious subject. Jonathan, animated not only by love of his friend, but by true patriotism, warned David of his danger, bidding him hide himself awhile until he had sounded his father, and tried to turn him from his evil purpose. Then he talked calmly with the morbid tyrant, reminded him of David's services, and of the great relief which he had himself felt at the youth's success, and implored him not to be guilty of shedding innocent blood. Saul, ever fickle, and still capable of generous emotions, relents at this intercession, and swears an oath that David's life should be spared: "As the Lord liveth, he shall not be slain." Nothing could be more solemn than such an asseveration. Jonathan was thoroughly reassured, and gladly communicating to David his father's more favourable disposition, brought his friend once more to the king, and he returned to his old footing at court. This reconciliation lasted some time, and David had resumed the terms of intimacy to which he had risen before the last outbreak, when a new cause awoke the king's slumbering jealousy to still greater fury. A fresh inroad of the Philistines was repelled by David with his accustomed vigour and success. This raised Saul's envy to the highest pitch. He made no attempt

---

[1] The translation of 1 Sam. xix. 1 in A.V. is erroneous: "spake to Jonathan . . . that they should kill David." It ought to be, "about killing David," *i.e.*, that he intended to kill him. So the Greek and Syriac versions.

to resist the evil temper; he encouraged and nurtured his malicious feelings, and was given over to the dominion of his own passions; so that it is again said: "an evil spirit from the Lord was upon him." This terrible fit of insanity was a judicial punishment of his impenitence and hardness of heart. While he was suffering under this mania, David came into his presence to soothe, if it might be, his mad excitement. But the time for such influence had passed away for ever. Here was his enemy unarmed, in his power; should he not avail himself of the opportunity and crush him at a blow? He seized his regal spear, and giving way to the murderous impulse, hurled it at the musician, aiming to slay him as he stood. David, keen, watchful, active, saw in good time the king's intent, avoided the threatening blow, and the weapon savagely sped was fixed harmlessly in the wall. But Saul, now inflexible in purpose, was not going to let the victim escape. David fled to his own home, thinking that the king was suffering from one of his usual paroxysms, and that when this was over he would be in no danger. Saul, however, was steadfastly bent on his destruction; he had his house carefully watched by armed emissaries, ordering them to fall upon him and slay him whenever he might come abroad. Josephus[1] deems that Saul meant to seize him and bring him to trial as a traitor, his condemnation being provided for; but, lost to all self-respect as the unhappy monarch now was, and having given the reins to his murderous jealousy, he was not likely to attend to any forms of law, but was sure to carry the matter with high-handed tyranny. By some means, perhaps through Jonathan's information, Michal became aware of the design against her husband's life; and as the doors were carefully watched, she let him down with cords from a window, as St. Paul was delivered at Damascus, and he escaped the ambush. That he might have time to get away safely, Michal exerted her woman's wit to delay the pursuit. She sent word that he had been very ill in the past night, and was still lying in his room sick and unable to move, making good her story by dressing an image in a bed to represent her absent husband. The deceit was soon discovered, but not before it had answered its purpose.

Meantime the fugitive, seeing that the court was no longer a

[1] "Antiq." vi. 11. 4.

home for him, made his way to his old friend and counsellor Samuel at Ramah. The prophet, though retired from active life, still retained much of his former influence, and could not only give David advice in this emergency, but also offer a refuge, where in peace and prayer he might calm his troubled spirit and find strength for future trials. In the neighbourhood of his home Samuel had erected some dwellings (called *Naioth* in our text) for the use of the students whose education he superintended. Here they lived a cœnobitical life, and learned the literary, religious, and political lessons which would fit them to play their own part in the world and to guide others aright. Received into this communion, David was for a time secure. But not for long. Saul was soon informed where David had found refuge, and regardless of the sacredness of his asylum, sent messengers to arrest him. But a stronger power than that of the tyrant interposed to prevent the execution of the design. The messengers arrived at "Naioth"; there was no attempt to hinder their approach; all was solemn, peaceful, religious. They enter the public hall, and what do they see? A company of reverent students; an ample, organized choir; a band of trained prophets, mature in age, devout in aspect; and presiding as leader the venerable Samuel himself, far advanced in years, but hale and efficient still—all engaged in chanting the praises of God, and in their enthusiastic worship utterly fearless of the presence of these armed intruders. Awe-struck for a minute the messengers stood, and then as the scene and its surroundings filled their imagination, as they listened to the noble melody that rose from the lips of these servants of God, and received into their souls the import of the words that were sung, a like enthusiasm fired their breasts; they cast aside their murderous purpose, and joined in the service with heart and voice. News of this proceeding was carried to Saul, and he sent other messengers to execute his will. The same thing occurred a second and a third time. The Spirit of the Lord came upon these emissaries; they took part in the religious exercise which they found going on, whether it were singing, or music, or dancing, or recitation, and, forgetting the hostile purpose with which they had set out, acted in all respects like persons who were themselves "sons of the prophets." At this frustration of his plans Saul was greatly enraged.[1] He had long done despite to

---

[1] So Sept., 1 Sam. xix. 22.

his conscience; nothing can now restrain him; he will violate the sanctity of the prophet's dwelling, break into the hallowed asylum, and himself lay hands on the offender. He immediately set forth for Ramah from his home at Gibeah. Arriving at a place which tradition still pointed out when the account was written, but which is not accurately identified—the great cistern in Sechu [1]—he inquired of the neighbouring inhabitants where Samuel and David were to be found. He was told that they were now in Naioth of Ramah, and proceeded thither. And now a wonderful thing happened. The spirit of prophecy suddenly fell upon Saul himself, as it had fallen on his messengers, and he went on his way reciting and singing in a state of the wildest excitement. As soon as he came to the school, he stripped himself of his ornaments, flung aside his royal robe, and attired only in his inner tunic, rushed into Samuel's presence, chanting, gesticulating, dancing, a victim to religious ecstasy. What was the meaning of this illapse of the spirit upon such a man at such a time? What brought about this change in the moody king? Even if we regard the effect as nothing supernatural, we find in it something very remarkable. The excitement under which he had long been labouring had culminated in conduct which we could scarcely have anticipated. The thought of meeting with his own estranged friend and guide, Samuel, was one element in his excitement; the feeling of vengeance soon to be gratified was another. Then the sight of Samuel at the head of the school of prophets, the sound of the strains once familiar to his ear, recalled that earlier scene when he was once before similarly affected; he seemed to be back in the old days and open again to holy influence: the remembrance overpowered him; mastered by uncontrollable emotion, he threw himself into the present circumstances like an Eastern fanatic, till exhausted by his feelings and bodily actions he lay like one dead upon the earth. Did this extraordinary ecstasy mark his reprobation, as the former had accompanied the inauguration of his reign? Or was it a last merciful pleading of the Holy Spirit in his heart, a powerful working of that better thing within him to lead him to repentance and amendment before it was too late? The outward effects were visible to all men, and occasioned a repetition

---

[1] It is supposed to be Kurbet Suweikeh, one and a half miles south of Beeroth. "Survey Memoirs," iii pp. 52, 126.

and confirmation of the proverb already noticed: "Is Saul also among the prophets?" If it was formerly a marvel that one so unlearned and untrained as Saul should be found among the prophetic band, much more wonderful was it now that one who had been vexed by an evil spirit, who had come with hostile intent to Ramah, bringing his profane wrath and murderous purpose into the very sanctuary, should experience the Divine afflatus and prophesy. And what lessons could he and his followers learn from this occurrence but these?—that God holds in His hands the hearts of men and turns them as He wills; that the Lord did not allow the destruction of David, and that in endeavouring to compass it they were fighting against God. The transient emotion past, Saul forgot the lesson; the warning took no hold of his fickle will, and, being disregarded, added to the hardness of his heart.

CHAPTER XII.

SAUL'S PERSECUTION OF DAVID.

Saul's intention towards David tested at the Festival of the New Moon; proved to be murderous—Jonathan informs David, who flees to Nob; is received and fed by Ahimelech—Doeg is present; informs Saul of what happened there—Massacre of the priests at Nob—Saul pursues David to Ziph—Disaffection in the land—Saul nearly entraps David at Maon—Is spared by David at Engedi—Affected by David's forbearance Saul professes reconciliation.

The occurrence at Ramah, together with Saul's trance which lasted a day and night, gave David time to escape his relentless enemy. He hastened to his friend Jonathan, and consulted with him as to the course which he should take under present circumstances. A partial reconciliation had, as it seems, been made, probably by the intervention of Samuel, and David found himself expected to resume his attendance at court; but he had no guarantee for the future, and his life hung on the caprice of a fickle tyrant. Jonathan, indeed, endeavoured to believe, and to persuade his friend, that his father's late acts were to be attributed to an access of his malady, and that when he came to himself no such danger was to be feared. David was not convinced of this. Saul had had no personal communication with him, had not assured him of any change of sentiment, and David naturally feared to trust himself in his presence after the late attempts on his life. A test of the king's intentions might be easily applied. It was plain that, knowing Jonathan's love for David, Saul would not impart to his son his design against David's life; but his feeling might be discovered in another way.

At the beginning of every month, the day of the new moon [1] was observed as a religious festival by all good Israelites, and by Saul as a great civil festival also, on which he gave a banquet, attended by his family and the chief men of the State. David, the king's son-in-law and a commander in his army, would be expected to be present on this occasion. If he absented himself, and Saul took it in good part, no danger need be feared; if, on the contrary, the king was violently incensed at his absence, then it was certain that recent events had not altered his feelings, and that he was still resolved on extreme measures. In this manner the question was to be settled.

Saul returned from Ramah cured of his frenzy and composed in mind. The monthly festival came round, ushered in by the blast of trumpets, and celebrated with the customary offerings and sacrifices. The royal feast took place and lasted two days. All the great officers were there arranged in due order. The king was in the seat of honour next the wall and farthest from the door; opposite to him was Jonathan, and at his side sat Abner. Saul immediately observed that David's place at the table was vacant, but he made no remark at the moment, thinking that there was a reasonable cause for his absence. But when David did not appear on the second day, he became suspicious that there was some special reason which kept him away. He turned to Jonathan, as most likely to know David's movements, and asked him why this "son of Jesse," as he called him in derision of his lowly birth, had not taken his place for these two days. Jonathan answered, as he and his friend had previously concerted, that David had been summoned by his eldest brother, acting as head of the family, to a public sacrifice at Bethlehem, and had asked permission to attend it. Such an excuse, whether true or not in this instance, was in itself entirely credible. But to Saul's suspicious temper the excuse suggested premeditation, and it incensed him because it deprived him of an opportunity of which he had intended to avail himself. At this feast, surrounded by his friends, and supported by a body of courtiers who had slandered the absent hero and hoped to reap benefit by his deposition and death, the king had fully intended to carry out his murderous design. Was he to be frustrated in this way, and that

[1] Numb. x. 10 ; xxviii 11 ff.

with the privity or at the instigation of his own son? He fell
into violent anger when he heard Jonathan's answer. "Thou
perverse rebel,"[1] he cried, "do not I know that thou hast chosen
the son of Jesse to thine own shame, and to the confusion of
the mother that bore thee? For as long as the son of Jesse
liveth upon the ground, thou shalt not be established nor thy
kingdom. Wherefore now send and fetch him unto me, for,"
he adds, casting aside all disguise, "he shall surely die."
Jonathan, thinking a soft answer turneth away wrath, pleaded
mildly for his friend, asking what he had done that he should
be thus condemned. Saul, seized with fury, has no patience
to explain. He felt that David was plotting against him,
endeavouring to supplant the friend who was interceding for
him, was a double-dyed traitor; and he was incensed beyond
measure at his son's partizanship. In ungovernable anger he
brandished his javelin in Jonathan's face, threatening to smite
him where he sat. Such an insult in the sight of the assembled
guests, and such injurious aspersions cast upon his innocent
comrade, Jonathan could not endure. With a fierce and
righteous indignation blazing in his generous heart, he rose
quickly from the table, left the chamber, and appeared no more
at that fatal feast. Nothing remained but to acquaint David
with the unhappy result of the concerted experiment. This he
proceeded to do in the morning, and, as David's only safety lay
in immediate flight, the two friends, with many tears and
poignant regret, took leave of one another, and Jonathan returned to the city, while David betook himself to Nob. Here
he was received by Ahimelech, the high priest, who fed him and
his followers with the hallowed shew-bread, which was removed
from the table on that day, and gave him the famous sword of
Goliath which was laid up as a trophy in the tabernacle. Un-

---

[1] The Authorized Version is: "Thou son of a perverse rebellious
woman," and the translation is supported by the consideration that in the
East it is the greatest possible insult to a man to abuse his mother. But
we do not see the probability that Saul would speak in this way when the
reflection would fall upon his own wife; nor could he, as in the latter part
of the verse, have vowed that even Jonathan's mother would be ashamed
of him for his treachery, if he had begun by calling her perverse and
rebellious. The expression is general, and has nothing to do with family
relations, being literally, "son of perversity of rebellion" *i.e*., perverse,
rebellious man.

SAUL'S PERSECUTION OF DAVID.

fortunately, one of Saul's most trusted and unscrupulous servants, Doeg, an Edomite, the chief of the royal herdsmen, was present at this meeting. It is strange to find this foreigner employed in the service of the king of Israel and highly trusted by him, and it is the first instance of such a thing in the whole history. He, we are told, was "detained before the Lord" at Nob, an expression capable of many interpretations. He may have been a proselyte who desired to be admitted into the community of Israel, and was then receiving religious instruction; or he may have been paying some vow, or engaged in some ceremonial purification. Some have thought that he was being examined for the cure of leprosy, others that he had committed some trespass, and was kept in close seclusion till he had offered the appointed sacrifice. Whatever was the cause that brought him there, David scented danger in his presence, knew that he was a creature of Saul's, and would be sure to report to his master what he had seen; so he made no stay there, but fled for refuge to some safer spot.

Meantime Saul's whole energies were now directed to the capture and destruction of his hated son-in-law, and he waited anxiously for news about his movements. He heard of him as taking refuge among the Philistines at Gath, where he could not follow him, then as having secured an asylum for his father and mother in Moab, whence his ancestress Ruth had come, and finally that he had been joined by a number of disaffected people, and was now somewhere in Judæa at the head of a disciplined band of several hundred men. At length information reached him that David and his men were encamped among the thickets of Hareth, a place now known as Kharas, that lay on the edge of the mountain-chain of Hebron, some three miles east of Keilah, on the road between Adullam and Hebron, from which it is ten miles distant in a N.N.W. direction. As soon as Saul heard this, he convened an assembly of his officers and adherents, men chiefly of his own tribe and attached to him by benefits received and expected, and, seated under a wide-spreading tamarisk tree, made a warm appeal to their feelings as loyal and grateful subjects. See him posted on the height above his own royal city, Gibeah, leaning on his spear, the symbol of his dignity, the valiant company arrayed in order around him, and over his head, and forming a beautiful canopy, the feathery branches of the tamarisk, not as in our climate, a mere shrub that is planted in maritime places because in its stunted growth it can endure the keen wind and salt spray of the ocean, but a tree as large as an oak, a most grateful shelter in a hot climate. "Hear now, ye Benjamites," he cries, "will the son of Jesse give every one of you fields and vineyards, will he make you all captains of thousands and captains of hundreds; that all of you have conspired against me, and there was none that disclosed to me when my son made a league with the son of Jesse?" And he adds, with a pathos which is truly affecting: "There is none that is sorry for me, or discloseth unto me that my son hath stirred up my servant against me, to lie in wait, as at this day." What could the officers reply to this appeal? The openly avowed favouritism which had secured all high posts for the king's tribesmen had not answered. Such partiality had begun to alienate the rest of Israel, and comparatively few followed his lead during the latter part of his reign. If he could bring himself to believe such things of his noble son and his gallant, trusty son-in-law, upon whom next might his suspicion fall? Who might be the next victim of the moody tyrant? While all were silent, the unscrupulous Doeg, who was present at the meeting and who took pleasure in ministering to his lord's vindictive passions, spoke and said: "I saw the son of Jesse coming to Nob, to Ahimelech, the son of Ahitub, and he inquired of the Lord for him, and give him victuals, and gave him the sword of Goliath the Philistine." By this malignant statement Doeg turned suspicion from the courtiers to the priests. Saul was quite ready to believe that they were in league with David, and, as though he had already determined on a general massacre, he sent to summon Ahimelech and all the priests at Nob to his presence. This Ahimelech was the great-grandson of Eli, and had succeeded his brother Ahiah in the pontificate, or had divided the office with him, one of them accompanying Saul to the camp, the other remaining with the ark or tabernacle. It was no great distance from Gibeah to Nob, and the sacerdotal family, to the number of eighty-five, were soon in Saul's presence. The angry monarch reproached Ahimelech with treachery and with conniving with David in his evil designs, recapitulating Doeg's three charges, that he had used the sacred oracle in his behalf, which was never employed but at the king's demand, that he had fed the fugitive and his followers, and that he had given him the giant's sword. Ahimelech did not deny the charge. He had done indeed as the king accused him, but he had acted in the innocence of his heart, with no malign intent, and quite unaware that he was thereby incurring Saul's displeasure. David, he said, the king's own son-in-law, the most faithful of all his servants, one who had the privilege of admission to the royal presence at any time, had come to him at Nob, representing that he was engaged in some secret service for the king, and seeking his advice and assistance. "Had I not then good cause," asked the priest ingenuously, "to inquire of God for him, as at thy own request I had done before?"[1] As for conspiring against thee, God forbid the thought! I have done all in perfect good faith. Of all that thou hast charged me with I know nothing little or great." The innocence of Ahimelech and the other priests was palpable; his exculpation was complete. Not so, however, in Saul's prejudiced eyes. He and his were all traitors together, and should meet the traitor's doom. His only answer to the high priest's defence is: "Thou shalt surely die, Ahimelech, thou, and all thy father's house." He regards them as dangerous rebels, because, as he chose to believe, they sided with David, and had not informed the king of his movements; and far from being deterred from vengeance by their sacred character, he is the more induced to deal summarily with them as giving example of contumacy in high place, and rendering his position even more insecure than he had deemed. Among their attendants, Eastern potentates are wont to have some who run by their side when they go abroad, and act as an escort. Such "runners" Saul had obtained for himself, as Samuel had foretold (chap. viii. 11), and they were among the most faithful of his followers and formed his body-guard. Having decreed the death of the innocent priests, the king ordered these "footmen" to slay them. But this ferocious, cold-blooded murder was something which revolted even these unscrupulous adherents. The king's atrocious conduct had weakened discipline, and even his authority could not enforce the execution of this bloody vengeance on the ministers of a religion which all professed to observe. They stood mute at the command. No one came forward to obey this barbarous order. The high priest and his servitors were in their eyes the representatives of Jehovah, and

[1] This seems to be the meaning of the much disputed phrase: "Have I to-day begun to inquire of God for him?"

not even loyalty to the sovereign or the strong feeling of deference to the head of their clan, could induce them to violate their conscience and incur the guilt of sacrilege. No such scruples affected Doeg, the Edomite. He had no sympathy with the religious aspect of the matter. To keep well with the king, to pander to his passions, to maintain his own position, and to enrich himself—this was his ambition; and when Saul, enraged at the disobedience of his body-guard, ordered him to execute the cruel command, he and his servants, foreigners, probably, like himself, at once fell upon the priests, undeterred by the sight of their sacerdotal vestments, and murdered them all to a man. Not content with this unparalleled atrocity, worthy of a Nero or Domitian, Saul extended his vengeance to the city of Nob. Treating it like a city of idolaters and accursed, he sent Doeg, who smote it with the edge of the sword, slaying therein men and women, children and sucklings, oxen, asses, and sheep, leaving nothing alive of all that dwelt there, save Abiathar, a son of Ahimelech, who by some means escaped from the general slaughter, and fled for refuge to David. Thus unconsciously Saul executed the judgment of God against the house of Eli. It was an inhuman and most impolitic deed. All good Israelites were horrified at the crime. An act so black alienated the affection of his most devoted adherents. Insanity does not account for it; there was method in it. Reasoning from his own nature, Saul could not realize David's innocence or the non-complicity of the priests. Though he cared little for the restraints of religion, and never guided his heart by holy motives, he liked to be thought to observe the externals of devotion; and when the spirituality turned against him he was furious, and at once made a terrible example of those who, as he fancied, took his enemy's side. He had set himself to oppose God; he refused to acquiesce in the selection of his successor; and now he could not retrace his steps; he must sink daily from bad to worse; the deterioration of his character went on continuously; the melancholy, morbid king became a ferocious, despairing tyrant, without pity, justice, or remorse. Henceforward his one object is to capture David, whom he fully believed was only prevented by weakness from seizing the kingdom from him. He had emissaries always on the watch to give him the earliest intelligence of David's movements, that he might entrap him in some difficult situation or overwhelm him by superior numbers in more open country.

David was heard of at Keilah, a town on the hills of Judah, overlooking the valley of Elah, about six and a half miles east of Beit Jibrin (Eleutheropolis), whither he had gone to deliver it from the hands of a marauding band of Philistines. Saul rejoiced to hear that David was shut up in a town, where he had friends who were quite ready to turn against their deliverer, and made sure of his capture. But before he could take measures to secure him, David left the place and roamed whither Saul could not successfully follow him. The evil king had deluded himself with the idea that Providence was on his side and had deserted his rival. "God," he cries, "hath delivered him into mine hand." But he reckoned foolishly. In driving Abiathar to David's side, he had given him the means of inquiring at the Divine oracle; and by the information thus given, David was saved on this and many other occasions.

After the retreat from Keilah, David is next found in the wilderness of Ziph, some four miles south of Hebron; and here at Horesh (Khoreisa)[1] he had his last interview with his gallant friend Jonathan, who, with his father, was encamped in the neighbourhood.

Saul possessed some thorough partisans among the Ziphites, and they were always ready to send him information concerning David's proceedings. Why they were so hostile to David we know not. There may have been some ancient feud between them and the family of Jesse; or more probably, regarding Saul as the legitimate monarch and disinclined to discuss David's claims, they simply acted as loyal subjects and discountenanced one who was in their eyes a rebel and an outlaw. They now send intelligence to the king, who was in his house at Gibeah, that David was concealed in the hill of Hachilah (El-Kolah), a ridge six miles east of Ziph, from which it is plainly visible, and eight miles south-east of Hebron, running towards the desert that extends to the Dead Sea. It is a dreary, desolate region of chalky ridges, scored by winter

---

[1] The English versions give "in a wood." But the soil of that district, says Conder ("Tent Work," ii. 89), could never have supported a growth of trees; and the word, *Horesh*, is doubtless the name of a town, recovered by Conder in Khoreisa, about two miles south of Ziph.

torrents, intersected by broad valleys, without a tree in all the prospect or a spring of water. In this pathless wilderness David and his six hundred men had taken refuge; and the Ziphites, who knew the country well, offered to guide Saul's troops in the pursuit of the outlaw. The king was well pleased to be thus seconded in his design. In his melancholy condition he grasps at any help, at any thing that may show him that he has sympathizers and that he is not left alone in his struggle against his enemy. "Blessed be ye of the Lord," he says to them; "for ye have had compassion upon me." But knowing David's warlike skill and prudence, how he would be sure to conceal his movements, to guard against surprise, and to leave an avenue of escape wherever he might be, Saul would not commit himself to the pursuit till he had the most certain intelligence. This soon reached him, and he at once followed his guides to the wilderness of Maon, where the fugitive was now posted. This place, now called Main, only about six miles from Ziph, lay on the edge of the Arabah, that singular depression which extends from the Lake of Gennesareth to the Dead Sea and beyond. Here, hard pressed and outnumbered by Saul's forces, David was in imminent danger of capture. The situation has been accurately examined and described by Conder,[1] who writes: "Between the ridge of El Kolah (Hachilah) and the neighbourhood of Maon there is a great gorge called 'the Valley of the Rocks,' a narrow but deep chasm, impassable except by a detour of many miles, so that Saul might have stood within sight of David, yet quite unable to overtake his enemy; and to this 'cliff of division' (*sela-hammahlekoth*) the name Malâky now applies, a word closely approaching the Hebrew *Mahlekoth*. The neighbourhood is seamed with many torrent beds, but there is no other place near Maon where cliffs such as are to be inferred from the word *sela* are to be found." Seeing David before him, Saul divided his forces so as to intercept the foe and cut off all hope of escape. Thus, although Saul would have had to make a detour of some miles in order to get round the gorge at either end, David's final escape was very problematical But at this moment, when the fate of the future king of Israel seemed decided, occurred one of those interpositions which men call chance, but which really are the effect of the wise ordering of Providence which makes the

[1] "Tent Work," ii 91, quoted by Dean Payne Smith.

SAUL'S PERSECUTION OF DAVID.

passions and plans of men work out its determined counsels. A messenger suddenly arrived in Saul's presence bringing the news that the Philistines had made a raid into the neighbouring territory, and urging him to hasten with all his forces to repel the invasion. This information could not be neglected. Private rancour must give way to public necessity. Saul let David escape this time, and withdrew his troops to combat with the hereditary enemy.

No sooner had Saul returned successfully from this expedition against the Philistines than he again set forth in pursuit of David. The latter had been tracked by the Ziphites to the vicinity of Engedi, "Fountain of the Goat," a warm spring, situated about the centre of the western shore of the Dead Sea, and some five hundred feet above its level. This fountain bursts forth in a copious stream from a narrow platform of bare limestone, and, rushing down the cliffs, scatters vegetation around, so as to form an oasis which is one of the most striking features of that otherwise desolate region. The cliffs surmounting the spring, which rise to the height of two thousand feet above the sea, as well as those that lead down to the shore, are seamed with ravines which are full of caves, even now used as sheep-cotes as they were in David's time. Taking with him three thousand picked soldiers, Saul followed his rival into this wild, rocky country. Here the advantage was on David's side, and had the monarch had a more unscrupulous foe to deal with, he would have here ended his career and atoned by death for his cruel persecution of the guiltless outlaw. It happened that while following the fugitive, Saul on one occasion, for privacy's sake, entered one of these caves, the gloom and coolness of which offered a refreshing contrast to the glare and heat of the bare rock outside. In this very cave David and a part of his followers were concealed. Looking from inside, they could see perfectly all that passed at the entrance, while to those outside the interior of the cavern was enveloped in impenetrable darkness. Saul thought that the place was empty, or if he heard any whispering or movement fancied that some of the shepherds by whom it was usually occupied were still lurking there, and took no further notice. With the utmost astonishment the outlaws beheld this arrival. He was immediately recognized, and a whispered intimation of the fact was made to David, and he was urged to take advantage of the opportunity, to rid himself by one blow of his tyrannical pursuer, and thus secure the kingdom for himself as it had been promised. If for one moment the wronged youth was inclined to revenge his many injuries, he did not succumb to the temptation. Though he held in his hand the sword of Goliath, and his followers were eager to fall upon Saul, he restrained them and himself. However cruelly Saul had behaved to him, he was still the Lord's anointed, his person was sacred. With a generosity unexampled in those barbarous days, he spared his great rival's life; at the same time he wished to show that that life had been in his power, thus proving his own innocence of any intention of injuring his person, and refuting the slanders of the courtiers who, by misrepresentation of his motives, fanned the embers of the king's animosity. On entering the cave Saul had laid aside his *meil*, the costly robe which he wore, and David, approaching silently in the gloom, cut off a corner of it unseen. Saul took up the injured mantle and left the cavern. David's companions were loud in complaint against their leader's ill-timed leniency; but far from feeling with them, his conscience reproached him for having failed in the respect due to the king's majesty, and for having even entertained a thought of injuring him. Watching the departure of the Israelite soldiers, and seeing Saul now almost alone in their rear, David came forth from the cave and called after him: "My lord the king." At the familiar voice Saul stopped and turned. He sees David on the rocky platform, bowing with his face to the ground, doing lowly obeisance, showing himself no rebel against lawful authority, but one who recognized in the monarch the personage whom he was bound to obey and reverence. And then he addresses Saul in touching words, asking why he listens to the calumnious insinuations of his enemies. To-day Providence had put the king into his power; he might have slain him with the greatest ease: see, here was a piece of the king's robe which he had cut off in the cave; the sword that had marred his mantle might have drunk his blood. Why should the monarch of Israel pursue with this unrelenting hatred one so insignificant and powerless as he? let the king learn from this day's adventure that he was utterly mistaken in attributing to him guile and treason. "The Lord be judge," he concludes, "and give sentence between me and thee, and see, and plead my cause, and deliver me out of thine hand." Saul could not hear this appeal unmoved. David's

SAUL'S PERSECUTION OF DAVID.

forbearance and his own surprising escape affected him keenly. In spite of his insanity and cruelty, he had human feelings which at times mastered his evil passions. And now he was quite overcome by mixed emotions, and he lifted up his voice and wept. Some of the old affection returned; he calls him, "My son, David," and overpowered by the generosity which had returned good for evil, prays God to reward him for the kindness which he had shown. Knowing that he himself had forfeited the throne, and strongly convinced that David was that neighbour better than he whom Samuel had announced as his successor, he makes a request, to which knowledge of the usual proceedings in the case of usurpers gives a painful significance.[1] "I know," he says, "that thou shalt surely be king, and that the kingdom of Israel shall be established in thine hand. Swear now therefore unto me by the Lord, that thou wilt not cut off my seed after me, and that thou wilt not destroy my name out of my father's house" The generous David at once gave the required promise, and they parted. Saul, for a time elevated to a better mind, returned to Gibeah and ceased from persecution; while David, unable to trust the fickle tyrant, continued to haunt the hill country where he had before found refuge.

[1] See 1 Kings xv. 29; xvi. 11; 2 Kings x. 7, 11.

CHAPTER XIII.

THE DEATH OF SAMUEL.

Samuel dies—His funeral and tomb—His services to Israel—His character—
His difficulties—His accomplished work.

IT was soon after the events narrated in the last chapter that Samuel, of whose later years we have no account, was called away. One verse tells us of his death and burial, the reticence of Scripture in such cases being noted. Here is the sole record: "Samuel died; and all Israel gathered themselves together, and lamented him, and buried him in his house at Ramah" (1 Sam. xxv. 1). He had arrived at a good old age; his work was done; the time for his reward had arrived. "So He giveth His beloved sleep." Though of late he had lived in retirement and had taken no part in public affairs, yet his death was felt as a public calamity, and all Israel, forgetting its rivalries and contentions, remembering only the mighty benefits he had conferred upon the nation, his unblemished life, his personal piety, assembled as one man to do him honour. "His moral excellence," says Josephus,[1] "and the esteem with which he was regarded, are proved by the continued mourning that was made for him, and the concern that was universally shown to conduct the funeral rites with becoming splendour and solemnity. He was buried in his own native place, and they wept for him very many days, not regarding it as the death of another man or a stranger, but as that in which each individual was concerned. He was a righteous man, and of a kindly nature, and, on that

[1] "Antiq." vi. 13. 5.

THE DEATH OF SAMUEL.

account, very dear to God." Such a public ceremony could hardly have taken place without the concurrence of Saul; probably he was foremost in doing honour to the prophet when dead, whose counsel he had so grievously neglected while living.[1] Some have thought that in a tardy burst of zeal, and feeling how much he had lost in the decease of his early friend, he tried to recover the favour of Jehovah by taking severe measures against offenders. Hence they refer to this time the overthrow of idolatry throughout the land, the destruction of wizards and necromancers, and the slaughter of the Gibeonites as enemies of the religion of Israel. Samuel was buried in the court or garden of his house at Ramah; not, of course, in the house itself, as that would have occasioned the place to be ceremonially unclean. Moslem tradition places the prophet's tomb on the conspicuous ridge of Neby Samwil, where is a mosque built on the foundations of an old Christian church. Jerome[2] asserts that his remains were transported A.D. 406 to Chalcedon (Kadi-Keni), at the entrance of the Bosphorus, and from thence, according to Callistus,[3] were transferred to Constantinople, and deposited in a church with great pomp. There was nothing unusual in the original place of his burial. Where there were no regular cemeteries, any suitable spot might be selected for a grave. King Manasseh is said to have been buried in the garden of his house; so Joab was interred, and our blessed Lord's sepulchre was in a garden.[4]

Well may the whole nation have mourned the loss of their great judge and prophet. Think what he was in himself, what he had done for them. Conspicuous in a rough, uncultured age, he stands forth as a witness for God and religion and education. Since Moses, none so eminent had arisen. The child of prayer, he is especially the man of prayer. A stainless boyhood passed in the tabernacle of God, and amid the solemnities of holy worship, prepared him for reception of heavenly inspirations. Severed from the outward world, parted even from the influence of domestic affections, he gives himself wholly to God and his country. He communes with the unseen, seeks no guide

---

[1] Hummelauer on 1 Sam. xxviii. 3.
[2] "Cont. Vigil." ii. 243 (Migne).
[3] "Hist. Eccl." xiv. 10. Gibbon, "Decline and Fall," ch. xxviii.
[4] 2 Kings xxi. 18; 2 Chron. xxxiii. 20: 1 Kings ii. 34; John xix. 41.

but the will of God, has no law but the law of the Most High. He is absorbed in his intercourse with heaven, and outward circumstances affect him but little. He began well, and he continued in the same path unto the end; he had set one great end before him and pursued it unflinchingly, undeterred by difficulties, and entirely uninfluenced by personal motives. His great strength was prayer; here was his refuge, his weapon, his support. Not only did he flee unto God in all great emergencies, before the face of powerful enemies, at the defection of Saul, but regularly at all times he practised the habit of devotion, and found calmness, comfort, and vigour in this communion with God. As it is said : " Moses and Aaron among His priests, and Samuel among them that call upon His name ; they called upon the Lord, and He answered them." But there was no dreaminess, no unreality in his devotion. All was thorough, earnest, practical, "one equable progression from beginning to end."[1] If he failed somewhat in sympathy, if he was hard and unbending in upholding the right, this apparent insensibility sprang from the unworldliness of his character and the intense appreciation of the utter importance of justice, truth, and piety. And if, as seems to have been the case, he was not skilful in reading character, and was apt to be deceived by outward appearances, it was his continued gaze upon God that turned him from the study of mankind, and made him no close investigator of men's mental and moral attributes. But this heavenly life taught him to shrink from anything mean, impure, unholy ; it led him to be inflexibly just, upright in all his dealings, observant of every duty, so that during his long administration no one had ever complained of his decisions, not a voice among all the people could impeach his impartiality and conscientiousness; so that he could say without contradiction : "I am old and gray-headed, and I have walked before you from my childhood to this day. Behold, here I am; witness against me before the Lord, and before His anointed." This made him patient under much discouragement, labouring long and unrepiningly with little outward success. This made him take such infinite pains to raise the tone of his countrymen, and to educate them for a higher life than they had been accustomed to lead. In his heavenward inspirations he has no room for thought of self.

[1] Wilberforce, "Heroes of Hebrew History."

THE DEATH OF SAMUEL.

What will bring men nearer to God? What will win the Divine blessing? What is the will of Providence?—these are his sole considerations. That his own position may be altered by a new state of things, that he may sink into an inferior grade, that some of his cherished designs must be frustrated—in all this he cheerfully acquiesces as soon as he ascertains that such is the Lord's purpose. A more unselfish man has never existed. His heart was filled with love for the Lord and His people; and what was best for them, that was his good pleasure also. That great heart, thus occupied, had no room for petty feelings. If a king could best head the people at this crisis of their history, let one be found; if he could be to them what Samuel himself had hoped to be, God speed him! All is cheerful, voluntary, dignified; there is no show of compelled submission; he sees what is best, and, without any consciousness of being slighted or superseded, he freely gives his friendship to the elect monarch, and by loving counsel, by stern rebuke, by solemn warning, by continued intercession, proves his interest in the new king, and his unselfish desire to make his reign a success. Good men can claim no immunity from trouble, but they have the secret of knowing how to meet it. He suffered many sorrows, he had to make many sacrifices, he saw the ruin of what he had loved, he lost his best and earliest friend, he was unhappy in his children, disappointed in the chosen king, disappointed in his fellow-countrymen; but in and through all these afflictions he bore a brave heart, staying himself on God, rising higher in the religious life as the waves beat against him, finding new occasion for prayer and devotion as every fresh distress fell upon his head.

But, while he prayed, he laboured. He had a great work before him, and he set himself diligently to do it. Practical religion had greatly declined during the time of the Judges; the high ideal which Moses had set forth was miserably defaced; priests and Levites exercised no authority, did nothing to elevate or unite the people. The principle of unity was lost, and the nation was degenerating into a collection of tribes, self-seeking, cruel, rapacious, forgetful of its destiny, ready to cast off its allegiance to Jehovah, and to sink in religion and habits to the level of surrounding heathens. Together with this degeneracy, and in punishment of its faithlessness, Israel fell under a foreign yoke. The raw, undisciplined, ill-armed levies of Israel were little able to withstand the mail-clad warriors of Philistia, who, through the culpable negligence of the Jews, were in possession of the seaboard, and could import arms and armour from Greece. It was the aim of Samuel's life to enable the people to reconquer their independence; but he saw that the first step towards gaining this end was a great religious reformation. This was the necessary preliminary to any national struggle for freedom. His mind was filled with the idea of the theocracy. The king of Israel was Jehovah, whose will was made known to His subjects by the intervention of priests and prophets; and he looked forward to the time when this great ideal should be thoroughly believed, and become the foundation of all public action. It was an arduous undertaking that lay before him. The degeneracy of the priesthood, of which from his boyhood he had been witness, the general low moral tone among the people, the apathy of the natural leaders, and the universal misery that was occasioned by the oppression of heathen invaders—these things might have driven one less faithful to despair. Samuel saw in these circumstances a power to raise his nation from their low estate. Thus they were taught that they were nothing without God. What had their long disaffection brought but sorrow and loss? Must they not learn that there was only one way to repair the mischief—the path of repentance? Thus terrible defeat at Aphek, and the destruction of Shiloh, a fatal blow which the annalists would fain have blotted out from the national records, caused the stricken people to turn to Samuel as the hope of the country, and to recognize in this young seer a worthy teacher and leader. Samuel used this confidence for their good. Year by year, patiently, quietly, hopefully, he went among them, preparing them for a great uprising by showing where their strength lay, teaching true, heart-felt religion, inspiring them to trust in the covenant Lord, who would never forsake His own inheritance. Then, when in confidence the whole nation turned to him as Judge and Intercessor, he led them to victory. Having thus secured a time of comparative peace, he thought to utilize this opportunity by establishing firmly the principle of theocratic government. His hopes were shattered by the demand for a king. How did he meet this request? At first confounded, dismayed, indignant, he sought to turn the people from their purpose; but laying the matter before the Lord, and finding what His Will was, he acquiesced in the demand, and only cared to fence the king's power with proper restrictions, and to choose a fit person for the new office. Here is magnanimity almost unparalleled. Disappointed in his highest hopes, made conscious that his people were unworthy of the great destiny offered them, displaced from his position as supreme guide of the nation, he accepts the situation with alacrity, and becomes the close friend of the man who supplants him. Without fiery enthusiasm, but firm and consistent, he never swerves from the most devoted patriotism. And when he is forced to own that the chosen king has forfeited his crown by flagrant acts of disobedience; when, in the highest interests of religion and government, he breaks off connection with the rebellious prince, he ceases not to pray for him; he loves the sinner still, and takes no overt action against him, upholding his authority and striving to repair any evil he might effect. He had found that the establishment of the kingdom was become a necessity, that the unity of the nation and its orderly development could only thus be secured, and he threw his whole energies into the prosecution of this idea. If the first monarch had proved a failure, he might train another who would more worthily carry out the Basileo-theocratic conception. In David he found one whom he could mould into the ideal king. If we look closely into the hints conveyed by the accounts of the period, and read them by the light of subsequent history, we find that Samuel founded a constitutional monarchy, restrained from falling into despotism by the checks of law and obedience to the revealed will of Jehovah. The rule which governed the life of the people, social, political, religious, was the Mosaic legislation; the king had to observe the same rule, and could never, while doing this, become an independent tyrant. It was Samuel's great business to guide the nation from the isolation, anarchy, and barbarism of the Judges, to consolidation and culture under a theocratic monarch, who would rule by law, be submissive to the voice of God, and aid the people to work out their sublime destiny. But the people had to be educated in order to profit by this constitution or to make it even feasible. Religion had to be restored and rendered real and practical; morality must be learned; youth must be instructed and trained. For this purpose Samuel founded the schools of the prophets, wherein not only were the young taught the rudiments of secular knowledge, how to take their part in religious exercises, how to serve God in Church and State, but a class of men were there brought up to exercise the office of prophet, to preach pure morality and the heart-felt worship of Jehovah, and to act along and co-ordinately with the priesthood and monarchy in guiding the state aright and checking all attempts at illegality and tyranny.

For one man to have inaugurated and methodized these two great innovations, constitutional monarchy and national education, and to have given them stability and permanence, is an unique proceeding which confers upon its author everlasting fame ; and, looking to the subsequent effects of these institutions, impels us to pronounce Samuel one of the great benefactors of the human race.

Of the books which bear his name, only a very small portion can with any probability be attributed to his composition. The two Books of Samuel originally formed one work called " The Book of Samuel." In the Septuagint and Latin Vulgate they are connected with the two following works, and are named respectively the First and Second Book of Kings. The materials from which the two Books were composed are distinctly enumerated in 1 Chron. xxix. 29 : " Now the acts of David the king, first and last, behold, they are written in (upon) the history of Samuel the seer, and in the history of Nathan the prophet, and in the history of Gad the seer." This seems to imply that Samuel himself wrote certain records of his time which were used in subsequent compilations. How far these annals were introduced into our two Books, or who was their compiler, we cannot accurately determine, nor need the matter be here discussed. That the work is collected from various authorities, not always very skilfully combined, is plain enough ; but the editor evidently believed in the authenticity of all the accounts which he used, and made one supplement the other, sometimes even repeating the same story with some slight variation or addition. It was long an opinion commonly held that Samuel was the author of the first twenty-four chapters of the first Book, the remainder of that Book and the whole of the second being written by Gad and Nathan. German critics have discovered four or five different authors, and as many dates, for various parts of the Books, considering them as founded more or less on contemporary documents, but disfigured by legends, and

THE DEATH OF SAMUEL.

compiled at different periods of Jewish history, some probably after the exile. The questions here introduced we cannot discuss. Thus much we may say as properly belonging to our subject. The First Book of Samuel, with which alone we are concerned, may be conveniently divided into three parts : I., the history of Samuel (chaps. i.-vii) ; II., the history of Saul (viii.-xvi.) ; III., the history of David as exile (xvii.-xxxi.).[1] The first seven chapters are probably the work of Samuel himself. There is a unity in them and a symmetrical arrangement which argue a single author, and that one who knows intimately what he describes, is reticent in his own praises, feels deeply the degradation of the sacerdotal order, and dwells largely on those matters which specially appertained to the interests and occupations of his life. Some facts, too, are stated which were only true at the time when the words were written ; *e. g*, chap. vii. 13 : "The Philistines were subdued, and they came no more into the coast of Israel"; whereas a very different condition of things obtained a few years later (comp. xiii. 19). Again, Samuel is said to have judged Israel all the days of his life, though he abdicated the office on Saul's assumption of the kingdom (chap. xii.). We can only suppose that the compiler inserted these chapters in Samuel's own words without making any change. The second Part, containing the history of Saul, seems to have been written partly by Samuel and partly by Gad. Some of its facts, as the anointing of Saul, were known to no one but the two actors. There is a tenderness in recounting Saul's errors, and a desire to display the noble parts of his character, which testify the regard of the narrator for the erring king. Gad was probably trained in one of the schools of the prophets, and must have been intimately acquainted with the events here narrated. He accompanied David in his wanderings, and is justly considered the author of the third part, which contains the account of Samuel's death and burial.

[1] Thus Hummelauer, p. 9.

CHAPTER XIV.

THE DEATH OF SAUL.

Saul again pursues David to Hachilah—His life spared a second time by
David—Saul's compunction—Philistines invade the country with large
forces—Saul encamps at Gilboa—Can obtain no Divine counsel—Consults a witch at Endor – Is answered by the spirit of Samuel—Warned
of his approaching defeat and death—Returns to his camp—Battle of
Gilboa—Defeat of Israel—Death of Saul and his sons—Their bodies
affixed to the walls of Bethshan ; removed and buried by the men of
Jabesh-Gilead—News of the catastrophe brought to David—His conduct thereupon—His funeral elegy—Summary of Saul's character.

ONLY once again did Saul and David meet ; and this meeting
was so similar in some respects to the last interview, that many
critics have considered the two accounts to be varying traditions
of one and the same event. But there are many circumstances
in the latter transaction which distinguish it from the former ;
nor is it in itself improbable either that in so small an area as
the desert of Judah the same scenes should be repeated, or that
Saul should have forgotten his temporary gratitude, and under
the influence of a fresh attack of his monomania, and aided by
the opportunity which was offered, should have again attempted
David's life, giving the latter another occasion for displaying his
remarkable magnanimity.

Relying somewhat on the reconciliation effected at Engedi,
David had returned to his old quarters at Hachilah, in the expectation that he would now be left in peace. But the Ziphites,
who well knew the king's feeling towards his powerful subject,
and were ready enough to gratify it, sent information of his
position to Saul, and urged him to set out at once and seize

THE DEATH OF SAUL.

him. Saul could not resist the opportunity. He had for many years kept with him a body of picked troops, which were called "the three thousand," whether in fact their numbers were more or less;[1] these were always prepared to undertake any minor expedition, and with them he immediately marched to seek David. Arriving in the neighbourhood of Ziph, he pitched his camp about six miles east of the town, on the ridge of Hachilah (El Kolah), by the side of the track which traversed the hill leading down to the south. David, who seems now to have been sufficiently powerful to feel no great apprehension at the proximity of his enemy, was kept well informed of Saul's movements, and having taken his post on higher ground, was able to watch all that went on below. Unwilling to believe that after all his protestations Saul himself had come out against him, he proposed to two of his most trusty followers, Ahimelech the Hittite, and Abishai his nephew, to make a closer reconnoisance of the Israelite camp. Ahimelech declined the hazardous enterprise; but Abishai agreeing to go, he and David at nightfall crept down the hill and approached the sleeping host. These had round them, as usual, the rampart of waggons, but no sentinels posted to watch their slumbers. The two adventurers easily penetrated even to the centre of the enclosure, and found Saul himself fast asleep, with the spear, the symbol of his kingly authority, fixed in the ground at his head. Urged by his companion to let him smite the king as he lay unconscious of danger, David, as before, refused to lift his hand against the Lord's anointed. But to show the king that he had again spared his life, he took his spear and the cruse of water that stood near at hand, and carried them away with him. Passing unheard and unperceived through the sleeping soldiers ("because a deep sleep from the Lord was fallen upon them"), David got back safely to the hill whence he had first reconnoitred Saul's camp, a gorge probably dividing the two positions. Having thus put a sufficient space between himself and the enemy, he called with a loud voice on Abner, the general of the army, and sarcastically upbraided him for not keeping better watch. Abner and his men deserved death for their carelessness in allowing their master to be in such jeopardy;

---

[1] Thus the famous cohort of the Persians was called "The ten thousand." Herod. vii. 55, 83.

for he might easily have been murdered by any one without the guards' knowledge. "Look for the king's spear and water cruse," he shouted. Saul, awakened by the cry, could see nothing amid the darkness, but recognized a well-known voice, and becoming conscious of the loss he had sustained, and remembering the outlaw's former generosity, he called aloud, "Is this thy voice, my son David?" And then David once more, as at Engedi, remonstrates with the king for his continued persecution of one so humble and insignificant, and withal so innocent of wrong as himself, adding with emphatic earnestness : "If it be the Lord that hath stirred thee up against me by permitting thine anger to get the mastery over thy better nature, He will accept an offering at thy hands and restore to thee thy right mind ; but if men have calumniated me to thee, cursed be they before the Lord ; for their slanderous tongues will force me to leave my native land, and to dwell among strangers and heathen." Touched with compunction, Saul cries : "I have sinned ; return, my son David; for I will no more do thee harm, because my life was precious in thine eyes this day." And then, vexed with himself for having again run his head into danger, and being again indebted for safety to the magnanimity of the son-in-law whom he had so wrongly judged and cruelly outraged, he adds : "Behold, I have played the fool, and have erred exceedingly." David bade him send an attendant to receive the spear and cruse which he had taken; and after reminding the king of the retribution which God dispenses to all, and silently rejecting overtures the insincerity of which he had now often experienced, he turned from the spot with the last words which he would ever hear from Saul sounding in his ears—words expressive rather of reluctant conviction than of willing appreciation : "Blessed shalt thou be, my son David ; thou shalt both do mightily, and shalt surely prevail." Saul returned to Gibeah, while David, despairing of safety in the land of Judah, sought a home beyond its borders, where the malice of his persecutor could not reach him.

And now we approach to the closing scenes in the life of the miserable Saul. Samuel, by whose perpetual intercession ruin had been averted from the royal house, had died two years ago. There was no prophet to take his place in the counsels of Saul ; the priests had been ruthlessly slain, and the only survivor had

THE DEATH OF SAUL.

carried the sacred Urim with him when he fled for refuge to David. The tabernacle was removed from Nob, and possibly a fresh ephod with its Urim was constructed; but the Divine oracle, when consulted, was silent. On the death of Samuel the people began to despair of the fortunes of Saul, and deserted his cause in great numbers. Many of his most valiant soldiers joined themselves to David, who had taken service with Achish, king of Gath. And now the Philistines had invaded the country with a large force, levied from all their cities and allies. No such combined movement had ever before been made. This was no mere border warfare, no mere raid organized by a band of marauders who might easily be defeated, but a most formidable expedition directed against the very centre of the territory of Israel. Marching northwards along the sea-coast, and gathering forces in their progress, they turned to the east and entered the plain of Jezreel or Esdraelon, the famous valley which runs from the Jordan in a north-westerly direction to the Bay of Acre. Crossing the plain, they encamped on the slope of the Little Hermon or Jebel Duhy range, which bounds it on the east, at a place called Shunem (Sulem), about 3½ miles north of Jezreel, celebrated in after time as the abode of the good woman who hospitably entertained the prophet Elisha.[1] To meet this invasion Saul gathered together what forces he could collect, and advancing from the south, where he had remained unmolested, pitched his camp on Mount Gilboa, the range which bounds the great plain on the south, bending out like a sickle from the hills of Samaria. Here, at a point where the valley is some four miles in width, he took up a position opposite to the Philistine encampment, and where from his greater elevation he could watch all the movements of the enemy. But his situation was extremely perilous; he was in imminent danger of being surrounded, for the Philistine general had marched a strong body of troops to Aphek, in the rear of Saul's army, and thus cut off all retreat to the south. Looking on the host opposed to him, and contrasting it with his own weak and dispirited army, Saul "was afraid, and his heart greatly trembled." Here was an enemy superior in numbers, in arms, and equipment, furnished with cavalry and chariots, with which he could not

[1] 2 Kings iv. 8.

contend on equal terms ; with this host, as he thought, the much wronged David was present, eager to avenge himself on his tyrannous oppressor ; his own army was thinned by the desertion of many of his most able warriors.[1] All these were very serious considerations. He was mistaken indeed about David, whom the jealousy of the Philistines had not permitted to take part in the expedition, but the other disadvantages were very real and formidable. Add to this, he felt himself abandoned by the Lord. The tabernacle had been set up at Gibeon, where Zadok, of the family of Eleazar, was acting as high priest, a new ephod having probably been made, though it is doubtful whether it was used in the present case.[2] Saul, in the extremity of his distress, endeavoured to obtain direction from the Lord by all known means, but in vain. The priests consulted gave no answer ; no inspired dreams intimated the future ; no prophet offered heavenly counsel. Impatient in his desire of supernatural information, not accepting his own iniquity which rendered him unworthy of such revelation, and falling a victim to the wildest and grossest superstition, he orders his servants to find him a woman possessed of a familiar spirit, that he may inquire of the future from her. Such pretenders to occult arts have been known in every age and country, and among them, as in modern days, women have been the chief professors or *media*. Saul himself, in an access of religious zeal, and probably immediately after the death of Samuel, had carried out the stern law of Moses,[3] and purged the land of wizards and necromancers. Now, in his desperation, he has recourse to one of these impostors to reveal to him what is about to happen. Who can tell the struggle in the proud king's soul before he could bring himself to ask 'the aid of a professor of those diabolical arts, so solemnly denounced by the law of God and sternly proscribed by his own re-enactments ? To what a depth of moral degradation must he have sunk to think thus to extort from hell the knowledge which heaven had refused ! Well may it be said : " Lo,

---

[1] 1 Chron. xii. 1 ff, 22.

[2] Compare 1 Sam. xxviii. 6 with ver 15. Urim is not mentioned in the latter passage, and very probably is named in the former as denoting one of the customary methods of obtaining Divine direction.

[3] Lev. xix. 31 , xx. 6. Deut. xviii. 10 ff.

THE DEATH OF SAUL.

this is a man that took not God for his strength," and was left by God to himself. There was at Endor, a town which lay at the foot of the northern face of the hills, about two miles from Shunem, where the Philistines were posted, a celebrated woman who possessed an *ob*, or familiar spirit, as it was termed, *i.e.*, who had the power of ventriloquism. Jewish tradition has represented this person as Abner's mother, which would account for her being spared at the time when the witches were exterminated ; but we know no grounds for such an improbable story. Endor was one of those places whence Manasseh had failed to expel the old tenants, and it was still inhabited by a mixed population, comprising many Canaanites, who retained their old superstitions, and were imitated by their Jewish fellow-citizens. Hence therein were to be found sorcerers and professors of the black art. The popular opinion about these necromancers is given by Josephus :[1] " Ventriloquists of this kind bring up the souls of the dead, and by their means foretell the future to those who inquire of them." Determined to seek forbidden knowledge in this unlawful way, Saul adopted every precaution to prevent his visit being discovered ; and taking with him only two trusty followers, whom again tradition asserts to have been Abner and Amasa, and disguising himself in mean attire, he set forth on his perilous journey in the early hours of the night. The distance between Gilboa and Endor was nearly seven miles, and as the camp of the Philistines lay between the two places, he had to make a detour round the eastern shoulder of the little Hermon, and avail himself of every inequality in the ground to escape the observation of the enemy's picquets. He, with his two companions, arrived safely at the witch's dwelling, and coming into her presence, at once requested her to use her magic powers of prognostication, and to bring up from Sheol, the abode of the dead, the soul of him whom he should name unto her. The woman, who knew not who her visitor was, and could never have supposed that the king would thus defy the law of God and infringe his own special ordinance, answered him, as she was wont to reply to all applicants, by reminding him of the penalty laid upon the practice of these secret arts, and the danger she would incur by assenting to his demand. This was said before she acknow-

[1] "Antiq." xiv. 6. 2.

ledged the possession of illicit powers, that she might extract from the inquirer an oath of secrecy, and thus be held safe from any evil consequences. Saul, now lost to all sense of religion and dignity, at once gives the desired promise: "As the Lord liveth," he swears, "there shall no punishment happen unto thee for this thing." Assured by this promise, the witch asks who it is whose presence Saul desires, much as the modern spirit-rapping impostors offer to put their dupes *en rapport* with departed spirits. Her question takes this form: "Whom shall I bring up for thee?" because the souls of the dead were popularly supposed to be located in some place beneath the surface of the earth. "Bring me up Samuel," answered Saul. In his hopeless despair the miserable man turns again to the guide and friend of his youth; he recognizes his pity and affection through all his sternness in condemnation; he would fain, even by means the most degrading, once more behold, once more converse with this tried and revered counsellor, and from his lips hear his doom. "Bring me up Samuel," he cries, fully believing that he would be visited by the prophet's spirit. The witch, removing herself to a distance, probably began her incantations with heaping incense on a brazier and causing a dense smoke to shroud her operations in the darkened chamber. Hardly had she commenced her spells when she uttered a fearful shriek. Something had appeared which she had not expected, something so awful and supernatural that even her hardened nature was appalled. She had intended to practise on the inquirer's credulity, and by her ventriloquial powers to make it appear that she held communication with a spirit. Or she may have been a clever clairvoyante, able to throw herself into an ecstatic state, and in this condition to answer questions propounded to her. Certainly the apparition which she beheld was wholly unexpected. She at once recognized Samuel in the figure that was visible to her; at the same time she perceived who her visitor was. Josephus says that Samuel informed her of Saul's presence; but this is unlikely. More probably the sight of his majestic stature and regal bearing, the fact that he had demanded the evocation of Samuel's spirit, and that the prophet had obeyed the summons, intimated the identity of the stranger; or in her state of clairvoyance she knew more than in her natural condition, and at once penetrated his disguise.

Perhaps, too, in the excitement of the moment the king dropped the robe in which he had muffled his face, and the witch saw who he was. This renewed her terror. She had exercised forbidden arts in the very presence of the monarch who had pitilessly put to death all who practised them. "Why hast thou deceived me?" she exclaims; "for thou art Saul." The king reassures her, bidding her fear not. He himself had seen nothing; he had heard the fearful shriek of the sorceress, but no vision had crossed his sight. With a thrill of horror he asked her what she had seen. That another person in the same room should behold a presence invisible to himself was a terrifying thought; and the woman's mysterious words increased the terror. "I saw," she answered, "a god-like form[1] ascending out of the earth." And on Saul asking, "What was his aspect?" she replied: "An old man cometh up, and he is covered with a mantle." The word for "mantle," *meïl*, is not appropriated to any special prophetic dress, but is used of a garment that had no official signification. Samuel in life seems always to have worn this; and now Saul, in his anxiety to converse with the prophet, and hearing that the apparition is that of an aged man, at once concludes that Samuel is present, and bends to the ground as in reverence of a superior being. In the conversation that ensued it has been questioned whether Saul himself heard Samuel's voice, or whether he was dependent upon the sorceress for his knowledge of what the shade uttered. Nothing is said of the woman's intervention, and it may be believed that as the spirit was present by Divine permission, so Saul was enabled to understand the message then delivered, whether it reached his outward ear or was subjectively received. The former is most likely, as the account in the text is probably derived from the information of the king's two companions, who also heard the words spoken. It is also not improbable that from this moment the form of Samuel became dimly visible. This awful interview between the fated king and the evoked spirit thus begins: "Why hast thou disquieted me," asks the Prophet, "to bring me up?" He speaks in accommodation to the popular idea of the abode of the dead, and complains that Saul's sin and his resort to wicked arts have bitterly grieved

---

[1] The Hebrew is *Elohim*, "gods," which is the plural of majesty, and does not denote a plurality of appearances.

his mind, disturbed his rest in the other world, and brought him up to deliver his woeful message. Saul's answer to his question is very pitiful and pathetic even in its inconsequence, as if forbidden arts could extort an answer refused by the regularly ordained *media* of communication. "I am sore distressed," he despairingly replies, "for the Philistines make war against me, and God is departed from me, and answereth me no more, neither by prophets nor by dreams." He does not mention the Urim, either from shame at the memory of the atrocious murder of the priests at Nob, or else for brevity's sake. "Therefore," he proceeds, "I have had thee called, that thou mayest make known unto me what I shall do." Samuel reproaches him for the inconsistency of this proceeding. With the stern straightforwardness which he had shown in life, he asks indignantly: "Why dost thou inquire of me, seeing that the Lord is departed from thee, and is become thine enemy? I am His prophet on earth or in Hades. And the Lord hath done to thee,[1] as He spake by me; for the Lord hath rent the kingdom out of thine hand, and hath given it to thy neighbour, even to David, because thou obeyedst not the voice of the Lord, nor executedst His fierce wrath upon Amalek." Here for the first time is David named by the Prophet's mouth as the person designated to supersede Saul. Though the latter had long known this, it was a cruel blow to hear the announcement under present circumstances. But there was more to follow. Not only was the king himself to be punished for his rebellion, which, as he was told at the time, was as heinous a sin as witchcraft (the crime he was now guilty of), but his people should be involved in his ruin. "Jehovah will deliver Israel also with thee into the hand of the Philistines, and to-morrow shalt thou and thy sons be with me; the Lord shall also deliver the camp of Israel into the hands of the Philistines." Thus the ruin would be complete, the army routed, the king and his sons slaughtered, the camp taken and sacked. It was a fearful doom. Heard in the darkness of that mysterious chamber, spoken by a visitant from another world, received under the influence of keen mental agitation and exhaustion consequent upon fatigue and want of food, it powerfully affected the miserable king. He fell at full length fainting on the floor. His condition roused the pity of

---

[1] So Sept. The Heb. is "for Himself."

the sorceress. She came to him, and as having a certain claim upon him for her attention to his wishes, entreated him to hearken to her and to take some food. This he at first refused to do, but urged by his two companions he at length rose from the ground, and sat wearily down on the divan that was set against the walls of the chamber, while the woman hastened to prepare a meal. She was the more willing to do this, not only because she saw his prostration and doubted if he could even return to his camp unless previously refreshed by food, but also from motives of policy, trusting that he who had eaten her bread and salt would not betray or punish her. An Eastern meal does not take long to prepare. A calf was killed and cooked, fresh bread baked, and all things were quickly made ready, as Saul sat resting in gloomy meditation, taking no heed of time. Having hastily partaken of the meal, Saul and his comrades retraced their steps, and arrived safely at the camp of Gilboa.[1]

Of Saul's feelings at this momentous crisis we can judge only by his recorded actions. He showed no repentance, no softening of the heart at the predicted ruin of all his hopes; certain of death, he shrank not from the contest; "in stolid desperation he went to meet his doom."

A day or two passed,[2] and some slight changes had taken

---

[1] I have given that view of the transaction at Endor which appears to me most reasonable. I cannot believe that the whole was deception; I cannot believe that the form and voice of Samuel were assumed by a demon; I cannot believe that all that then passed was a subjective illusion in Saul's diseased mind. I think that Samuel, by God's command, not in response to the witch's spells, did appear as really as did Moses and Elias at the Transfiguration. I am of the opinion of the son of Sirach who says of Samuel: "After his death he prophesied, and showed the king his end, and lifted up his voice from the earth in prophecy, to blot out the wickedness of the people" (Ecclus. xlvi. 20). The addition made in the Greek version of 1 Chron. x. 13 seems to me to be justified: "So Saul died for his transgression which he committed against the Lord, even against the word of the Lord, which he kept not, and also because he asked counsel of one that had a familiar spirit, to inquire of it, *and Samuel the prophet answered him.*" The arguments on the various views taken may be seen in the commentaries, *e.g.*, in Keil, Wordsworth, and Hummelauer.

[2] The "to-morrow" in 1 Sam xxviii 19 ("to-morrow shalt thou and thy sons be with me") must not be pressed to mean the very next day, but taken in a wider sense—"time immediately succeeding"

place in the situation of the Philistines and the Israelites. The former had moved somewhat to the west in order to have more favourable ground for their cavalry and chariots, and to threaten the enemy's post on its most exposed side. The Israelites had come down from Mount Gilboa, and taken a strong position near the spring which is in Jezreel at the base of the mountain. Jezreel itself, says Captain Conder,[1] is situated on a knoll five hundred feet high, and is now called Zerin. The site, which has never been lost, is peculiar, "for whilst on the north and north-east the slopes are steep and rugged, on the south the ascent is very gradual, and the traveller coming northward is astonished to look down suddenly on the valley with its two springs, one (Ain Jalud) welling out from a conglomerate cliff, and forming a pool about one hundred yards long, with muddy borders; the other (Ain Tubaun), the Crusaders' Fountain of Tubania, where the Christian armies were fed 'miraculously' for three days on the fish which still swarm in most of the great springs near." It was in the neighbourhood of the former of these springs, the "Fountain of Goliath," that the Israelites were encamped. Here they were attacked by the Philistines in overwhelming force. Weakened by defection, dispirited by the consciousness of inferiority, they were driven from their station to the mountain behind them, and here on its steep ridges made their final stand. The details of the battle are wanting; the narrator found it a bitter task to write the events of that fatal day. But everywhere we see the figure of Saul towering above the sea of heads, the royal crown encircling the helmet, the royal bracelet glittering on his arm, followed by his brave sons, performing prodigies of valour. Oppressed by the chariots in the plain, surrounded by the archers on the hill-side, amid the showers of stones hurled from the rude engines, he combats undaunted, continuing the desperate fight long after success had been rendered impossible. The brave Jonathan fell at his side; his two other sons, Abinadab (or Ishui) and Melchishua, were slain in his defence; the flower of his guard lay dead; the troops were flying in disorder. The enemy gathered around him, intent on slaying or capturing their powerful adversary; none were found to cope with him hand to hand, but the archers from a safe distance aimed their arrows at him, and Saul was

---

[1] "Tent Work," i. 124.

sore distressed. Wounded and weakened, deserted by God, hopeless of safety, he calls in his agony to his trusty armour-bearer (whom tradition asserts to have been Doeg the Edomite) to take his sword and slay him, lest he fall into the hands of the uncircumcised Philistines and be by them mocked and maltreated ere he was put to death. But the armour-bearer could not bring himself to comply with the terrible request. His love for his master withheld the blow. He himself was sore afraid; he was in some sort answerable for his lord's life; he could not without guilt raise his hand against the Lord's anointed. Hard pressed the king would not delay to expostulate, but dropping his spear, and taking the heavy sword from his servant, he fixed the hilt firmly in the ground, and threw the whole weight of his ponderous body upon the upturned weapon. The point pierced his heart, and he fell dead on the blood-stained field. The armour-bearer, unwilling to survive his master, followed his example, and slew himself in the same way; and when night fell, none were left alive of the gallant band who had fought so bravely round their leader. It was a fatal day for Israel. The king and nearly all his house were cut off; the defeat was complete; in utter panic the people fled; they stopped not in their headlong flight, but, abandoning their homes, took refuge in the country beyond the Jordan, and the Philistines came and occupied the forsaken villages. Returning from the pursuit, the Philistines on the next day visited the field of battle to strip the slain and collect booty. Then the full importance of their victory was made known to them. Amid a heap of his bravest warriors they found the corpses of Saul and his three sons. Though the former had been despoiled of his royal ornaments, he was easily recognized by his great stature, and his face was doubtless known to many among them. The news of his fall spread rapidly around, and was proclaimed in every city of the Philistines with joy and exultation. Respect to an enemy's body was not part of the Philistine code. They had feared Saul while living, and now they wreaked their vengeance on him when dead. They cut off his head and those of his sons, stripped their bodies of their arms and armour, which they placed as trophies in the great temple of Astarte at Askelon, sent Saul's head to the temple of Dagon at Ashdod, and the others to some of their chief towns, grim tokens of victory, and fixed the decapitated bodies to the walls of Bethshan, a city whose Canaanitish inhabitants would naturally rejoice at indignities offered to their ancient enemy. This town, known afterwards by the name of Scythopolis, and now as Beisan, stood in a commanding situation on a spur of rock overlooking the valley of Jezreel on the one side, and on the other the valley of the Jordan, from which it was about four miles distant. The river Jalud, which drains the eastern portion of the Plain of Esdraelon, passes close under this hill on its way to the Jordan, forming the Wady Jalud, a great highway between east and west, and debouching nearly opposite a ford called pre-eminently Abarah, The Ford. On the slope of the hills of Gilead, facing Bethshan at some twelve miles distant, lay Jabesh Gilead, the town so gallantly rescued by Saul in tne early days of his kingdom. The news of the terrible disaster that had befallen their countrymen, and of the maltreatment of the corpse of their king, poignantly affected this grateful people. They at once determined to show that they had not forgotten what they owed to the deceased monarch; his body should not be left as a laughing-stock to his enemies, a prey to foul birds and insects. So the bravest men of the city set out by night, crossed the Jordan, arrived unmolested at Bethshan, took down from the wall the four corpses, and bore them reverently to their city. There, as the flesh by this time was corrupted, and the bodies were mutilated, and the usual custom of embalming could not be practised, they burned the bodies, and buried the remains under a tamarisk tree which grew beside the town. And to mark their sorrow they fasted seven days, mourning as for a beloved and honoured friend. Some years after, David removed these remains and interred them in the family burying-place of Kish, at Zelah in Benjamin.[1]

Intelligence of the defeat of the Israelites and of the death of Saul and his sons was brought to David by an Amalekite, who gave correct details of the events that had occurred, but, to win the favour of David, represented himself as having slain Saul at the king's own desire, confirming the truth of his narrative by offering him the royal crown and bracelet of which he had despoiled the dead monarch. Far from rewarding the self-accusing murderer, David gave orders for his immediate execution for having sacrilegiously lifted his hand against the

[1] 2 Sam. xxi 12 ff.

anointed of the Lord. In the utter abandonment of grief at this great national calamity, and at his own loss thereby, he rent his clothes, and commanded an universal mourning to be observed; " and they mourned and wept and fasted until even for Saul, and for Jonathan his son, and for the people of the Lord, and for the house of Israel; because they were fallen by the sword." And then, forgetting all the ills that he had suffered at Saul's hands, remembering only the noble traits of his character, the bravery and skill of his military enterprises, his feats of arms, his manliness, his beauty, his goodly stature, recalling with mournful tenderness the virtues of Jonathan, his fleetness of foot, his dexterity in the use of weapons of war, and most of all the warmth and loyalty of his love, David uttered a pathetic elegy, which has been preserved in the unknown " Book of Jasher," and is here inserted by the historian [1] :—

> "Thy glory, O Israel, is slain upon thy high places!
> How are the mighty fallen!" &c.

We need not linger long on the delineation of Saul's character. The course of our history has clearly displayed it; its early promise, its gradual deterioration, its ruinous fall. Among all his contemporaries chosen as the fittest to receive the royal dignity, possessing personal beauty, animal courage, commanding stature, warlike skill, gifted with energy, perseverance, and a high regard for the honour of his nation, Saul entered upon his new and untried office under most favourable circumstances. Though he was not what we should call a religious man in the highest sense of the term, yet he at first exhibited a sincere zeal for the worship of Jehovah and the customs of which it formed the moving power. He repressed with a strong hand infringements of the ancient code; he would sacrifice his gallant son for a breach of a religious vow. A skilful commander and organizer, he raised a band of heroic warriors, with whose aid he carried on successful wars, of which that with the Amalekites is only an example of one out of many. To him must be ascribed the

---

[1] 2 Sam. i. 17 ff. The clause translated in Revised Version: "And he bade them teach the children of Judah the song of the Bow," is thought by some to be the title found in the Book whence the ode was taken, and transferred to the historian's text, and should run thus: "And he said: 'For the children of Judah to learn by heart *the Bow*, from the Book of Jasher.'" Then follows the dirge. So "Speaker's Commentary."

foundation of that empire which reached its culminating point under his immediate successors. There was much in him that was lovable; he certainly won the affection of his people so that they followed him willingly, and in spite of his later folly and madness, never conspired against him. To what then are we to attribute his failure, which led to his rejection? It was not that he was impetuous and thoughtless; it was not that he was jealous and suspicious; such faults he had, but though they contributed to, they were not the primary cause of his fall. That is to be sought in the feeling that the standard set before him, the ideal to which he ought to attain, was quite beyond the desire of his heart or the bent of his will. To know what is right, and yet to resist it wilfully; to find no comfort in resistance, and yet to persist in opposition, is a state of inward conflict which may well cloud the brightest mind with gloom and depression. The prophet's voice represented an external conscience to which he gave only partial heed, and which excited his jealousy and troubled his peace. Aware that his sovereignty depended upon his allegiance to Jehovah, he would not realize the fact in his daily conduct; he rebelled against such constraint, and at times let the irritability thus occasioned get complete mastery, so that he acted as a madman, losing all sense of justice, law, and humanity. And when at length he finds that he cannot be wholly independent, that the warnings and restraints of the Divine voice cannot be safely dispensed with, instead of trying to retrieve the past by timely repentance and submission, he falls into the depths of a miserable despair, and his religion is merged into a debasing superstition. The progress of his declension has been sketched in the previous narrative. Surface religion is no support in great mental crises. It fails entirely in Saul's great need. He feels remorse, but not repentance; dissatisfied and angry with himself, he vents his humour on others; he can ill brook reproof even from the power for which he had some respect; headstrong and self-willed he takes his own course, though conscious that that course leads him farther from God, and alienates him from his truest friend. In his inmost soul he knows this, and the knowledge occasions vexation and agony; he broods upon it; night and day his meditation is occupied with his own rejection and his unknown rival; the latent insanity in his mental constitution is stirred into activity by this dark melancholy, and he becomes subject to outbreaks of maniacal fury. And when his gloomy forebodings and vague surmises received a definite object from the women's laudation of David, the hatred and suspicion of this youthful warrior became a rooted passion, and goaded him to reckless cruelty, so that the once generous, high-minded ruler changed into a gloomy, vindictive tyrant; his old heroic spirit failed; he felt powerless to contend against his destiny; and though at the fatal battle of Gilboa he fought bravely and disdained to fly, his was the energy of despair, the hopeless struggle of one who feels himself forsaken of God, and the fitting end was suicide.

The fate of Saul, once chosen of the Lord, the pride of the people, possessed of many noble qualities which endeared him to the wisest and best of the age, then rejected, haunted by evil spirits, the prey of gross superstition, despairing, dying by his own hand, teaches surely that high privileges must be used aright, must lead to a high and holy life, or they become curses and increase condemnation; teaches that acting against conscience is fatal to the soul's life, hardens the heart, alienates from God; that religion must be real and vital, if it is to make a man strong to resist evil, ready to meet temptation, able to fight the Lord's battles against enemies within or without. And it has a lesson also for the nations; it warns them not to trust in outward endowments, in strength of arm, in multitude of warriors, but to see that their cause is righteous, to act with justice and humanity, and to leave the issue with confidence to the Lord of hosts.